UNDERSTANDING HAPPINESS

We all want to be happy, and there are plenty of people telling us how it can be achieved. The positive psychology movement, indeed, has established happiness as a scientific concept within everyone's grasp. But is happiness really something we can actively aim for, or is it simply a by-product of how we live our lives more widely?

Dr Mick Power, Professor of Clinical Psychology and Director of Clinical Programmes at the National University of Singapore, provides a critical assessment of what happiness really means, and the evidence for how it can be increased. Arguing that negative emotions are as important to overall well-being as the sunnier sides of our disposition, the book examines many of the claims of the positive psychology movement, including the relationship between happiness and physical health, and argues that resilience, adaptability in the face of adversity, psychological flexibility, and a sense of generativity and creativity are far more achievable as life goals.

This is a book that will fascinate anyone interested in positive psychology, or anyone who has ever questioned the plethora of publications suggesting that blissful happiness is 10 easy steps away.

Mick Power is Professor of Clinical Psychology and Director of Clinical Programmes at the National University of Singapore. He has previously worked in universities and hospitals in London, Tromsø, Milan, Beijing, Edinburgh and Lisbon. For many years he has worked with the World Health Organization to develop a measure of quality of life, the WHOQOL, that is now in widespread use throughout the world.

UNDERSTANDING HAPPINESS

A critical review of positive psychology

Mick Power

Routledge
Taylor & Francis Group

LONDON AND NEW YORK

First published 2016
by Routledge
2 Park Square, Milton Park, Abingdon, Oxon OX14 4RN

and by Routledge
711 Third Avenue, New York, NY 10017

Routledge is an imprint of the Taylor & Francis Group, an informa business

British Library Cataloguing in Publication Data
A catalogue record for this book is available from the British Library

Library of Congress Cataloging in Publication Data
Power, Michael J., author.
Understanding happiness : a critical review of positive psychology /
Mick Power.
pages cm
Includes bibliographical references and index.
1. Positive psychology. 2. Happiness—Psychological aspects. I. Title.
BF204.6.P69 2016
150.19'88—dc23
2015023177

ISBN: 978-1-138-92923-4 (hbk)
ISBN: 978-1-138-92924-1 (pbk)
ISBN: 978-1-315-68133-7 (ebk)

Typeset in Bembo
by Swales & Willis Ltd, Exeter, Devon, UK
Printed in Great Britain by Ashford Colour Press Ltd

To Irina

Happiness is no laughing matter.

(Richard Whateley)

Happiness
Look! The shimmering pool of happiness
hovers always on the road's horizon.
Like God and the Good and this book
it's only there
to help us move forward together, so
do not suppose, dear reader, that you
can stay in any such place
anytime soon or ever, because happiness is
a place forever not here or there
in a time that has never been nor will come.
But look! it's still there. So, onward, as Brummies say
better the expectant, hopeful, affectionate pose
treat the cycle of life like a cyclist
who only moves by balancing
and only by balancing, keeps moving.

(Mick Quille)

CONTENTS

PREFACE

Let me start with a confession. I normally find books written about happiness and how to be happy extremely irritating. A rehash of some bland and obvious dos and don'ts, though I do like the quote from the Hungarian-born actress Zsa Zsa Gabor 'I've been poor and I've been rich, and I'd rather be rich and unhappy than poor and unhappy'. Notwithstanding Zsa Zsa, if I were to pick up this book in a bookshop and was suffering from amnesia so that I had forgotten writing it, there would be a risk of dropping it faster than a hot potato in case it was yet another illusion-filled Wizard of Pos guide to the Yellow Brick Road. So let me reassure sceptics like myself that this book is not another superficial rehash, but, instead, is designed to look behind the curtain and to look for the truth in philosophy, psychology, and the science of well-being and suffering at what we really should be aiming for in our lives.

Now friends are starting to get worried about me. In my previous book, *Adieu to God*, I gave up on god and the afterlife, and now in this book I am giving up on happiness. 'Surely you must be completely depressed and nihilistic without any of life's props?' they ask. On the contrary, I reply. Life has never felt better. Now I have a feeling of liberation because I have thrown off the shackles of all those strange beliefs that even as a child were no more convincing than any other fairytales. Letting go of the delusions leads to a feeling of freedom.

As a word, 'happiness' has to be one of the most misused and misleading sequence of letters in the English language. It is simply the name for a brief emotion state that lasts for a few seconds or minutes and then disappears. It is one of a panoply of other such emotions, all of which play important functions, but none of which become ends in themselves – 'the pursuit of happiness' should sound as strange as 'the pursuit of guilt' or 'the pursuit of anger', if they were to be posited as basic goals in life.

So this book is premised on a very simple proposal – that 'happiness' has come to be used mistakenly as an end to be aimed for rather than being merely an ephemeral emotion. It is time to drop the illusions and delusions that are a consequence of such an impossible pursuit. Instead, we need to pursue our valued roles and goals, our relationships, and our hobbies in and of themselves. Meaningful work, connection through relationships and the occasional holiday in Italy go a long way to making life tolerable, and then dealing as best you can with the adversities that inevitably come at you. If your pursuits offer fleeting feelings of happiness, and of course many other emotions along the way, so be it. However, this proposal will not sit well with those who make their money from the happiness industry – those who attempt to market it, to bottle it, and to prescribe it. The American-led positive psychology movement will not be at all happy, especially when along the way I challenge some of their cherished proposals, such as criticising their claims about the supposed importance of optimism. However, it is important to note that the positive psychology movement is not just a one-coloured coat that simply promotes the pursuit of happiness, which it can be mistakenly portrayed as from the outside, but it is a coat of many colours and there are many points of commonality, especially in its consideration of the 'virtuous life'.

When it comes to thanking my own family, friends and colleagues, perhaps I should start with my son Liam, a philosopher by training and a musician by trade, who, I hope, is soon to step into considerable musical success, and who frequently reminded me of how much us moderns are merely recycling Ancient Greek ideas. To colleagues, students and friends over many years for those many stimulating discussions – Charlie Sharp, Tim Dalgleish, Andy MacLeod, Eleanor Sutton (especially for Chapter 2), Augustina Skoropadskaya, Lorna Champion, Dave Peck, Ann Green, Kath Melia, Mick Quille – to name but a few, I give thanks. I have also had the good fortune to be part of the World Health Organization WHOQOL Group for the study of quality of life and well-being since the early 1990s, for which I thank a succession of WHOQOL coordinators, including Norman Sartorius, John Orley, Rex Billington and our current WHO minder, Somnath Chatterji. Through the WHOQOL Group, I have visited parts of the world that I did not even know existed, and I have met and worked with an extraordinarily hospitable and talented group of people – Kathryn Quinn, Monika Bullinger, Lajos Kullman, Martin Eisemann, Eva Dragomirecka, Svetlana Akolzina, Olga Kishko, Miyako Tazaki, Yuantao Hao, Jiqian Fang, Don Bushnell, Marcelo Fleck, Neusa Sica da Rocha, Willem Kuyken, Ramona Lucas, Eduardo Chachamovich and Marianne Amir (who has sadly passed away). I must especially thank Martin Eisemann and his colleague Knut Waterloo for the many adventurous trips to Tromsø in Norway, where last winter I finally gazed in wonder at the Northern Lights.

I must also thank my brother Ken for his insights into the financial world and all of its disasters, which helped with much of the material for the final chapter in the book. Finally, my heartfelt thanks to my wife Irina for her support and warmth and for her challenges to my half-spun ideas – don't ever stop. We share a love of bad jokes. Let me tell you another one . . .

1

HAPPINESS

An overview

The word 'happiness' should be retired because it's so ambiguous.
(Daniel Kahneman, 2012)

Introduction

The world's greatest living psychologist (at least according to his friend Steven Pinker) and only living psychologist to have won the Nobel Prize for economics, Daniel Kahneman, is on record to have declared himself a pessimist (Kahneman, 2011). However, many people might still be puzzled at Kahneman's declaration that 'happiness', at least as a word, should be abandoned and replaced with something more useful given how much time, effort and money people spend on the pursuit of happiness. Perhaps, you might think, that is taking pessimism just a bit too far. But let us consider a few facts and figures.

In relation to tourism and happiness, in 2013 the World Tourism Organization (see www.unwto.org) estimated that there were over 1 billion international travellers worldwide who spent over US$1.4 trillion in order to travel. In relation to alcohol and happiness, in the UK alone the expenditure on alcohol has been estimated for 2012 at approximately £38 billion (Institute of Alcohol Studies, www.ias.org.uk). Similarly, in the week leading up to Christmas 2011 UK shoppers had spent £8 billion in shops by Christmas Eve at a rate of an estimated £2.5 million every minute, with the total expenditure for Christmas in the UK coming in at a staggering £69.1 billion (*Daily Mirror*, 19 December 2011, accessed at www.mirror.co.uk). There are bucketloads of such figures that could be rolled out, but they all lead to the one question: What is it that we are trying to buy? Haven't we been told that money can't buy love? That money can't buy happiness? So why do we seem to behave as if the opposite were true?

To return to the world's greatest living psychologist, what is even more puzzling about Daniel Kahneman is that as a self-confessed pessimist he moved from Israel to work in the United States. If there is one country in the world that has elevated the pursuit of happiness to a major cultural preoccupation, then it has to be the US. Enshrined in the American Declaration of Independence are the immortal words:

> We hold these truths to be self-evident – that all men are created equal; that they are endowed by their Creator with certain inalienable rights, that among these are life, liberty, and the pursuit of happiness.

Those of us who are a little sceptical of such high ideals might suggest that Americans have been more preoccupied with the pursuit of wealth than the pursuit of happiness, given that more than half of the world's billionaires live in the US (Wilkinson and Pickett, 2010). However, a more constructive response might be to point to the development of the positive psychology movement in the US and to argue that surely this movement follows in the great tradition begun in the Declaration of Independence. The founder of this movement, the psychologist Martin Seligman, describes its origins to have taken place in his back garden when his 5-year-old daughter Nikki asked him why he was always so grouchy. As Seligman writes:

> Nikki . . . was throwing weeds into the air and dancing and singing. Since she was distracting me, I yelled at her, and she walked away. Within a few minutes she was back, saying, 'Daddy, I want to talk to you.'
>
> 'Yes, Nikki?'
>
> 'Daddy, do you remember before my fifth birthday? From when I was three until when I was five, I was a whiner. I whined every day. On my fifth birthday I decided I wasn't going to whine anymore. That was the hardest thing I've ever done. And if I can stop whining, you can stop being such a grouch.'
>
> This was an epiphany for me. In terms of my own life, Nikki hit the nail right on the head. I was a grouch.
>
> *(Seligman, 2002, p. 28)*

This insightful question from a wise 5-year-old seems to have led to a mid-life crisis in which the inventor of Learned Helplessness, a state that would surely make anyone a grouchy old man, rediscovered his inner positive self and then wrote, as it states on the front cover, *The New York Times* Bestseller *Authentic Happiness* (2002), and a whole truckload of similar books besides.

One crucial point that we must make about the positive psychology movement (we will return to it frequently in later chapters) is that surely it must be annoying to older generations to see some of their ideas repackaged and recycled? Wasn't that a positive psychology movement back in the 1950s when the great (and, of course, subsequently very rich) Norman Vincent Peale wrote classics such as *The Power of Positive Thinking*, *The Power of Positive Living*, *The Amazing Results of Positive Thinking*, *The Power of Positive*

Thinking for Young People, and, my favourite title of all, *Stay Alive All Your Life*? I guess you begin to get the idea. Anyway, Norman's conquest of positive thinking includes examples that sound just like Seligman in his back garden:

> Altogether too many people are defeated by the everyday problems of life. They go struggling, perhaps even whining, through their days with a sense of dull resentment at what they consider the 'bad breaks' life has given them. . . . By learning how to cast them from the mind, by refusing to become mentally sub-servient to them, and by channelling spiritual power through your thoughts, you can rise above obstacles which ordinarily might defeat you.
>
> *(Peale, 1953, pp. vii–viii)*

On the basis of this continual pursuit of happiness and all things positive, you might naively assume that Americans should come top of the happiness league tables that are now generated from large-scale surveys of how people feel. Absolutely not!

An extremely insightful and highly recommended book by Richard Wilkinson and Kate Pickett, *The Spirit Level: Why Equality is Better For Everyone* (2010), includes a wealth of charts and figures demonstrating why the US, of all the developed coun-tries, typically comes bottom on almost all indicators that are relevant to health, well-being and quality of life. Figure 1.1 presents the case, showing that of all the developed nations, the US has the greatest income inequality, which in turn is linked to a variety of negative indicators such as the Index of Health and Social Problems.

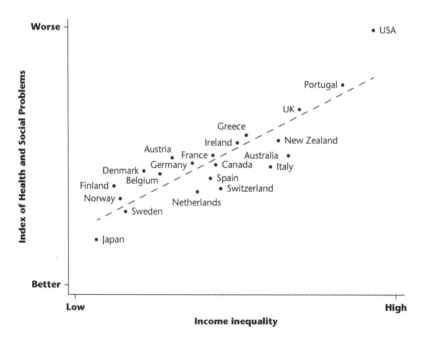

FIGURE 1.1   Income inequality and the Index of Health and Social Problems.

Source: Wilkinson and Pickett (2010). Reproduced with permission.

In order to understand the consequences of such an unequal society whilst being bombarded by positive thinking and the pursuit of happiness, Wilkinson and Pickett point to the work of the US psychologist Jean Twenge, who, in publications such as *Generation Me* (2006), has identified some worrying longitudinal trends in the US. In a summary of studies carried out between the 1950s and the 1990s, Twenge found that there has been a continuous upward trend in the levels of anxiety over those 40 years for both men and women in the US. Over a similar time period, studies also seem to show that people in the US report increasingly positive levels of self-esteem on standardised measures of esteem. The paradox therefore seems to be that Americans are becoming both more anxious and more positive about themselves at the same time, which seems to present a puzzling scenario. In explanation, Twenge has argued that high self-esteem can come in two varieties: the first is a genuine healthy style that is open to experience and to feedback from others; in contrast, the second is a type of defensive egotism or narcissism that is not open to experience or to feedback from others, but which provides a defence against social-evaluative threats. We will examine this defensive self-esteem and a number of other similar problems in detail in Chapter 2. However, it is important to point out the possible links to the 'Have a nice day – Have a nice life' think positive movement with which the US is currently preoccupied.

The problem with all such simplistic philosophies is that they come with a psychological blindness that can put people at risk, whilst leading to the apparent paradoxes such as why we are wealthier but not happier, or why we think more positively but act more negatively. In Chapter 3 we will consider more sophisticated psychological models such as our own SPAARS model (Power and Dalgleish, 2008) and Kahneman's (2011) arguments for two major systems: System 1, which operates largely automatically and outside of awareness, and System 2, which is largely conscious and controlled. However, at this point we will just note the entertaining book by Barbara Ehrenreich *Smile or Die: How Positive Thinking Fooled America & The World* (2009) (published in the US under the title *Bright-Sided*). In a nutshell, Ehrenreich argues that the think positive movement is just one of the many tricks by which the rich enjoy being rich but try to keep the poor, the infirm, the unemployed and the disabled quiet about their situations: 'Just think positive and you too could be President!' However, and just to set the balance straight, we are certainly not arguing that positive psychology is all bad, but that in the popular press unfortunately it has become synonymous with a simplistic happiology industry; in later chapters we will examine many of the plusses, including issues about strengths and virtues, the importance of forgiveness, gratitude and acts of kindness in our interpersonal relations, and the assessment and improvement of our quality of life. The issue for us is that the positive psychology movement in its popular presentation appears to throw the baby out with the bathwater. For example, so-called 'negative' emotions, which got such a bad press in Seligman's writings at the beginning of the movement, are essential parts of us and, when used in the appropriate way, also add to our strengths, virtues, and improve the quality of our interpersonal relationships (see Chapter 3).

Popular conceptions and misconceptions of 'happiness'

One of the puzzles of modern economics is that, despite the genuine increase in the wealth of the developed nations, there has not been an equivalent increase in the happiness of people populating those nations (e.g. Diener and Biswas-Diener, 2008). One interpretation has been that although physical capital has increased, there has been a concomitant decline in social capital, that is, in the quality of the social support and social networks with which we all enrich our lives. Although the reasons for the decline in social capital are likely to be complex (Layard, 2011), we can take one simple example: the impact of television over the past 50 years has been considerable. A study of television's impact in the Kingdom of Bhutan, located to the east of Tibet in the Himalayas, has come up with some dramatic results. The Kingdom of Bhutan has taken a unique approach to the state of its population in that it has introduced an economic population measure known as Gross National Happiness (GNH), which sits alongside other economies' preoccupation with Gross National Product (GNP). In the time since television was introduced into Bhutan in 1999, there has been a dramatic decline in social capital, or GNH, to the extent that the Bhutanese Government is likely to cut down the number of TV channels and the amount of TV coverage that will be available in the future (Layard, 2011; MacDonald, 2003).

One of the problems that economists struggle with is the relationship between objective and subjective indicators of states such as happiness; our emphasis throughout this book is very much that it is not the objective event or situation but the subjective appraisal of an event or situation that is more important in determining the consequent emotional state (see Power and Dalgleish, 2008). Although there may be thresholds below which material deprivation and poverty do impact on happiness (Diener, 2003), above these thresholds the impact on happiness and on quality of life is likely to be more subjective or appraisal-based (e.g. Power, 2003), which is why the relationship between health and well-being indicators with income inequality emerges in the wealthy developed nations.

A second issue that the economic approach to happiness raises is that the type of happiness referred to by economists, that is, the type that might relate to how many zeros there are in your income and how many cars are parked outside your house, is not the same as the brief momentary states of happiness that are the equivalent of states of anxiety, anger or sadness. The term 'happiness' is an umbrella term that needs to be divided into at least two different meanings (e.g. Argyle, 2001): one refers to brief transitory emotions such as joy, amusement or ecstasy, and the other refers to concepts such as meaning in life, self-actualisation, life satisfaction and a mood-like state of continuing contentment (e.g. Layard, 2011). The second type should not be labelled 'happiness', as we will argue throughout this book, because of its confusion with the first type of 'happiness'. Authors' opinions vary as to the extent aspects of these two general categories should be included under each heading, but, allowing for these differences, these two types of happiness have also been referred to as the hedonic and eudaimonic approaches respectively (e.g. Ryan and

Deci, 2001), or a related distinction between 'experienced well-being' and 'life satisfaction' by Daniel Kahneman (2011).

Samuel Franklin, in his elegant *The Psychology of Happiness* (2010), also argues that it is the eudaimonic rather than the hedonic by which we should lead our lives, and he suggests, with others, that the 'pursuit of happiness' enshrined in the American Declaration of Independence refers to this virtuous form of happiness. Although the primary focus in this book will be on the more permanent states variously referred to as life satisfaction, contentment, actualisation and so on, nevertheless, some of the discussion will inevitably spill over into considerations of the transitory emotions of happiness when we consider states such as romantic love (see Chapter 2). We are also mindful of the fact that the distinction between hedonic and eudaimonic may be more a theoretical than a practical one. Paul Dolan, for example, has argued in *Happiness by Design: Finding Pleasure and Purpose in Everyday Life* (2014) that we should not see pleasure and purpose as separate but rather as two sides of the activities we engage in and that the best activities may give us a sense of both.

Happiness – temporary emotion versus permanent state

So, what is 'happiness'? Attempts to define happiness within the psychology literature generally reflect the breadth of scope that, according to Averill and Moore (2000), is so mocking of analysis. For example, Wessman and Ricks (1966) proposed that happiness:

> Appears as an overall evaluation of a quality of the individuals own experience in the conduct of his vital affairs. As such, happiness represents a conception abstracted from the flux of affective life indicating a decided balance of positive affectivity over long periods of time.
>
> *(pp. 240–241)*

Similarly, Veenhoven (1984) suggests that happiness is 'the degree to which an individual judges the overall quality of his life-as-a-whole favourably' and is 'not a simple sum of pleasures, but rather a cognitive construction which the individual puts together from his various experiences'.

It seems clear that conceptualisations of happiness such as these are referring, as we noted above, to a different type of construction that are not the same as brief states of anger, sadness, fear or disgust. Clearly, there are positive emotions that are circumscribed in the same way as the ones we have discussed: the emotions of joy, exhilaration, ecstasy and so on are most usually about the achievement of a particular valued goal and, indeed, the term happiness is also frequently used in this way. However, we must also distinguish happiness as an emotion from pleasure that results from drive satisfaction, consistent with the distinction that we have made previously between emotions, drives and sensations (Power and Dalgleish, 2008; Power, 2014); thus, the satiation of food, thirst, sex or other drives may be accompanied by feelings of pleasure, which may in turn lead to the appraisal of happiness, but could lead under many circumstances to appraisals other than happiness (e.g. Rozin, 1999). In this chapter, therefore, we will begin by briefly examining circumscribed positive emotions such as joy before proceeding to a more detailed discussion of happiness as defined above by authors such as Veenhoven and Wessman and Ricks.

Joy may be conceptualised as the emotional state related to an appraisal that a valued goal has been achieved, or that movement towards such an achievement has occurred. So, for example, somebody might feel joy when she is able to go and book her summer holiday. Such an analysis of joy clearly distinguishes it from what is called life satisfaction. Joy is very much an emotional reaction to a specific goal in a specific domain, whereas life satisfaction, it seems, casts its appraisal net much wider. It is perfectly feasible for an individual to experience joy with respect to a specific goal whilst not being generally happy when all goals in all domains are considered together (cf. Fredrickson, 2005); similarly, it is possible for an individual to be happy in general, that is, high in life satisfaction, whilst also feeling some fear, anger or sadness as a result of appraisals concerning specific goals in specific domains.

The circumscribed positive emotion of joy is very much the antithesis of the negative emotions, though it can contribute to the experience of emotional conflict. Descartes, in his *The Passions of the Soul* (1649/1989), recounts the tale of a man who, whilst being sad at his wife's death, was also unable to contain his joy at his new-found freedom because she was no longer alive to trouble him. Such conflict between feelings of joy at the achievement of goals that we may feel uncomfortable with and negative emotions towards those goals is frequently the subject of therapeutic work (see Power, 2010). Much of this conflict not only incorporates our own goals but also those of others, such as in the experience of the wonderful German emotion of *Schadenfreude*, which is very much the opposite of envy, and which involves joy at another's misfortune, and can often prove distressing. Whether it involves being secretly pleased that one of our classmates did not succeed in getting a distinction in his exams, or feeling a surge of exhilaration when someone's perfect relationship breaks down, feelings of *Schadenfreude* can disturb us because they reveal wants, needs and goals that we perhaps did not realise we had and that feel uncomfortable and incongruent with our idealised models of our selves.

In the Introduction we noted several definitions of the broad emotional state of happiness. Although these attempts at definition capture some of the breadth of the concept, research into the nature of happiness has, for the most part, been conducted outside of such definitional guidelines or theoretical frameworks. Such research has tended either to ask people what they feel makes them happy, or has examined the correlates of happiness in people who claim to be happy (e.g. Veenhoven, 2000). The findings from these approaches have revealed a number of issues and paradoxes that, in our view, underline the need for a carefully thought-out, theoretical framework before we can achieve any measure of understanding of the concept of happiness. In the sections that follow we consider some of this research and some of the issues that it has generated. We must note, though, that in order to assess whether or not individuals are happy, researchers have devised a number of fairly straightforward self-report measures, but because of the wide-ranging nature of the concept, it is not always happiness that these inventories actually measure. There now exist questionnaires that look at 'positive affect', 'subjective well-being', 'satisfaction with life', 'quality of life' and a number of other related constructs. Although there are clearly debates about the relationships between these different concepts, it is our broad assumption in this chapter that they are all more or less intended as synonyms for the concept of happiness when taken in its broadest sense, but which we take to mean life satisfaction and quality of life (e.g. Layard, 2011).

On the prototypical happiness questionnaire, the respondent is asked, on a single- or multiple-item scale, how happy he or she is. Examples of such questionnaires include the Satisfaction with Life Scale (Diener *et al.*, 1985), the Depression-Happiness Scale (McGreal and Joseph, 1993), the Memorial University of Newfoundland Scale of Happiness (Kozma and Stones, 1980) and the Oxford Happiness Inventory (Hills and Argyle, 1998) (see Argyle, 2001, and Larsen and Fredrickson, 1999, for reviews). Convergent validity for such measures of happiness is surprisingly good. For example, Sandvik *et al.* (1993) found a strong relationship between self-reports of emotional well-being and interview ratings, peer ratings, reports of the average ratio of pleasant to unpleasant moods, and an index of a memory for pleasant and unpleasant events. Furthermore, such measures are claimed to be uncontaminated by social desirability (Diener *et al.*, 1991), and show structural invariance across time and cultural group (e.g. Vitterso *et al.*, 2002).

However, when looked at more closely, there may be fundamental limitations with the approach and with the conclusions that are reached. For example, the most famous of the happiness researchers is Ruut Veenhoven in the Netherlands, who has established the World Database of Happiness, and who is founder of the *Journal of Happiness Studies* (see www.worlddatabaseofhappiness.eur.nl). Veenhoven's surveys are typically based on a single item along the lines of:

All things considered, how happy would you say you are these days?

This question is typically rated on a 4-point scale that runs from Unhappy to Very Happy, though his website lists about a thousand variants of this and related questions that range from 3-point to 10-point rating scales. We will consider later in the section on quality of life why such single-item questions are weaker in terms of reliability and validity in comparison to multiple-item scales, especially when they are translated across different languages and cultures in which the term 'happiness' has very different interpretations. For example, on the basis of these single questions, Veenhoven has argued that individualistic cultures are happier than collectivist cultures and that income inequality does not affect happiness. In direct contradiction to these conclusions, we know from the work of Wilkinson and Pickett (2010) (see Figure 1.1 above and Figures 1.2 and 1.3 later) that income inequality really does matter for health, well-being and happiness, and that many collectivist cultures (e.g. Japan) score very highly on the relevant indicators. The moral, as we argue throughout this book, is that because of its multiple ambiguities, surveys with single items that ask you to rate 'happiness' are fraught with conceptual and empirical problems and should be avoided except where 'happiness' refers to the brief emotion state and, in English, is better referred to as 'joy' or 'elation' or something similar.

Pleasure versus pain

The possibility that happiness might be definable as the absence of pain and the presence of pleasure has engaged philosophers from the Greeks onwards (see Darrin McMahon's *The Pursuit of Happiness*, 2006, for an entertaining account) and, more recently, has provided the backbone that underlies both psychoanalytic and behavioural approaches within psychology. But to begin with the philosophers, if there is one philosopher who still lends his name to indulgent pleasures, then it has to be Epicurus. Epicurus says 'The pleasure of the stomach is the beginning and root of all good, and it is to this that wisdom and over-refinement actually refer' (Long and Sedley, 1987, p. 117). Even during his life, Epicurus was misunderstood because of such remarks, and misrepresented as an orgiastic hedonist, but to quote further from him:

> But when we say that pleasure is the end, we do not mean the pleasures of the dissipated and those that consist in having a good time . . . but freedom from pain in the body and from disturbance in the soul.
>
> *(p. 114)*

If we are in any doubt that pleasure does not equate with hedonistic indulgence for Epicurus, then the following quote surely seals it:

> For what produces the pleasant life is not continuous drinking and parties or pederasty or womanizing or the enjoyment of fish and other dishes of an expensive table, but sober reasoning which tracks down the causes of every choice and avoidance, and which banishes the opinions that beset souls with the greatest confusion.
>
> *(p. 114)*

In fact, Epicurus comes close to the philosophers of the virtuous life, to whom we will return in the next section. This was just an opportunity to put the record straight for poor old misunderstood Epicurus.

In his *Nicomachean Ethics*, Aristotle makes the point that, just as slaves cannot be happy if they are denied the opportunity to pursue virtuous activities (higher order goal fulfilment), neither can the victim of torture be happy merely by virtue of being a good person (that is, because of the lack of fulfilment of lower order biological goals). These are contentious points; the first seems to be an argument against any form of hedonism, whilst the latter seems to provide objections to certain forms of spiritualism or religious happiness.

The principal objection to taking an entirely bottom-up approach to happiness (that is, that happiness can derive from the fulfilment of low-level goals in the various goal domains) is that individuals seem to habituate fairly rapidly to such events (e.g. McIntosh and Martin, 1991). So, events that at one time seem very positive come to be perceived as less positive when people get used to experiencing those events. For example, the brand new Alfa Romeo sitting in the driveway may be a source of great joy; however, after a few months the owner will become used to seeing the car parked outside and it will no longer be a source of such positive affect. Or the first time you try the Anglo-Indian dish chicken tikka masala you might be overwhelmed with pleasure, but try and eat it every day and you are soon likely to grow tired of it and perhaps even nauseous at the thought of it. This habituation process suggests that the path to happiness does not lie with increasingly indulgent satisfaction of such low-level goals, but requires also the satisfaction of higher level, less materially dependent, more psychologically important goals and needs. The circle returns to Epicurus.

What about the possibility of happiness when there is no such fulfilment of low-level basic goals and needs? It seems unlikely that the biological and psychological systems, with their evolutionary imperatives to satisfy basic goals and needs such as hunger, thirst and physical comfort, could be continually short-circuited such that the absence of satisfaction of these needs is not an impediment to the individual's overall happiness. As Aristotle retorts: 'Those who say that the victim on the rack or the man who falls into great misfortune is happy if he is good are . . . talking nonsense' (*Nicomachean Ethics*, 1153b, 19). This notion of the fulfilment of basic needs prior to the achievement of higher order aims is central to a number of theories in humanistic psychology (e.g. Maslow, 1968) and is central to the more recent development of the measurement of quality of life (e.g. Power, 2003), which we will return to later in this chapter. However, we will step briefly back into the recent history of psychology where the ideas of pleasure and pain have played a much more significant role than perhaps they do in modern academic psychology.

Behaviourism was the dominant force in psychology throughout much of the twentieth century, especially in the US, although the development of the computer and cognitive science has led to its substantial decline. At the core of behaviourism are the principles of pleasure and pain, which provide the conditions for learning through either classical conditioning (identified by Pavlov) or operant conditioning (identified by Skinner and others) (see Power and Champion, 2000). For example, in the famous Pavlov studies of the conditioning of salivation in dogs, the dogs learned that the sound of the dinner-bell led to the pleasure of food, so that eventually they salivated just at the sound of the dinner-bell even when no food was presented. Equally, in conditioned emotional responses, if a painful stimulus such as an electric shock occurred after the dinner-bell instead of the pleasurable lunch, then the dogs would show signs of distress at the sound of the bell because they learned to associate it with pain. Skinner extended this analysis to show that we can also learn through oper-ant conditioning that if behaviour leads to the termination of a painful stimu-lus such behaviour is quickly learned through so-called negative reinforcement. However, one of the main turning points in psychology came when Skinner applied the behavioural pleasure–pain analysis to 'verbal behaviour'. Skinner's book *Verbal Behavior* (1957) was shredded by a young linguist, Noam Chomsky, in a couple of pages of review in 1959, in which Chomsky argued that it would be mathematically impossible to learn a language with only pleasure–pain-based learning mechanisms. As Chomsky demonstrated, most of what we say or write consists of unique utterances and sentences that we could not have learned previ-ously (though, in support of Skinner, I have one or two academic colleagues who seemed to have learned their lectures Skinnerian style). Chomsky's proposed solution was that we have an innate universal grammar- or language-acquisition device, from which our spoken language develops with the minimal language input that it receives in social interaction (Chomsky, 1965). However, Chomsky's solution has in turn been heavily criticised (e.g. see Eysenck and Keane, 2015). The important point to make here is that, although pleasure and pain mechanisms are of importance in much of what we do, the developments in language and other areas of cognitive science have highlighted that they cannot provide the whole story and that much of what we do is not motivated simply by seeking out pleasure or avoiding pain, as any sado-masochist would tell you. We will consider more general frameworks later in this chapter when drive-related pleasure and pain are considered as one level in complex hierarchical structures that may provide a more adequate approach to well-being and quality of life.

Finally in this section, we note the well-known thought experiment that the political philosopher Robert Nozick presented in his book *Anarchy, State and Utopia* (1974), which is often cited against simple models of hedonism and, in its more recent Jeremy Bentham form, utilitarianism. Nozick imagined a sci-ence fiction scenario of an Experience Machine that would offer its user the possibility of non-stop pleasure for the rest of his or her life. Would you choose to spend the rest of your life in such a state of perfect pleasure? No, answered Nozick, an answer that demonstrates that simple hedonistic models must be wrong. However, although Nozick's conclusion perfectly suits our argument in this book, and in a perfectly biased world we would simply rest our case at this point, in fact the situation is not quite as straightforward as Nozick would have us believe. In a series of classic studies in psychology, Olds and Milner (e.g. 1954) carried out brain stimulation studies in rats, in which they found an area of the brain, the lateral hypothalamus that, if directly stimulated with a small electri-cal current or chemical substance, led the rats to seek out constant stimulation in preference to food, water or the opportunity to copulate, to the point where the rats died from a lack of food and water. Olds and Milner, therefore, had previously carried out the experiment that Nozick simply imagined. Of course, you might argue, ok, just because it works like that for rats, it is not like that for us humans. Although this may be true for the majority of humans, unfortunately there are a minority who become addicted to drugs and alcohol in a way that leads to deterioration in their health, just as the rats continued the brain stimulation until they died. Perhaps Aristotle had already answered this question.

Back to philosophy and the virtuous life

Aristotle's concept of eudaimonia provides a key starting point in any discussion of happiness. In his *Nicomachean Ethics* (1095a, 15–22), Aristotle says that eudaimonia means 'doing and living well'. One important move in Greek philosophy to answer the question of how to achieve eudaimonia is to bring in another important concept in ancient philosophy, *arete* (that is, 'virtue'). Aristotle says that the eudaimonic life is one of 'virtuous activity in accordance with reason', to which, as we noted earlier, even Epicurus subscribed. Socrates presented a more extreme version of the virtuous life with his disagreement with those who thought that the eudaimonic life is the life of honour or pleasure, and he criticised the Athenians for caring more for riches and honour than the state of their souls. The Stoic philosophers developed this Socratic viewpoint with Stoic ethics presenting a strong form of eudaimonism. According to the Stoic philosophers such as Zeno, virtue is necessary and sufficient for eudaimonia. To quote from Stobaeus, the fifth-century CE compiler of writings from Greek philosophy:

> The bastion of Stoic ethics is the thesis that virtue and vice respectively are the sole constituents of happiness and unhappiness. These states do not in the least depend, they insisted, on the possession or absence of things conventionally regarded as good or bad – health, reputation, wealth etc: It is possible to be happy even without these.
>
> *(Long and Sedley, 1987, p. 357)*

The Stoic philosophers thereby denied the importance to eudaimonia of external goods and circumstances, in contrast to what Aristotle had proposed. He thought that severe misfortune (such as the death of one's family and friends) could rob even the most virtuous person of eudaimonia.

The proposals of Aristotle and the more extreme versions of eudaimonia from Socrates and the Stoic philosophers have had a considerable influence on modern proposals, with writers such as Maslow on self-actualisation and Erikson on adult development, which we will examine in more detail in the section on quality of life later in the chapter. However, to give away the punch-line first, we have to side with Aristotle because we believe that it is only for some people under special or extreme circumstances that the denial or excessive control of basic needs and drives can provide a sense of 'virtue' and goodness (as we will examine in Chapter 6 with some extreme religious practices). However, for the majority of us ordinary folk, who are neither saints nor martyrs, we achieve the virtuous life through continuing satisfaction of the basic needs in addition to whatever higher ideals we might possess.

The hedonic treadmill

There exists a plethora of research findings concerning the relationship between measures of happiness on self-report measures, such as those described above, and a variety of demographic and resource variables (see Argyle, 2001, and Layard, 2011, for comprehensive summaries). To overview briefly, we will start with the very complex and changing views on the possible relationship between income and happiness. It has been found that income is related to well-being, though for some time it was assumed that this relationship was only significant below a minimal level of income and was therefore much stronger in poorer countries (Vitterso *et al.*, 2002).

The effect seems possibly to be to do with relative income compared to others in a community or culture rather than the absolute level of income (Wilkinson and Pickett, 2010). However, more careful analyses by Deaton (2008) of the extensive Gallup World Poll data from 132 countries showed that when the logarithm of income or GDP is used rather than the raw value, no such threshold occurs in the data when country log income per person is plotted against life satisfaction. Kahneman and Deaton (2010), in further detailed analyses of 450,000 US respondents in a subsequent Gallup survey, replicated the positive relationship between life satisfaction and log income, but in contrast showed that a measure of current emotional well-being did show a threshold effect at about US$75,000. That is, with an income below $75,000 in the US, respondents' emotional well-being increased with income, but then plateaued at around this value with no further increases in current well-being. As Kahneman and Deaton demonstrate, the question 'What is the relationship between income and happiness?' needs to be deconstructed into which type of 'happiness' (current affect or life satisfaction) and into which type of income variable (log income, relative income, income inequality). A more recent analysis of longitudinal Gallup World Poll data across 135 countries by Diener *et al.* (2013) showed similar findings for log GDP data, with the strongest effects being for life evaluation. When they used household income, effects were also obtained for current well-being, but they found that the effects were primarily mediated by material possessions, optimism and financial satisfaction, and that they did not adapt across time.

Other variables have been less well studied than the income question. Age and education show only small correlations with subjective reports of happiness (Diener, 1984). Okun and George (1984) found a surprisingly small correlation between health and reports of happiness when objective measures of health are employed, though there is a small but clear effect (Power *et al.*, 2005). Finally, unemployment has been a predictor of unhappiness in some studies (e.g. Clark, 2003), and marriage has been a consistent but weak positive predictor of subjective reports of happiness, with married individuals being reportedly happier than single individuals (e.g. Helliwell and Putnam, 2005). Even putting aside basic methodological issues, for example, that perhaps it is happy people who get married, rather than married people who are happy (though recent evidence suggests that both statements may be true to some extent: see Lucas *et al.*, 2003, for summary findings from a longitudinal German study), the general lack of positive correlational findings between what objectively might be thought of as desirable resources or qualities and subjective reports of happiness requires explanation.

It seems that objective life situations and resources are, at best, only weak predictors of happiness. Indeed, this has been starkly illustrated in some comparative studies; for example, in a classic study, Brickman *et al.* (1978) found that recent lottery winners are often no happier than control participants, only slightly happier than recently paralysed accident victims, and no happier than they were before they won the lottery. Overall, Andrews and Withey (1976) found that age, sex, race, education, income, religion, occupation, employment status and size of city only accounted for approximately 11 per cent of the total variance in subjective judgements of happiness. Similarly Kammann (1982) concluded that objective life circumstances routinely account for less than 5 per cent of the variance in subjective judgements of happiness.

One of the attempts to account for how both highly negative events and highly positive events affect levels of happiness in the medium to long term was suggested by Philip Brickman and his colleagues in their classic study of lottery winners versus accident victims. They suggested that, as with many physiological processes, there are important adaptational psychological processes that impact on us. Brickman and colleagues argued that, equivalent to these physiological adaptation processes, hedonic adaptation occurs through similar homeostasis, such that we return to our original level of happiness as we 'recover' from both highly positive events such as winning the lottery, and highly negative events such as serious traffic accidents.

In his book *Happiness: Facts and Myths* (1990), Michael Eysenck referred to this adaptation process as the 'hedonic treadmill', and this is the term that has come to be widely used. The proposal is that we all have a 'happiness set-point', such that like on a treadmill, we always return to the point at which we started whatever happens in the intervening period. Eysenck presented numerous examples that, included increasing wealth, increasing achievement and increasing sporting ability, in all of which the expectations change such that an athlete could be happier after winning his school 100 metre championships than after coming second in the Olympic Games. The failed hope or expectation in the Olympics from not winning gold can be viewed even in a negative manner with second place being seen as a failure. Or, perhaps, to give a current example from the world of banking, the banker who receives million dollar bonuses every year will simply come to expect these as normal, with 'happiness' only occurring if the bonus is several times more than expected. Of course, the same bonus dropped into an African Shanty Town and shared between 10,000 would give such a level of utilitarian happiness that would make even Jeremy Bentham cry with joy (preserved as he is in his glass case in University College London). The important point that Brickman, Eysenck and others made is that happiness is simply a temporary state from which we all recover relatively quickly, perhaps even returning to a set-point to which we are genetically shackled.

The conclusions from the 'hedonic treadmill' theory would be very tempting for the approach that we take in this book, in which we argue that chasing happiness is as likely to be successful as chasing the pot of gold at the end of the rainbow or the mirage in the desert. As conducive to our own argument as this theory is, we must, however, point to some weaknesses in the theory that mean it has to be modified (cf. Diener *et al.*, 2006). In the next section, we will consider some of Seligman's and others' work on the contribution of circumstances and activity to levels of happiness, which runs counter to hedonic treadmill theory, but at this point we just want to note the work of Laura Carstensen (e.g. 2006) on so-called 'socio-emotional selectivity theory'. The theory argues that, as time horizons reduce with age, people become increasingly selective, investing greater resources in emotionally meaningful goals and activities. Ageing becomes associated with a preference for positive over negative information in both attention and memory (the 'positivity effect'). Older adults often spend more time with familiar individuals with whom they have had rewarding relationships, which increases positive emotional experiences and reduces emotional risks as individuals become older. At the same time, older adults report that they are better able to regulate their negative emotions compared to when they were younger, so typically report fewer and less extreme 'downs' in comparison to younger people. The net effect is that people are often surprised at the wisdom and emotional capacity that they develop with age, as we have shown in our studies on attitudes to ageing (Laidlaw *et al.*, 2007), to which we will return in Chapter 3. The important point to make here is that there may actually be a slow drift upwards in the 'set-point' across the lifespan, even if in the short to medium term the Brickman treadmill model has some validity for some types of life events for some of the people some of the time. Overall, however, the hedonic treadmill theory does not account for why some life events do change our happiness levels upwards or downwards, nor why people on average become more positive across their lifespan.

Martin Seligman

Another major area of criticism of the hedonic treadmill approach to happiness comes from the work of Martin Seligman and colleagues. For those who have reached the age of consent, you can log onto Seligman's website at www.authentichappiness.sas.upenn.edu, where you can join a community claimed to be 2 million users worldwide, who regularly complete positive psychology questionnaires, presumably because if you know the right answers you will get positive feedback and feel good about yourself!

Seligman and colleagues, such as Sonja Lyubomirsky, Mihalyi Csikszentmihalyi and others, have produced what they have called the 'happiness formula' (e.g. Seligman, 2002):

$$H = S + C + V$$

In this formula, H refers to the enduring level of happiness that you experience, S refers to the genetic or biological set-point, C refers to the conditions or circumstances of your life, and V refers to the factors under your voluntary control. Seligman has summarised a range of studies of twins and adoptees to show that behavioural traits have a relatively high amount of genetic determination, such that 50 per cent of our personality comes from our genetics. However, in contrast to the hedonic treadmill approach, which basically assumes that all personality is predetermined, Seligman and colleagues have included two factors that contribute the remaining 50 per cent to levels of happiness and that can be changed; namely, the circumstances and voluntary control of activities factors.

The circumstances in the formula include factors such as income and wealth, marriage, fulfilling social lives and religious belief. These factors all have extremely complex relationships to enduring happiness, which any examination of the relationship between money and happiness indicates. For example, in his book *Authentic Happiness* (2002), Seligman summarised analyses of surveys of income and national happiness such as those from the World Values Survey in the 1980s and 1990s, which demonstrated that there is a threshold in income below which you do find a positive correlation between income and happiness, the threshold being at about US$8,000 in the 1990s, though the more recent figures provided by Wilkinson and Pickett (2010) suggested that this threshold had increased to about US$25,000. Above these thresholds, Seligman and others have summarised the income data to show that there is no correlation between income and happiness, which leads Seligman to conclude erroneously that income redistribution is unnecessary because it does not make the poor any happier once they are at this minimum threshold. However, we now know from the more recent work of Deaton (2008), Diener et al (2013) and Kahneman and Deaton (2010) summarised earlier that when log income data is used there is no threshold effect and that, contrary to Seligman, there is a continuing increase in life satisfaction and experiential well-being with increases in income. A second problem, as we showed earlier in Figure 1.1, is in relation to health and social problems; it may not be absolute income that is crucial in relation to indicators of health and well-being in a society, but the inequality in income.

Figures 1.2 and 1.3, taken from Wilkinson and Pickett's analyses, dramatically demonstrate the differences between absolute income and income inequality. These figures show the impact in developed nations of income (Figure 1.2) versus income inequality (Figure 1.3) on the UNICEF index of child well-being in the world's 22 richest nations. Figure 1.2 clearly supports Seligman's claim that there is no relationship between absolute income and child well-being in the world's rich nations, despite the wide income range covered, from Portugal at the lowest to the US at the highest.

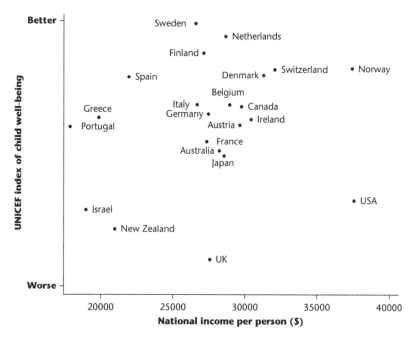

FIGURE 1.2 Absolute income and the UNICEF index of child well-being.

Source: Wilkinson and Pickett (2010). Reproduced with permission.

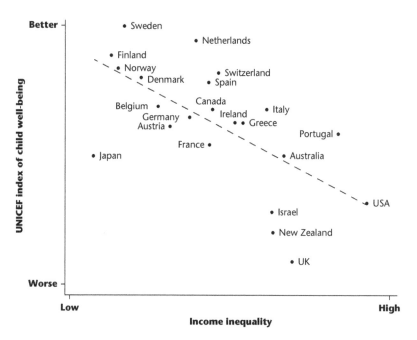

FIGURE 1.3 Income inequality and the UNICEF index of child well-being.

Source: Wilkinson and Pickett (2010). Reproduced with permission.

Figure 1.3 highlights what happens when absolute income is replaced by income inequality. Now there is a strong relationship with child well-being revealed, with the highest level of income inequality in the US being associated with low child well-being, and the low income inequality, especially in the Scandinavian countries, being associated with high levels of child well-being. Seligman and his colleagues need to rethink and re-analyse their data, as well as their politics.

The final element in the Seligman equation is the 'V' or voluntary control factor. Again, this is a wide-ranging concept, and it originally included directives from Seligman such as 'Do not dwell on the past', 'Get rid of your negative emotions', 'Forgive and forget' and 'Increase your optimism'. This earlier work of Seligman could be seen to contribute to the split in the American psyche that Jean Twenge, as we noted earlier, has identified with both the increase in self-esteem and the concurrent increase in anxiety and depression. Contrary to Seligman, you do not need to walk away from your negative emotions and from your past as if you were merely a piece of computer hardware that could be reformatted and the disk wiped clean (cf. Kashdan and Biswas-Diener, 2014). Fortunately, more recently Seligman himself and many within the positive psychology movement have shifted away from this one-coloured coat and now wear a coat of many colours; thus, the excellent *Oxford Handbook of Positive Psychology* edited by Lopez and Snyder (2009) presents a much more diverse approach, with many thoughtful analyses of topics such as wisdom, resilience, emotion expression, courage and humility that we will return to throughout this book (especially in Chapter 7) and with which we are in agreement.

Well-being, quality of life and other abstract states

Some years ago in Britain the newspapers carried a story of a man who committed suicide when he realised that he had not won the National Lottery. The situation was this: the man in question had selected a set of numbers that he entered into the lottery each week, subscribing six or seven weeks in advance. Eventually, he hit lucky and his numbers matched those drawn out of the hat for the maximum jackpot. However, on checking again the following day after a night of celebration, he found that his lottery entry was not valid because his advance subscriptions had lapsed the week before. Unable to cope with having thought that he had won millions of pounds when he had actually won nothing, the man committed suicide. What is perhaps most puzzling about this case is the fact that, prior to his false lottery win, the man concerned was reportedly very happy. The objective circumstances of his life that had previously made him happy were no different and were exactly the same after his false win; however, it seems that the man's goals and dreams in various domains of his life had shifted in line with his supposedly new-found fortune and the inability to attain these new goals and needs seems to have led to desperate unhappiness and his suicide.

The proposal that life satisfaction and well-being may be a function of goal fulfilment across various domains and levels, even allowing for the fact that individuals can invest more heavily in one domain or another, entails that such states are necessarily dynamic, with the possibility of change, even after long periods of apparent stability. A sense of satisfaction and well-being lasting minutes, hours, days, weeks or months will arise out of a process of psychological negotiation in which the goals and needs in one domain are pursued and realised. As Diener and Biswas-Diener have emphasised in their book *Happiness: Unlocking The Mysteries of Psychological Wealth* (2008), our sense of satisfaction is often more about the process than it is about the end-point of that process. As anyone who has children will recognise, even if earlier in life having children might have seemed like the end-point of a goal, having children is in fact just the beginning of a process of being a parent that never actually comes to an end. As with many goals, one apparent end-point merely opens up a new set of goals and processes. To take a different example, imagine that your goal had been to be a professor in a university. Once you have achieved that goal, there is then a whole new set of goals and processes that open up, such as walking around absent-mindedly, wearing different coloured socks and having a hairstyle that looks like you dress in front of the Van de Graaff generator every morning before you go to work. Joking, of course.

In order to understand how people make judgements about their position in life and their sense of satisfaction or dissatisfaction with their life, we have been working for many years to understand what is known as 'quality of life'. The phrase 'quality of life' is used in many different ways, and a major issue that faces this area of work is how the term should be defined and conceptualised. One of the key distinctions that has been made is that between health-related and non-health-related quality of life (e.g. Spilker, 1996). The starting point for a number of the health-related definitions has been the well-known World Health Organization (WHO) (e.g. 1958) definition of health as: 'a state of complete physical, mental and social well-being and not merely the absence of disease or infirmity'.

The inclusion of the phrase 'well-being' in the WHO definition has led some researchers to focus too narrowly on self-reported psychological well-being, or the even more restricted notion of 'happiness', as being the only aspect of quality of life of importance (e.g. Dupuy, 1984). However, 'well-being' and 'happiness' have to be seen as the narrower terms that may be important aspects of quality of life, but which are not the only aspects to be considered. The challenge has been to specify the range of health-related and non-health-related aspects of quality of life that should also be included, such that 'quality of life' is not simply another term for 'well-being'.

The original WHO definition of health provides us with an excellent starting point for defining quality of life (WHOQOL Group, 1995), but it leaves open two key questions. First, what other areas should be included in addition to the physical, mental and social? And, second, should the conceptualisation include, for example, objective characteristics of the individual in addition to the individual's subjective evaluation? Other definitions and measures of quality of life take many varied approaches to these two questions. Nevertheless, there may now be an emerging consensus for both of these key issues. In addition to the physical, mental and social aspects, there is now a recognition that spiritual and religious aspects need to be included in health-related quality of life (e.g. Power et al., 1999; see Chapter 6), and a range of aspects of the individual's physical environment needs to be included in non-health-related quality of life.

In relation to the second issue of the objective and the subjective, although many of the earlier measures of quality of life included both objective characteristics (e.g. being able to run for a bus or walk up a flight of stairs) and subjective characteristics (e.g. rating satisfaction/dissatisfaction with level of physical mobility), the more recent measures have focused solely on the subjective (WHOQOL Group, 1998a). It seems to make sense now that subjective and objective indicators should be kept separate. To give an extreme example, how can an individual living in poverty in a village in India report a higher level of happiness and quality of life than a multi-millionaire in Manhattan? This problem has led economists such as the Nobel-prizewinning Amartya Sen (Sen, 2001) to suggest that subjective indicators should be rejected because of their discordance with objective economic indicators. However, as psychologists within the positive psychology movement would agree, the discordance between the objective and the subjective is crucial and often provides a testament to how the human spirit can overcome and even flourish under adversity.

Our starting point, therefore, was to agree a definition of quality of life as follows:

> individuals' perception of their position in life in the context of the culture and value systems in which they live and in relation to their goals, expectations, standards and concerns. It is a broad ranging concept affected in a complex way by the persons' physical health, psychological state, level of independence, social relationships and their relationship to salient features of their environment.
>
> *(WHOQOL Group, 1995, p. 1404)*

A series of focus groups were then carried out in 15 different centres worldwide in order to generate different items and facets for the different domains of health, relationships and personal environment that were included in the definition. A pilot measure was developed after analysis of the focus group material, which was then tested and further refined in a series of field tests (WHOQOL Group, 1998a, 1998b). The resulting domains and facets are shown in Table 1.1 and these have been found in subsequent studies to be the important domains and facets that apply across the adult lifespan in over 40 cultures that have now been tested (e.g. Power, 2003).

One of the opportunities that data collected in this way offered was the possibility of examining the actual structure and content of quality of life. Partly inspired by Maslow's (e.g. 1968) original hierarchy of needs and subsequent work in personality theory, a number of influential approaches have conceptualised

TABLE 1.1 WHOQOL domains and facets

Physical domain	Pain and discomfort
	Energy and fatigue
	Sleep and rest
Psychological domain	Positive feelings
	Thinking, learning, memory and concentration
	Self-esteem
	Bodily image and appearance
	Negative feelings
Level of independence	Mobility
	Activities of daily living
	Dependence on medical substances and treatments
	Work capacity
Social relationships	Personal relationships
	Social support
	Sexual activity
Environment	Physical safety and security
	Home environment
	Financial resources
	Health and social care: accessibility and quality
	Opportunity for new information and skills
	Recreation and leisure activities
	Physical environment (pollution/noise/climate)
	Transport
Spirituality/religion/personal beliefs	

Source: WHOQOL Group, (1998a, 1998b).

quality of life as a hierarchical structure or pyramid with overall well-being at the top, broad domains (such as physical, psychological and social) at the intermediate level, and then specific facets or components of each domain at the bottom (e.g. Spilker, 1990). This overall hierarchical approach was adopted by the WHOQOL Group. As a preliminary test of this predicted hierarchy, a table of facet and domain inter-correlations was produced. The most notable finding was that, whereas the experts had relegated sexual activity to the physical domain (facet-to-corrected-domain $r = 0.16$), the data showed that respondents considered sex to be part of the social relationships domain ($r = 0.41$), to which it was moved. The difference may of course tell us something about experts versus real people! On a variety of psychometric criteria (see WHOQOL Group, 1998a), five of the facets (sensory functions, dependence on non-medicinal substances, communication capacity, work satisfaction, and activities as a provider/supporter) were dropped from the generic measure. (It was noted, however, that some of these might need to be included in subsequent illness-specific or group-specific modules.) With these deletions, there were now 24 specific facets and several items measuring overall quality of life. In deciding on the number of items to choose for each retained facet, the decision was taken to select four items per facet, because four is the minimum number required for the scale reliability analyses that were carried out in subsequent psychometric testing of the instrument. These decisions led to the selection of 25 × 4 = 100 items (including the four general items); thus, the revised field trial WHOQOL became known as the WHOQOL-100.

The hierarchical model of quality of life that we have developed since the early 1990s in the form of the WHOQOL provides a much more complex multidimensional view of Aristotle's eudaimonia than do one-dimensional approaches that simply measure 'well-being' or ephemeral emotion states of 'happiness'. However, one of the important early questions that happiness proponents directed at us was whether or not our complex account of quality of life could, at the end of the day, simply be reduced to happiness and that a Veenhoven-type single-item measure of happiness (such as the 'All things considered, how happy would you say you are these days?' noted earlier) would do just as well as our 100-item WHOQOL. There is the technique of multiple regression that can tackle such a question at least from the statistical point of view. To this day, I can remember sitting in my office at WHO in Geneva in September 1995 when John Orley, the then coordinator of the WHOQOL, asked me to run the analysis based on the data from our first 15 centres to see if there really was more to quality of life than mere 'happiness'. It was with some trepidation that I loaded up the statistics package, SPSS, and carried out the multiple regression analysis.

The outcome of the statistical analysis is summarised in Table 1.2, a revised version of the equation which uses data from our field trial study (WHOQOL Group, 1998a) from 7,701 respondents in 19 different centres worldwide. The basic assumption of the analysis in Table 1.2 was that if 'happiness' (a facet covered in the psychological domain as 'positive feelings') were to explain all of quality of life, then only this facet would be significant when all the remaining 23 WHOQOL-100 facets were subsequently included in the analysis. However, the actual analysis showed that a further 19 of the facets continued to offer a significant contribution (as shown in the column labelled 'Sign.' standing for 'significance level' in Table 1.2) to the statistical account of overall quality of life, even when the positive feelings facet was included first in the multiple regression. That is, all of the different domains, including physical, psychological, relationships, independence, environment and personal beliefs, make a separate but important contribution to our overall assessment of our own quality of life. The statistics provided powerful support for both our own conceptualisation and the information that came back from focus groups worldwide that 'quality of life' is a far broader concept than the notions of happiness or well-being and that it is not reducible to these one-dimensional concepts.

As mentioned above, the concept of quality of life was construed initially as a useful adjunct to traditional concepts of health and functional status. An overall health assessment, therefore, would have included a single measure of the person's physical health, a measure of functioning and a measure of quality of life. Early attempts at assessments that went beyond physical health status sometimes took the form of a rating on a single scale, but, as we have stated, these

TABLE 1.2 Regression equation for happiness and quality of life

Model	Beta	t	Sign.
Positive feelings	.136	12.119	.000
Energy	.157	13.565	.000
Sleep	.034	3.514	.000
Think	.029	2.613	.009
Esteem	.145	12.165	.000
Body image	−.091	−8.708	.000
Neg feel	−.062	−5.978	.000
Mobility	.040	3.838	.000
Daily activities	.039	2.890	.004
Work	.166	15.466	.000
Relationships	.122	9.932	.000
Support	.025	2.533	.011
Sex satisfaction	.055	5.992	.000
Home	.089	8.135	.000
Finances	.070	6.978	.000
Social services	.096	10.346	.000
Leisure	.140	13.024	.000
Environment	.024	2.490	.013
Transport	−.093	−9.036	.000
Meaning	−.038	−4.401	.000

scales unfortunately condensed a complex multidimensional concept into a single dimension. To devise a measure of quality of life that is both reliable and valid, a broad range of potentially independent domains covering all important aspects of quality of life is necessary. Furthermore, to devise a measure that is reliable and valid cross-culturally requires a different approach to instrument development (e.g. Bullinger et al., 1996). Our collection of data from a large number of different cultures has allowed the question to be asked, therefore, of whether or not there is something universal about the aspects of our lives that contribute to our overall sense of well-being and quality of life. Although the term 'quality of life' itself does not translate well into all languages, our analyses across a wide variety of cultures suggest that there are universal aspects of this concept that may well be linked in to other universals in areas such as language, emotion and social relationships (e.g. Power and Dalgleish, 2015). As the saying goes, not only should we add years to life, but we should also add life to years.

Finally, one very straightforward question to ask cross-culturally is whether or not the confusion that occurs in English between 'happiness' – the brief emotion state – versus 'happiness' – the long-term state of satisfaction with life – also occurs in other languages. For example, in German, the word *Gluck* shares the same problem as the English word happiness in that it can refer either to the momentary state or to long-term satisfaction. In Spanish, there is a similar problem with the word *felicidad*, which also refers to both, but which is then distinguished by which verb (*ser* or *estar*) accompanies the noun. In Portuguese, *alegria* is more likely to be used for the momentary state, and *felicidade* for long-term satisfaction, but again it is acceptable to use either word to refer to both. But our favourite is in Russian in which счастье ('little happiness') refers to the momentary state of happiness and счастливый ('big happiness') refers to the permanent state of well-being. It is both reassuring and worrying at the same time, therefore, that languages other than English share some of the confusion between the two types of 'happiness', even if they do not always have a word or phrase for 'quality of life'.

The HAS and the HAS-nots

In order to conclude this chapter and line up some of the key issues for the forthcoming chapters, we can attempt to summarise some of the main points from what we have said so far together with their implications for the understanding of well-being and quality of life. One simple formula for what counts and does not count in life may be to categorise people into the HAS and the HAS-nots:

1. H = Healthy lifestyle
2. A = Adaptability
3. S = Sociability.

The first point is that having a healthy lifestyle in general contributes to well-being and quality of life. We will consider in later chapters how factors such as physical exercise, good diet, good sleep habits, avoidance of smoking and low to moderate alcohol use can all help towards a positive state of physical and mental health. And we emphasise healthy lifestyle as opposed to simply a state of health because the increasing numbers of chronic diseases that occur in our ageing affluent societies mean that many people are living longer but with accompanying chronic conditions such as diabetes, arthritis, high blood pressure and so on. The point is that it is possible to manage these chronic conditions well or badly such that many people with chronic conditions still report good quality of life, as we have found in our international studies of older adults (Power *et al.*, 2005).

The second feature that we have noted is adaptability or flexibility, which refers to the capacity of an individual, a family or a larger group to cope well with significant changes in the conditions of their lives, whether these changes affect just those individuals or the larger group as a whole. The story of how *Homo sapiens* colonised Europe and survived through an ice age is indicative of just how adaptable or flexible our species has proven to be, and we will return to this issue in Chapter 6. However, there is still considerable variation between individuals and groups in how well they adapt. In Chapter 3, when we consider the range of negative emotions, we will be particularly interested in individual differences that people have in dealing with their negative emotions and how problems in emotion and emotion regulation can cause difficulties both physically and psychologically for individuals, and also impact on the quality of relationships, as we will explore in Chapter 2.

The third feature for the HAS is sociability. We do not imply a one-size-fits-all model of sociability, but note that for healthy sociability there are considerable variations. In Chapter 2, we will examine the importance of an intimate confiding relationship for everyone, whether or not that is a heterosexual physical relationship or some other intimate relationship. Equally, good sociability includes a range of other types of relationships that serve different social support functions. Now we are not denying that it may be possible for an ascetic monk to live alone quite contentedly in a cave on a remote island rock such as Skellig Michael, miles off the coast of Kerry in south-west Ireland. In fact, such a monk would be motivated to live such a life because of his relationship to an imaginary being, and, as we will see in Chapter 6 on religion, there can be many benefits from a deep commitment to such belief systems. The problem is how you cope if your god appears to abandon you and does not provide the support that a real person should.

Finally, we know that the world is full of HAS-nots, and maybe even one or two of you have got as far as to start reading this book. Although we have not set out to write a self-help guide on how to be a HAS rather than a HAS-not, and in contrast to the shelf-loads of such books that fill all popular psychology bookshops, there may nevertheless be plenty of suggestions buried beneath all the evidence that we will examine. Undoubtedly, there will be pointers provided on how to avoid the excesses of too much or too little and how, instead, to take the 'good enough' route through life that will maximise your opportunities without being sunk by the chains of perfectionism, nor defeated by the sibyls of unrealistic pessimism. If we convert even one HAS-not into a HAS along the way, there would be much proverbial rejoicing in the positive psychology heaven. However, throughout this book we also want to present the other side of the argument with the case for the HAS-nots. Our species has become the most successful to date because of its diversity and its capacity to be creative. If we all wandered around smiling and making lemonade out of lemons, we would probably still be living in caves and telling ourselves how lucky we were just to be there. Oh what a beautiful cave!

Dissatisfaction with what we have has been a great motivator for invention – for tools that are more powerful and sharper than the previous ones, for modes of transport that are more efficient and faster, for social organisations that freed some people up from subsistence existence to be creators and inventors. Progress in technology and progress in social organisation have resulted from complex and multiple different types of motivation, not simply the pursuit of happiness. We must acknowledge, therefore, that our cultures and societies have benefited as much from the HAS-nots as from the HAS. You need only to read the biographies of the great contributors to science, such as Copernicus, Darwin and Newton to say that by positive psychology standards they might well have been discarded into the bucket of the HAS-nots. This proposal is not to deny that the extremes at the negative end of H, A and S are problematic, but equally problematic are the extremes at the positive end, the people whom the French writer Gustav Flaubert referred to as the 'stupid happy'. The stupid happy score 10 out of 10 on all the authentic happiness scales, but, as we will show in subsequent chapters, they are just as likely to develop illnesses and die younger than the people who score low on these scales. Ultimately, however, our argument is in favour of diversity, for societies in which Prozac does not have to be put into the water for all. There are situations under which it is better to anticipate the worst outcome rather than the best, because terrible things do sometimes happen, when the illusion that we control our universe is readily shattered, as we will show in subsequent chapters.

2

LOVE AND MANIA

Disorders of happiness

> After a lover has really entered into the court of Love he has no will either to
> do anything except what Love's table sets before him. . . . Such a place may be
> compared to the court of hell, for although the door of hell stands open for all
> who wish to enter, there is no way of getting out after you are once in.
>
> *(Andreas Capellanus)*

Introduction

We begin this chapter with a quote from Andreas Capellanus's *The Art of Courtly Love*, first written towards the end of the twelfth century in about 1186 and the book which many would point to as the beginnings of our modern conception of romantic love. If positive psychology and the pursuit of happiness are as good and as simple as some of their proponents would have us believe (reviewed in Chapter 1), then romantic love in all its varieties and all the other extremes of positive emotions and positive personality traits ought to stand at the pinnacle of its claims. Therefore, we will begin in this chapter with an examination of what love really is and compare it to the Hollywood 'happily ever after' idealisation that many would have us believe. Our aim is not to dissect and destroy love like some psychopathic scientist who has never been in love, but rather to point to both the art and the science of love in order to examine its complexity and its wonderfully dangerous seductions. The overall aim of the chapter is to ask the question: Can we have too much positive – is too much positive a bad thing?

Love is famously blind, so we will also spend some time in this chapter examining the evidence for and against this claim, though we will extend the examination of biases caused by emotion states into a more general consideration of the emotions of happiness and how they relate to issues such as the pursuit of wealth and power. First, however, and in the spirit of Andreas Capellanus's love-is-hell proposal, we will consider how love has been presented in the arts, because poets and novelists are often the most insightful psychologists of all.

The art of love

The nature of love is reflected in our common use of expressions such as 'being madly in love', 'to be crazy about someone' or 'to be lovesick'. Love is commonly referred to as an incurable illness. As Tom Scheff (2001) observed in his study of love in popular songs, many songs express the idea of love as a mental impairment with powerful imagery of the craziness or insanity in mental disorders. Indeed, many songs virtually equate love with mental disorder (see Table 2.1 for examples).

This tradition of love sickness has been present at least since the writings of Plato, with subsequent descriptions of characters afflicted with a madness rooted in love abounding in literature and poetry.

> When a lover is at hand the non-lover should be more favoured, because the lover is insane, and the other sane. For if it were a simple fact that insanity is an evil, the saying would be true; but in reality the greatest of blessings come to us through madness, when it is sent as a gift of the Gods.
>
> *(Socrates: Plato, Phaedrus)*

Shakespeare commented frequently on the irrationality of love and its potential to 'make fools of us all', *A Midsummer Night's Dream* being perhaps the most humorous illustration of love's many facets:

> Lovers and madmen have such seething brains,
> such shaping fantasies, that apprehend
> more than cool reason ever comprehends.
>
> (A Midsummer Night's Dream: *Act V, Scene 1*)

TABLE 2.1 Examples of love and disorder in songs

The highs and lows of love's roller coaster	'Helter Skelter', Lennon and McCartney, 1968 'Love Gives Love Takes', The Corrs, 1997
Love as a form of insanity	'Crazy For You', Madonna, 1985 'Crazy', Aerosmith, 1992
Love as an obsession	'Every Breath You Take', The Police, 1983
Physical impairment	'Addicted to Love', Robert Palmer, 1986 'All Shook Up', Elvis Presley, 1957
The despair of unrequited love	'Without You', Nilsson, 1971 'Nothing Compares 2U', Sinead O'Connor, 1990

Adapted from Scheff (2001).

In *As You Like It*, Rosalind makes an extraordinary observation that takes love close to perversity:

> love is merely a madness, and I tell you, deserves as well a dark house and whip as madmen do: and the reason why they are not so punished and cured is, that the lunacy is so ordinary that the whippers are in love too.
>
> (As You Like It: *Act III, Scene 2*)

Even in the great love sonnets, Shakespeare highlights both sides of love:

> For I have sworn thee fair and thought thee bright
> Who art as black as hell as dark as night.
>
> *(Sonnet 147)*

Love's similarity to one particular type of 'madness' – mania – is exemplified in the writings of Robert Louis Stevenson (1876/1988), who wrote:

> it seems as if he had never heard or felt or seen until that moment; and by the report of his memory, he must have lived his past life between sleep and waking . . . a very supreme sense of pleasure in all parts of life, in lying down to sleep, in waking, in motion, in breathing, in continuing to be – the lover begins to regard his happiness as beneficial for the rest of the world and highly meritorious in himself.
>
> *(pp. 8–9)*

The Kama Sutra (Vatsyama, trans. 1962) lists the following degrees of love: (1) love of the eye, (2) attachment of the mind, (3) constant reflection, (4) destruction of sleep, (5) emaciation of the body, (6) turning away from objects of enjoyment, (7) removal of shame, (8) madness, (9) fainting and (10) death. With the exception of the sixth degree, these could be read as a list of some of the features of hypomania.

Parallels between love and madness can also be drawn from the academic literature. Psychoanalytic writings on love frequently refer to love as a form of madness: Ross (1991) in an essay on the psychoanalysis of erotic love refers to falling in love and being in love as 'a sense of abiding danger, pleasure and ecstasy, divine madness'; Freud (1914) wrote that 'love . . . is a sort of sublime madness'; Green (1993) described love as 'a private madness'. Prosen *et al.* (1972) have observed how the so-called 'middle age crisis' in men can trigger the search for an idealised woman, a search which can reach 'hypomanic' intensity based on the hope of finding fusion with the distantly remembered fantasy mother of childhood (which he never finds). Another example comes from a paper on the nature of love, desire and infatuation: 'the paradox of erotic love is that although it always speaks the language of the eternal and the infinite, it is in reality always temporal and limited' (Colman, 1994), an astute observation that many will recognise and agree with when recollecting past infatuations.

So what is love?

It would be unforgiveable, of course, to write a book on happiness without spending some time talking about the most compelling and sought after emotional state of all. An excellent and entertaining review is provided by Frank Tallis in his book *Love Sick: Love as a Mental Illness* (2004). Although we would disagree with Tallis's fundamental thesis that love should be seen as a mental illness, in the same way that we point to people who can experience panic attacks and other passionate states without being ill (Power, 2014), we concur that, at the extremes and under certain circumstances, love sickness can drive a person to despair. We will return to disorders of love later, but first we consider love in all its glorious beauty.

Any trip to the popular psychology shelves of the local bookshop will reveal the central place that love, intimacy and attachment have in our emotional lives. However, along with a host of books on how to fall in love and how to love the same person for the whole of your life, we are also invited to browse books on women who love too much or on pathological love or on erotomania or whatever. Such a cursory content analysis of the bookshelves raises a number of interesting questions: Is there just one type of love? Is the love that we feel when we love someone for the whole of our lives the same as the love we yearn for when we are trying to fall in love? Does the person who is seen as 'loving too much', or who loves 'pathologically' simply choosing the 'wrong' partners or is he somehow in love in the 'wrong' way? We will endeavour to explore some of these mysteries of love and offer some thoughts about how different aspects of love might be conceptualised. Embarking on such an exercise, it is well to bear in mind Valéry's caveat (cited in Rilke, 1986) to aspiring poets: 'that in the making of a work an act comes into contact with the indefinable'.

Several researchers have proposed typologies for the varieties of love. These typologies typically start with the distinct systems based on the sexual drive and on the attachment system and how they might (or might not) be combined into one relationship. The modern Western ideal of romantic love and courtship attempts to fuse these two distinct systems following the rules set out, as noted above, in *The Art of Courtly Love* written in the twelfth century by Andreas Capellanus (1186) with instructions on how knights should behave towards noble ladies (see also Tallis, 2004). Hatfield and Rapson (1993) contend that two kinds of love can be distinguished: passionate love (sometimes called obsessive love, infatuation, love sickness or being in love) and companionate love (sometimes called fondness). Other researchers have been more elaborate; for example, Lee (1976) described six love styles: Eros (romantic love), Ludus (game-playing love), Storge (friendship love), Mania (possessive love), Pragma (logical love) and Agape (selfless love). In tandem with these taxonomies, a number of questionnaire measures of love have been developed; for example, the Passionate Love Scale (Hatfield and Sprecher, 1986) and the Love Style Questionnaire (Mallandain and Davies, 1994).

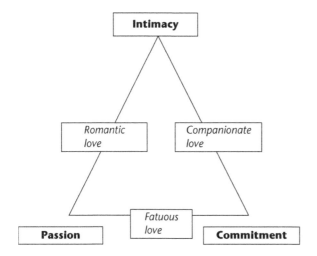

FIGURE 2.1 Sternberg's triangular theory of love.

Source: Sternberg (1986, 1988).

One influential theory of love has been Sternberg's (1986, 1988) so-called triangular theory (Figure 2.1). Sternberg proposed that there are three key dimensions involved in love that include intimacy, passion and commitment. Different combinations of these three dimensions lead to different types of love: for example, romantic love is the combination of intimacy plus passion; companionate love is intimacy plus commitment; and consummate love is intimacy plus passion plus commitment. Again, Sternberg's passion dimension maps onto the sexual drive, and intimacy and commitment map onto the attachment system. In this section, therefore, we shall talk briefly about passionate love, which we equate with Lee's concept of Eros, and which we see as the emotion system's incorporation of the sex drive, and in more detail about companionate love which we equate with Lee's concept of Storge, and which we see as primarily based on the attachment system. Finally, we shall touch on varieties of so-called pathological love, some of which are related to Lee's other love styles.

Passionate love

Hatfield and Rapson (1993) have defined passionate love as follows:

> a state of intense longing for union with another. Reciprocated love (union with the other) is associated with fulfilment and ecstasy. Unrequited love (separation) is associated with emptiness, anxiety, or despair. Passionate love

is a complex functional whole including appraisals or appreciations, subjective feelings, expressions, patterned physiological processes, action tendencies, and instrumental behaviours.

(p. 5)

It is clear from this attempt at a definition that Hatfield and Rapson conceptualise passionate love as consisting of the same types of components that we and others have argued constitute all emotional states: appraisals, subjective feelings, physiological change, action tendencies and interpretations (see Power and Dalgleish, 2008). But what type of emotion is passionate love? The problematic nature of such a question is well illustrated by a cross-cultural study carried out by Shaver *et al.* 1991). They interviewed students in the United States, Italy and China about a variety of emotional experiences, including happiness, love, fear, anger and sadness. There was a considerable degree of cross-cultural agreement concerning all of these emotions except for one – love. The participants from the US and Italy tended to equate love with happiness and other positive emotional states. However, the Chinese students had a far more negative view of love. In Chinese there are few ideographs that correspond to happy love words from Western languages; instead, love is associated with sadness and other negative emotions. The Chinese participants associated passionate love with ideographs that translate as 'infatuation', 'unrequited love', 'nostalgia' and 'sorrow love'. When Shaver and colleagues informed the participants about the views of love in the other cultures, both the Eastern and Western groups regarded each other's visions of love as 'unrealistic'.

Perhaps both cultural groups are correct. Is not passionate love a combination of exhilaration and despair, joy and sadness, with healthy doses of shyness, jealousy, anger, ecstasy and insecurity thrown in? Indeed, Tennov (1979), who interviewed more than 500 lovers, concluded that almost all of them took it for granted that passionate love is a bitter-sweet experience – the biggest and most frightening emotional roller coaster of them all.

An important point that Hatfield and Rapson miss in their attempt at definition is in fact the very passionate nature of passionate love. Like anger (see Power and Dalgleish, 2008), the ability of passionate love to overwhelm individuals provides a vehicle by which the individual can be absolved of the responsibility for their behaviour. Such passions, it is argued (e.g. Tallis, 2004), enable the individual to take on a role in which they can do things that are out of the ordinary. Oatley (1992) cites the example of Anna Karenina who, by falling passionately in love, left her suffocating marriage, was separated from her child, was rejected by her friends and lost all of the support offered by her previous way of living, all of which eventually led to Anna's suicide. In an evolutionary sense, falling passionately in love clearly has functionality. It provides the momentum for binding two people together to form a relationship, to have children and to raise their children together (e.g. Buss, 2001). One can even go further than this: Oatley (1992) suggests that emotions often function when rational solutions are unavailable, the implication being that the only way you could find yourself entering into a mutual plan as momentous as a life-long marriage, is if you are carried there by overwhelming passion.

Companionate love

Companionate love is a far less intense or dramatic emotion than passionate love, though it involves feelings of deep attachment, commitment, sharing and intimacy. As with passionate love, Hatfield and Rapson (1993) have attempted a definition. Companionate love is:

> the affection and tenderness we feel for those with whom our lives are deeply entwined, companionate love is a complex functional whole including appraisals or appreciations, subjective feelings, expressions, patterned physiological processes, action tendencies, and instrumental behaviours.
>
> *(p. 9)*

Again, this definition is perhaps not quite adequate. Many of these definitions of passionate love and companionate love are word for word the same and there is very little explication of how one differs from the other. Is companionate love, in Hatfield and Rapson's eyes, merely passionate love that has lost its intensity? Certainly, companionate love seems more approachable in theoretical terms than its passionate counterpart. It seems that companionate love, can be conceptualised in a similar way to the analysis of happiness presented earlier. The crucial difference is that the goal domains and levels that drive the emotion of happiness are essentially those of the individual, whereas, for the emotion of companionate love, it is necessary to apply a dyadic framework. Companionate love is a function of not only having an investment in one's own goals but also an investment in the goals of our partner in the various domains of self, other, and self plus other. Furthermore, requited companionate love involves the sense that our own goals across various domains are shared by our partner. This sharing of goals leads to the sense of feeling understood and accepted, sharing a sense of union and feeling secure and safe, important characteristics of companionate love.

Perhaps discovering the potential for such sharing of goals across different domains is what is happening in passionate love. One can speculate that passionate love is the enthralling, desperate, exciting whirlwind of emotions that arises from the discovery that here is someone who I can potentially share goals and needs with and who can share his or hers with me. Perhaps, as Oatley suggests, such monumental mutual planning is so daunting a prospect that we need something like passionate love to blind us to all the possible pitfalls!

A note on love, sex and death

The traditional Christian location of the 'sin of sex' in women, who are viewed as constantly trying to lead astray those otherwise innocent spiritual men, would lead one to predict that most sex crimes should be committed by women (Power, 2012).

But what does the evidence on crime show us? Just to set the context, recent figures from the US Federal Bureau of Investigation (see www.fbi.gov/ucr/cius2009) show that of 15,760 murders committed in the US in 2009, in only 7.6 per cent of cases was the murderer female. If we look specifically at murder in marital partners, 141 husbands were murdered by wives, but 609 wives were murdered by husbands (a ratio of 4.3 to 1 for male to female murderers). Similarly, 138 boyfriends were murdered by girlfriends, but 472 girlfriends were murdered by boyfriends (a ratio of 3.4 to 1 male to female murderers). Crimes of violence in intimate partners were 82,360 incidents for male victims, but 564,430 incidents for female victims (a ratio of 6.9 to 1 for male to female perpetrators of violence), and in the case of sexual assault and rape there were 55,110 female victims but no male victims. These figures are just the tip of the iceberg about so-called love relationships, which have to come with a serious health warning, especially for women.

If we ask specifically about the crime of incest, the situation is equally horrific. A variety of factors mean that incest figures are notoriously unreliable and likely to be considerable underestimates of the true figures. Nevertheless, a national study in Canada was published by Statistics Canada in 2001 called *Family Violence in Canada: A Statistical Profile* (see www.statcan.gc.ca). Figures for children aged 0–15 years showed that 69 per cent of the victims of sexual abuse were girls and 31 per cent were boys. The perpetrators of sexual abuse were in 3 per cent of cases the biological mother, 2 per cent a stepmother, 8 per cent the biological father and 8 per cent a stepfather. In 44 per cent of cases the perpetrator was an older male sibling, uncle, grandfather or other relative.

Overall, what these figures for murder, violence, sexual assault and incest show dramatically is that men are many times more likely to be the perpetrators of such crimes, whereas women are many times more likely to be the victims of these crimes, and, moreover, that these men are likely to be in a 'loving relationship' with the girls and women that they kill, batter or abuse. Any patriarchal religion such as Christianity that attempts to locate sexual sin in women has got it completely the wrong way round, as we have argued elsewhere (Power, 2012). The majority of crimes, especially those of a sexual nature, are carried out by men, not by women, and are carried out against the women they supposedly love.

Disorders of love and happiness

Theoretical writings on the nature of love, particularly passionate or erotic love, bear a remarkable similarity to the nature of mania, in so much as one could often substitute the word 'love' for 'mania' and the observations made about either state would often remain within context. In order to test this possible link between love and mania empirically, one of my doctoral students, Eleanor Sutton, interviewed a group of healthy participants about a recent experience of infatuation, and compared them to a group of recovered bipolar disorder patients who were interviewed about a recent manic episode but using the same structured interview that has been designed to assess manic episodes (Cavanagh *et al.*, 2009). Although the bipolar patients tended to score higher across most of the items, there was a high correlation (Spearman rho = 0.72) between the rank order of the items for the manic episode and the love episode, especially when items such as increases in anxiety, sleep disturbance and feelings of pressure that reflected a 'mixed state' rather than simply a 'hyper-positive state' were included. The pattern of similarity between the 'symptoms' of love and the symptoms of mania can be seen very clearly in Figure 2.2, in which 'symptoms' such as elated mood and sexuality are in fact just as high in the infatuated state as they are in mania. The overlap is so considerable that it does lead one to speculate that mania might be a state of disordered attachment, but that is another story for another time and place (see Power and Dalgleish, 2015).

The concept of happiness 'disorder' is rarely discussed in the emotion literature and almost never in the literature on positive psychology. Perhaps this bias arises because, in Western society, we are more tolerant of variations and extremes within the parameters, both cognitive and physiological, that define a particular individual's positive emotions and are thus less likely to 'label' the emotion as disordered in comparison to the case of extreme variants of negative emotions such as anger, fear or sadness (see Chapter 3). In certain other, mainly non-Western cultures, happiness or joy are sometimes regarded as far less socially acceptable than in the West. For example, the Ifaluk, a group who inhabit a small island in the South Pacific, equate happiness with a tendency for the individual to disregard others and the needs of the social

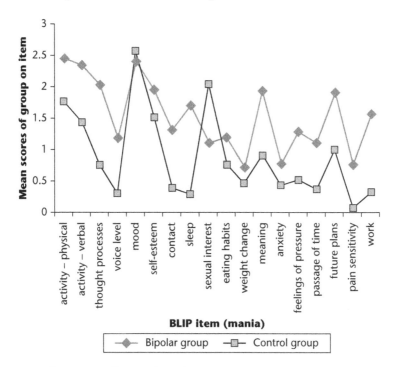

FIGURE 2.2 Symptoms of love and mania.

group (see Lutz, 1988). For the Ifaluk, then, happiness is a negative emotion which is socialised out of children from about the age of 5 onwards, whereas emotions such as sadness are encouraged as positive emotional states because of their functions in social relationships. The same approach to the sins of pride and happiness can be observed in some extreme forms of Scottish Calvinism, where even the pleasure of hanging your washing out to dry on a Sunday is banned, as I discovered to my cost whilst on holiday on the Scottish Hebridean Island of Harris. Despite the paucity of discussion in the literature on abnormal happiness, we propose that extreme variations in the cognitive or physiological parameters that contribute to the emotion of happiness may be usefully conceptualised as types of 'happiness disorder'. It is these varieties of happiness disorder that we discuss in the present section, and, again, the aim is to provide some pointers rather than any comprehensive analysis.

Hypomania and mania

The disorders that seem most clearly to be disorders of happiness or positive mood are hypomania and mania, as we noted earlier. The central features in these disorders are elevation of mood, hyperactivity and grandiose ideas about the self (e.g. Jauhar and Cavanagh, 2013). Manic individuals often seem cheerful and optimistic when their mood is elevated and have an infectious gaiety. However, other manic individuals can be irritable rather than euphoric and their emotions are extremely labile, so that the simmering irritability can easily translate into anger. There is often diurnal variation in the individual's mood, whether it is of an irritable or euphoric variety. However, this variation does not normally conform to the regular patterns of other depressive disorders (see Power and Dalgleish, 2015). Even in patients who are elated, it is not unusual for their periods of elevated mood to be interrupted by brief episodes of depression and, in fact, these 'mixed state' presentations in mania, in which there may be a range of emotions present, seem to be much more typical than previously considered in the literature on mania (Cassidy and Carroll, 2001; Cavanagh et al., 2009).

The manic individual's choice of clothing can often reflect the prevailing mood – there is an emphasis on bright colours and ill-matching garments. In more severe cases of mania, individuals often appear untidy and dishevelled. Manic persons are highly active, often leading to physical exhaustion. Furthermore, many activities are started but seldom finished as new activities become more tempting; speech is often rapid and copious and, in more severe cases, there is a marked flight of ideas such that it is difficult to follow the train of thought of the manic person's discourse. Sleep is often impoverished or even absent, appetite may be increased, as are sexual desires such that sexual behaviour may become uninhibited. The manic individual may also attempt to lengthen the high and reduce any negative features through the use of alcohol and other drugs, which, over time, may lead to substance disorders in addition to mania itself.

Finally, manic individuals commonly experience expansive ideas. They can believe that their thoughts and ideas are original, their opinions important and their work of the most outstanding quality. Occasionally, these expansive themes merge into grandiose delusions in which the individual believes that he or she is a religious prophet or a famous person. Such grandiosity and expansiveness also manifest in extravagant behaviour; manic individuals often spend more money than they can afford, and they can make reckless decisions, give up good jobs or embark on schemes and ventures that have little chance of success. Such problems are compounded by impaired insight in many cases. Manic individuals will often see no reason why their grandiose plans should be reined in or their extravagant expenditure curtailed. Manic individuals rarely think of themselves as having an emotional problem or needing any kind of help.

In mania and hypomania, it appears that the individuals' dominant schematic models of self are highly self-serving, leading to the setting of unrealistic and overly optimistic goals. The achievement of these goals, or the belief that they have been achieved, is a source of joy and elation, though, as June Gruber (2011) has noted, there are many situations in which bipolar disorder individuals seem to experience too much positive emotion which persists for too long. There seems to be little or no access to the representations of the goals of others and, most notably, the shared goals of self and others – the social standards that are so important for setting limits on behaviour and that become incorporated into emotion-regulation strategies (see Chapter 3 for a more detailed exploration of emotion regulation). I recall, as a young clinical psychologist, sitting in a ward round in the Bethlem Hospital in South London when the manic patient who we were discussing strode into the room, walked straight over to the professor of psychiatry who was running the ward round, sat on his lap and proceeded to be extremely flirtatious with him. Needless to say, it livened up an otherwise dull Monday morning. On another occasion, one of the male manic patients on the ward decided that the fire safety procedures clearly were not up to standard, so he went out and bought a second-hand fire engine together with a fireman's uniform for himself and then drove the fire engine to the hospital and parked it outside the ward, just in case.

However, allied with these Spike Milligan-like comic interludes (Spike as well as being a famous comedian suffered from manic depression, or bipolar disorder as it is now called) is the manic person's tendency to switch from periods of extreme gaiety to periods of intense anger or depression. It seems that different configurations of self-related schematic models come to dominate and regulate the system, such that at one moment everything is all rosy and the next it is all black. The tendency for mania and hypomania to co-occur with depression provides a difficult challenge that no biological or psychological theory has yet effectively accounted for. One might speculate that, first, if the self becomes predominantly organised around issues of success versus failure, appraisals of goal attainment versus goal failure for a highly invested domain are very likely to occur at different points (e.g. Johnson, 2005), so the person may swing between the emotions of joy, sadness and self-disgust accordingly. Second, one of the findings that distinguishes bipolar disorders from other disorders of depression is the substantial genetic component in the bipolar disorders (Macritchie and Blackwood, 2013); perhaps this genetic component influences the development of the basic emotions early on, so that they are more likely to be unintegrated with each other. This proposal would suggest that this would be true not only for the basic emotions of sadness and happiness, but for the other basic emotions as well.

SPAARS and bipolar disorders

A specific application of the SPAARS (Schematic, Propositional, Analogical and Associative Representational Systems) model developed by Tim Dalgleish and myself (Power and Dalgleish, 1997) to bipolar disorders was proposed by Jones (2001) and further extended by Power (2005). Jones proposed that the starting point in bipolar disorders is often at the analogical level, for example through a disruption to normal circadian rhythms, through increased energy, through the experience of a positive event and so on. Positive schematic models of such changes can lead to positive feedback loops which further increase the level of disruption, and also lead to a range of automatic appraisal biases at the automatic level. Power (2005) has further proposed that positive feedback loops can also occur through the coupling of emotions such as happiness and anger, and that the organisation of the components of the self-concept into extremes of positive versus negative valence further adds to the exacerbation and maintenance of the manic state, at times when a normal individual would downregulate (Power et al., 2002).

It is a testament to the power of passionate love that, when it goes unrequited, the rejected individual can be driven to suicide and more. This is one way in which love can go off the rails; we can fall in love with people who may be inappropriate in that either they are unlikely to return our love or that somehow they would not make good companions in a relationship. Such unrequited love is, in fact, at the core of the mediaeval origins of romantic love (e.g. Tallis, 2004). It seems possible, then, for love to be 'disordered' with respect to who we love. However, it is not just who we love but the way we love that is fraught with danger, for are not the 'women who love too much' of bookshelf fame also viewed as exhibiting 'disordered love'?

Both of these aspects of love, it has been argued, can be understood more clearly in terms of attachment theory (e.g. Bowlby, 1969, 1973, 1980). Bowlby proposed three styles of attachment in infancy: avoidant, secure and anxious/ambivalent, though a fourth style of disordered attachment has been added subsequently (Main and Solomon, 1986). Hazan and Shaver (1987) have proposed that these infant attachment styles manifest themselves in adulthood in the way that the adult attaches in the loving relationship. They proposed that children with secure infant attachments, who are allowed to be both affectionate towards, and independent of, their mothers, are likely to mature into secure adults who are able to engage in comfortable intimate relationships with trust and a healthy level of dependence on their partners. Children with anxious/ambivalent attachment relationships to their mothers have learned to be clinging and dependent or fearful of being smothered, or both. Such children, Hazan and Shaver suggest, are likely to become anxious/ambivalent adults. They will fall in love easily; they will seek extremely high levels of closeness and intimacy, and they will be terrified that they will be abandoned. The love affairs they have are, thus, likely to be very short-lived. Finally, the avoidant child who has been abandoned early on in infancy is likely, it is suggested, to become an avoidant adult. He or she will feel uncomfortable about getting too close, will have a fear of intimacy and will have difficulty depending on others. Shaver and Hazan (1988) have amassed considerable support in favour of this formulation and similar formulations have been proposed by other authors (e.g. Bartholomew, 1990).

The idea that our 'choice' of lover is also somehow a function of our attachment processes is clearly not a new one. It is a fundamental concept in psychodynamic psychology. For many people, this choice is likely to be a functional one. The potential lover often has qualities that would also make them a good partner in a loving relationship over the long term. However, for other individuals, the people who rouse their passions are exactly the sort of people whom their rational thoughts tell them should be avoided. Furthermore, as we have mentioned above, for the majority of individuals the choice of lover is partly a function of the likelihood that the chosen person will reciprocate our feelings. However, for others, there is often a pattern of falling in love with people with whom the chances of a reciprocated loving relationship are small or even non-existent. This problem is manifest, in its most extreme form, in the disorder of erotomania or De Clerambault's syndrome, in which individuals fall in love with public figures or famous personages whom they are unlikely even to meet (see Franzini and Grossberg, 1995). The sobering example of this disorder is the case of John Hinckley, who attempted to assassinate Ronald Reagan in 1981 as a last ditch attempt to impress the actress Jodie Foster with whom he reported being desperately in love.

Biases of happiness

There is a growing body of research into biases associated with the emotion states, particularly when the material to be processed is affectively valenced in one way or another. The line we have taken towards this evidence (Power and Dalgleish, 2008) is that processing biases are not exclusively the preserve of mood-disordered individuals, but rather occur as ways of selecting and ordering personally relevant information for all of us. This suggests that none of us are inherently free of bias (cf. Kahneman, 2011). However, we have further suggested that different emotional states may be associated with different profiles of processing biases across a range of tasks. For example, anxiety seems to be associated with attentional biases in which threatening material is more likely to be detected, whereas sad mood can lead to biases of memory in which we are more likely to recall negative or upsetting events from our past (see Chapter 3). These particular profiles of processing bias for different emotions are a consequence of being in that particular emotion state; that is, they are a function of the reconfiguration of the entire psychological system once a particular emotion state becomes predominant, something that we have referred to as the current dominant schematic model in terms of the SPAARS approach that we have developed (Power and Dalgleish, 1997, 2015).

The majority of research with sad and anxious moods has focused on fundamental cognitive processes such as memory, attention and perception. In contrast to this, much of the research on cognitive processing and positive affect has looked at higher order processes such as decision-making, creativity and judgement. We have reviewed the literature on mood biases and memory and attention elsewhere (Power and Dalgleish, 2015), so here we will concentrate on the effects of positive mood on higher order processes, though we note with interest the research based on Fredrickson's broaden-and-build (Fredrickson, 2005; Fredrickson and Branigan, 2005) approach, which gives preliminary support for a broadening of attention effect during positive mood (but see Chapter 6 for a detailed critique of recent problems with Fredrickson's theory, which also includes a summary of work on positive psychology interventions). We will first consider some of the factors that interact with positive mood to influence an individual's performance on such higher order tasks, and will then look at some examples of research which have used such tasks to examine the role of positive affect in information processing. We will necessarily be selective in this process, so the reader is referred to excellent detailed reviews by Alice Isen (e.g. 1999, 2008) for a more comprehensive discussion of these issues.

There are four factors that are important to consider in any analysis of the effects of positive mood on processing tasks. These factors are (1) a basic memory bias for positive material; (2) the interest level and importance of the task at hand; (3) the tendency of the psychological system to maintain positive affect (see above) and (4) the association between the use of heuristics and stereotypes in processing and the existence of positive affect.

A number of studies have indicated that the presence of positive feelings is likely to cue positive items in memory, thus making access to such material easier (e.g. Isen et al., 1978; MacLeod et al., 1994). For example, MacLeod et al. (1994) asked subjects to provide self-ratings of positive and negative affect terms and to retrieve personal memories associated with those terms. Self-rated positive affect was associated with the latency to retrieve positive affect memories but not negative affect memories. Similarly, self-rated negative affect was associated with the latency to retrieve negative but not positive affect-related memories. This dissociation of the effects of positive and negative affect on memory has been a ubiquitous finding. Furthermore, a number of studies have also noted an asymmetry between the two types of emotional state; that is, although positive affect is an effective retrieval cue for positive material in memory, negative affect is not always found to be an effective cue for negative material (see the review of depressive realism research in Chapter 3). A study by Storbeck and Clore (2005) used the Deese–Roediger–McDermott paradigm in which the subject is given a list of words (e.g. bed, pillow, rest, awake, dream) that share a non-presented 'critical lure' (i.e. ' sleep' in this example). The findings showed that induced positive mood increased the likelihood that critical lures would be recalled in comparison to negative mood induction. The researchers interpret the findings as further evidence for an increase in connections and global processing with positive affect, though such processes can lead to increased errors under certain conditions. The important point is that in such studies positive mood states are more likely to lead to memory biases and may therefore be less realistic and less accurate in their impact on memory.

The memory bias effect is clearly likely to be an important factor when trying to understand any research involving the effect of positive mood on higher order processes such as thinking and reasoning, especially when these tasks involve valenced material. A related factor to this, according to Isen (1999, 2008), is that because positive material is more extensive and diverse than other material in memory in healthy subjects, the cognitive context is more complex when a person is feeling happy because a broader range of ideas is cued. This proposal is also central to the broaden-and-build approach (Fredrickson, 1998, 2005; see Chapter 6). Consequently, positive affect may influence the context within which any information-processing task is carried out and there is clear evidence that such context also influences thinking and decision-making (Kahneman, 2011).

The second factor that is important when considering the influence of positive affect on information processing is that the precise effect that positive feelings have seems to be a function of how interesting or important the task is to the individual. Individuals in whom positive affect has been induced show a number of information-processing differences in comparison to controls, but usually only on tasks or with material that is relatively interesting or important to them (e.g. Isen et al., 1991).

The third factor, and one that we have discussed above in the section on the relationship between schematic models and goals, is the configuration of the emotion system which attempts to maintain positive affect in healthy individuals. Consequently, individuals who are experiencing positive affect may avoid difficult or unpleasant tasks or materials, and may opt to work with more pleasant items instead (e.g. Isen and Reeve, 1992), though Isen and Reeve (2005) found that positive affect individuals could better distribute their time between enjoyable and less enjoyable work tasks. As Anthony Storr (1979) noted, the best therapists may be those with a tendency towards depression, because they are more tolerant of and better able to work with the distressing and difficult material that their clients present them with. Jolly happy 'have a nice day' therapists might not actually survive very long under the weight of the world's suffering, but might be better off writing self-help books on pop psychology instead!

The final factor to consider when analysing the effects of positive affect on cognitive processes is the increasing body of evidence that individuals experiencing positive affect are more likely to recruit heuristics or stereotypes when faced with task demands, as opposed to systematically processing the various options available. For example, Bodenhausen et al. (1994) report four experiments that examined the effects of happiness on the tendency to use stereotypes in social judgement. In each experiment, the participants in the induced happy mood rendered more stereotypical judgements than those participants who were in a neutral mood. However, when the participants were told that they would be held accountable for their judgements, the stereotypic thinking bias disappeared. This finding that, although there is some evidence for the use of stereotypes and heuristics in individuals with positive affect, they can nevertheless still engage in more systematic processing of the material when required, has been repeated in a number of other studies (see Isen, 2008, for a review).

Having considered a number of important factors that bear on an understanding of the influence of positive affect or happiness on processing tasks, it is useful to look at one or two examples of experiments from the literature that implicate these factors in various ways. Isen *et al.* (1992) carried out a series of studies to examine the influence of positive affect on categorisation. The participants were requested to rate the degree to which atypical examples of positive or negative categories of people (e.g. 'bartender' as a member of the category 'nurturant people') fit as members of that category. Positive affect participants rated atypical members of positive categories as fitting better in the category than controls rated them; however, this effect was not present for the negative person categories (e.g. 'genius' as a member of a negative category 'unstable people'). Isen's explanation of these findings indicates the ways in which the various factors we have discussed above might interact. She argued that:

> although an underlying process (increased elaboration) is postulated to occur, this process is expected to be different for different kinds of material in the situation described. Since positive affect cues positive material, the elaborative process would be expected to occur with positive material (for all subjects) or for positive-affect subjects working with neutral material.
>
> *(Isen, 1993, p. 265)*

Furthermore, as suggested above, the positive affect participants may make a choice not to deal with and to avoid the negative material.

Finally, a number of studies have investigated the influence of positive affect on complex decision-making. Briefly, the studies suggest that individuals who are experiencing positive affect are both more efficient in decision-making, but at the same time are also able to be more thorough if the task demands require such increased effort. For example, Isen *et al.* (1991) asked medical students to choose the patient most likely to have a diagnosis of lung cancer from six descriptions of patients varying with respect to each of nine health-relevant labels (e.g. cough, chest X-ray, and so on). The participants were assigned to one of two groups – a positive affect group or a control group. Both groups performed similarly with respect to their ability to make the correct choice of patient. However, the positive affect subjects made the choice significantly earlier in their protocols. In addition, the positive affect subjects went on to do much more with the materials they were presented with; they proposed working diagnoses for the other (control) patients in the study and started to make suggestions concerning treatment plans.

In summary, therefore, we are not denying that there can be clear benefits of positive mood, as these types of studies show and as emphasised in Fredrickson's (e.g. 2005) broaden-and-build approach. What we are arguing against is any naive assumption that positivity is all good, when in fact there is a tendency for positive mood states to lead to characteristic biases in psychological processes such as memory, thinking and reasoning, and that under certain circumstances such biases may be dangerous and even life-threatening, a theme that we will return to constantly throughout this book. As Gruber *et al.* (2011) have elegantly summarised, too much happiness can be bad, especially in the wrong contexts, if it is pursued incorrectly, and it is socially or culturally inappropriate. In Chapters 6 and 7 we will point to the importance of psychological flexibility, which can sometimes look positive but at other times looks negative, as being of most benefit, a capacity that positive psychologists such as Sonja Lyubomirsky (see *The Myths of Happiness* published in 2013) and others have also come to recognise.

The repressive coping style

Another topic that deserves inclusion in any chapter on disorders of happiness concerns individuals who maintain their self-esteem or happiness by denying the existence of negative material in their lives. Although usual analyses of this so-called 'repressive coping style' (e.g. Derakshan *et al.*, 2007) conceptualise it as the avoidance of anxiety, it is equally feasible to consider the motivation to be the maintenance of a state of positive affect though at a price; thus, it is an as yet unanswered empirical question as to whether repressive coping only relates to anxiety avoidance or whether other aversive emotions such as anger and disgust are also avoided.

The term *verdrängt* (repressed) is forever associated with the work of Freud and was first employed by him in *Studies on Hysteria* (Breuer and Freud, 1895). From that point on, Freud's use of the term repression was varied and sometimes contradictory (Power and Brewin, 1991). The consensus of opinion is that Freud's conceptualisation of repression varied throughout his writings from a narrow view of a single defence mechanism to a broader definition of many types of defence mechanism. As Singer and Sincoff (1990) in their own chapter in the edited book *Repression and Dissociation: Implications for Personality Theory, Psychopathology and Health* have stated:

> Freud began by describing repression as motivated forgetting, as an intentional failure to access information stored in memory. As his theory of the defences developed, the concept of repression absorbed these developments and began to represent defence mechanisms in general rather than forgetting in particular. . . . Repression eventually came to denote the systematic avoidance, through any variety of mechanisms, of potentially threatening material in thought or social experience.

(p. 474)

This confusion as to the exact meaning of the term repression in Freud's writings is compounded by Freud's refusal to be explicit about whether repression is an unconscious or a conscious psychological process. Indeed, Freud used terms such as suppression (a conscious process) and repression (either a conscious or an unconscious process) interchangeably throughout his career (see Erdelyi, 2006). Despite these sources of confusion, it is clear that by using the term repression Freud was broadly referring to psychological processes involved in keeping disturbing material at a distance from consciousness; for example:

> the motive and purpose of repression was nothing else than the avoidance of unpleasure. . . . If a repression does not succeed in preventing feelings of unpleasure or anxiety from arising, we may say that it has failed.
>
> *(Freud, 1915, p. 153)*

More recently, there have been numerous attempts to operationalise the concept of repression and to treat it as an individual difference variable. Furthermore, a number of self-report and questionnaire measures have been developed to measure an individual's tendency to employ a so-called repressive coping style. The basic premise behind most of these scales (e.g. the Byrne Repression–Sensitization Scale, Byrne, 1964; Weinberger Adjustment Inventory [WAI], Weinberger *et al.*, 1979) has been to conceptualise individuals as high in repressive coping style if they show elevated scores on a measure of social desirability and low scores on a measure of anxiety. There is considerable debate in the literature about the relative merits and intercorrelations of the different scales. For example, Weinberger *et al.* (1979) argued that the Byrne Repression–Sensitization Scale does not discriminate between truly low anxious individuals and repressors. However, Turvey and Salovey (1994) compared six common measures of repression and found that all of them were highly inter-correlated and, furthermore, all loaded on a single factor. This psychometric literature is reviewed in detail by Myers (2000).

This definition of repression as a function of the pattern of scores obtained from self-report measures of anxiety and defensiveness (social desirability) suggests that, for some individuals at least, a sense of happiness and high self-esteem may be maintained through the denial and defence of distressing information, as we commented in Chapter 1 in relation to Jean Twenge's (2006) findings in the US. Furthermore, it suggests that these individuals are likely to differ in a number of ways from individuals who are happy without seeking to deny the existence of distressing information. In this section we will review selectively some of the research that has looked at the type of information that repressors might deny, the type of emotions that repressors report experiencing, the information-processing research using repressors and controls, and finally we will attempt to conceptualise the concept of repression within ours SPAARS framework.

Weinberger *et al.* (1979) have suggested a fourfold classification of individuals with respect to their scores on measures of anxiety and defensiveness: namely, low anxious (low anxiety – low defensiveness); repressor (low anxiety – high defensiveness); high anxious (high anxiety – low defensiveness) and defensive high anxious (high anxiety – high defensiveness). Initial attempts at a validation of this system have indicated that repressors report the lowest level of subjective distress, even though a variety of physiological measures (e.g. heart rate, spontaneous skin resistance, forehead muscle tension) and behavioural measures (e.g. reaction times, content avoidance, verbal interference) reveal that they are more stressed than the low anxious groups. Weinberger *et al.* concluded that repressors employ a coping style that involves:

> an avoidance of disturbing cognitions . . . supported by . . . denial of cog-
> nitive (relative to somatic) anxiety and . . . decreased trait anxiety following
> a stressful experiment . . . [the] repressors claim of having less trait anxiety
> than the lowest group is contradicted by three measures of their behaviour
> for three of their physiology.
>
> *(p. 378)*

These findings have been replicated in a number of studies, including those by Derakshan and Eysenck (2001) and Gudjonsson (1981).

Numerous additional research findings (e.g. Davis, 1987) have indicated that repressors do not differ from non-repressors in terms of the self-reported intensity of emotional experience for primary, dominant emotions in response to memories or events. However, significant group differences are found for non-dominant or secondary emotions to such events or memories. For example, Weinberger and Schwartz (reported in Schwartz, 1982) asked groups of repressors and non-repressors to rate the levels of emotional intensity to hypothetical scenarios, such as discovering that their car had been broken into. Repressors reported similar levels of intensity for anger (the primary, dominant emotion) when compared to the low anxious subjects; however, with respect to secondary emotions such as depression, the repressors reported experiencing less intense affect than did the low anxious controls. Similar results have been found by Hansen (e.g. Hansen *et al.*, 1992). Furthermore, Sincoff (1992), using groups of school children and undergraduates, showed that repressors at all educational grades reported lower levels of mixed feelings and significantly greater certainty about their feelings than did control groups.

As we have discussed above, in definitional terms, repressors do not differ from low anxious subjects on scores for anxiety measures (e.g. the Spielberger State Trait Anxiety Inventory; Spielberger *et al.*, 1970). This has clear implications for the research on information-processing biases and anxiety in that the groups of supposed low anxious subjects in many research studies, because they are selected on the basis of self-report questionnaire measures, are likely to include individuals who are not genuinely low anxious at all but who are in fact so-called repressors. These implications are few if there are no information-processing or cognitive-processing differences between repressors and genuine low anxious individuals. However, a number of experimental investigations have shown that this is not the case. Research in this area was pioneered by Penny Davis and her colleagues (e.g. Davis and Schwartz, 1987; Davis, 1987, 1990; Davis *et al.*, 1988). In the first of these studies (Davis and Schwartz, 1987), the participants were asked to free-recall personal experiences from childhood. Repressors recalled fewer negative memories than non-repressor controls. Furthermore, the age of the subject at the time of the first negative memory recalled was substantially greater in the repressor group. Similar findings in studies in which response bias has been ruled out in various ways have been reported by Davis (1987), Davis *et al.* (1988) and by Myers (Myers, Brewin and Power, 1992; Myers and Brewin, 1994; Myers and Derakshan, 2004).

As with all autobiographical memory tasks, the question arises as to whether the repressors actually experienced fewer negative events in childhood or are merely failing to recall those negative memories. Myers examined this question by using semi-structured interviews with groups of repressors and controls in which the participants were asked detailed questions about their childhood (Myers *et al.*, 1992; Myers, 1993; Myers and Brewin, 1994). She found that repressors' accounts of their childhood were more likely to be characterised by paternal antipathy and indifference and that the repressors were less likely to record an emotionally or physically close relationship with their fathers. It seems, then, that repressors do have negative events in their autobiographical past, but that access to those events is difficult in simple recall scenarios. Myers has further demonstrated a possible mechanism for this effect through the use of the Directed Forgetting Task, in which participants are instructed to forget a set of words but which they are subsequently later asked to recall (Myers *et al.*, 1998). This task showed greater inhibition of to-be-forgotten negative trait adjectives than positive adjectives in the repressor group, thereby demonstrating a retrieval inhibition effect for negative self-related material in repressors.

In addition to research that has investigated mnemonic biases in repressors, there are a number of studies that have looked at attentional processes. For example, Fox (1993) used the attentional deployment paradigm of MacLeod *et al.* (1986) to investigate the allocation of attention in groups of repressors and controls. Fox's results showed that high anxious subjects seem to shift their attention towards socially threatening words, whereas repressors shift their attention away from such words and the low anxious subjects showed no consistent biases. Similar findings were reported by Derakshan and Eysenck (2001). Consistent results have also been obtained using a dichotic listening task (Bonnano *et al.*, 1991), the modified Stroop task (Dawkins and Furnham, 1989) and a negative priming task (Fox, 1994). Taken together, these studies suggest that repressors are able to orientate their attention away from unwanted material and, furthermore, that there is an automatic attentional bias that serves to screen out socially threatening material.

We have gone into some detail about this research on repressors in order to make an important point. As Twenge (2006) found in her review of longitudinal studies in the US, there are an increasing number of individuals who report themselves to be 'happy', who report that they are well satisfied with their lives and that their childhoods were wonderful. However, these individuals also display a variety of other problems and issues that simply do not add up. Even though these individuals score maximum on an item such as Ruut Veenhoven's 'How happy are you these days?' (see Chapter 1), when you probe just below the surface, which the range of experimental and other tasks that we have highlighted in this chapter allows psychologists to do, you find a level of problems and misery that may be actually damaging to health. For example, repressors are more likely to suffer from a range of psychosomatic disorders such as circulatory disorders and cancer because of the inhibited but heightened levels of physiological arousal that they demonstrate (see Chapter 6). The psychological and social pressures that some people experience and cope with in this repressive style are sufficient in themselves to lead one to be concerned about the pressures to be positive in the groups followed by Twenge. When combined with the other disorders of happiness, such as hypomania and mania that we discussed earlier in the chapter, the pursuit of happiness really can become a very dangerous obsession. However, in case you thought you could escape the health warnings, in our final section in this chapter we will consider some of the everyday excesses that people resort to in their pursuit of happiness, whether these are excesses of money, of greed, of power or of drug-induced ecstasy. All of these excesses surround us, and all of them are fraught with danger.

Happiness and excess

The pursuit of happiness is fraught with danger, a message that is worth repeating. Many people, for a variety of reasons, come to equate long-term happiness with a narrowly defined goal such as being wealthy or being famous, or with more mundane versions of greed such as excessive overeating, smoking, gambling, sex or drug and alcohol use. These excesses reflect the simplistic approaches that many people take in their illusory constructions of what would make them happy, especially when the actual data are considered that put people's naive theories to the test.

Let us begin with one of the most tragic excesses, that of dependence on drugs and alcohol, when the dependence leads to a lifestyle that is constructed around obtaining the next 'high'. The drug high is a temporary state that lies somewhere in the range between peaceful calm and ecstasy, depending on the particular individual, the drug and the circumstances in which the drug is taken. Drug users go to extremes to maintain or continue these 'highs' to the extent that, given the choice, and like the rats in the classic Olds and Milner (1954) studies mentioned in Chapter 1, even the risk of physical impairment and death may not be sufficient to prevent them from continuing to induce them. For example, an internet survey carried out by Looby and Earleywine (2007) identified a group of 610 respondents out of a sample of over 6,600 who had used methamphetamine in the past year. Figures show that the amphetamines are the most widely used illicit drugs worldwide, besides cannabis, and that users typically state that feelings of euphoria, increased confidence and self-esteem are the main reasons for use of the drugs. In their survey, Looby and Earleywine measured levels of depression, satisfaction with life and a short, 4-item measure of happiness (from Lyubomirsky and Lepper, 1999). They found that the methamphetamine users reported significantly higher levels of depression, higher levels of apathy, lower levels of happiness, lower levels of satisfaction with life and lower overall subjective well-being in comparison to the drug non-users. This study, and many others like it, highlights how the pursuit of drug-induced happiness and drug highs actually lead to the opposite consequences in the longer term, that is, more misery and reduced longevity.

A similar story can be told with any of the other excesses noted above. Gambling, like drug addiction, can be pursued to excess, in which the aims are the excitement and highs from risk and unpredictability combined with the hope for easy wealth and riches. With an estimated US$335 billion spent worldwide on legal gambling alone and a rapid increase in online gambling, it is no surprise that recent years have seen an increase in the number of problem or pathological gamblers. Research on these problem or pathological gamblers shows that they typically have poor impulse control and an inability to delay gratification in preference for immediate gratification (e.g. Michalczuk *et al.*, 2011), but that both positive and negative emotion states can significantly enhance the impulsivity control problems, such as the illusory belief 'I'm feeling good, so I know I'm going to win' (Power and Wykes, 1996).

The recent 'casino banking'-driven financial crisis has highlighted how many of the world's pathological gamblers have found their niche in the financial world, whilst creating chaos for the rest of us (see Chapter 7 for further discussion). The crisis has certainly provided a rich opportunity to examine the impact of disgust-based reactions, with the contemptuous use of the word 'greed' to describe the actions of bankers towards other people's money and towards their own bonuses. Our ambivalence towards money is highlighted by phrases such as 'filthy lucre', 'dirty money' and 'money laundering', such that medium- to long-term reactions to the crisis should, one would predict, lead to an increased use of ethical investments, ethical banking, regulatory impositions on the banking sector and an increased stigmatisation of the financial sector. But let us turn to our favourite banker, Sir Frederick Goodwin (perhaps his surname, Good-win, should now be changed to Bad-loss?) and the Royal Bank of Scotland (RBS). A review of the RBS share price on the *Financial Times* website (see markets.ft.com) shows that when Sir Fred took over as CEO in January 2001 the share price had been rising from about 25p in the 1980s to 454p. Aggressive expansion and acquisition saw RBS shares at over 600p per share by March 2007, but then a steady decline set in with further expansions in China and the acquisition of the Dutch bank ABN-AMRO in October 2007. On 19 January 2009, the so-called 'Blue Monday Crash', the share price fell 67% in one day to 10.9p per share following Sir Fred's announcement of expected losses of £28 billion for the year, the biggest ever in UK corporate history. Sir Fred announced his resignation and left on 31 January 2009, having described the government's attempts to shore up RBS as like a 'drive-by shooting'. However, the public announcement of his £700,000 per year pension from RBS led to widespread public, media and government condemnation. Vince Cable, the former coalition government Business Secretary, stated that Goodwin 'obviously has got no sense of shame'. We would, of course, concur: shame as an emotion has important regulatory and moral functions, the absence of which makes the financial sector vulnerable to individuals who are motivated by short-term financial gain in the context of a culture that encourages such greed.

Further points and conclusions

The biases that come with happiness and optimism can, of course, at times have advantages for the individual, but, equally, they can lead to disaster when they are unchecked. Norman Dixon (1976), in his study of military incompetence, argued persuasively that many of the great military disasters arose from optimism and over-confidence, as in the case of Pearl Harbor:

> Sunday, December 7th, 1941, had been set aside by Admiral Kimmel (Commander-in-Chief of the Pacific Fleet) for a friendly game of golf with his colleague General Short, ninety-six ships of the American Fleet slept at anchor in the harbour, American planes stood wing-tip to wing-tip on the tarmac, American servicemen were off duty enjoying week-end leave. By the end of the day Pearl Harbor, with its ships, planes and military installations, had been reduced to smoking ruins, 2000 servicemen had been killed and as many more missing or wounded.
>
> . . . the neglect of intelligence reports and gross underestimation of enemy capabilities, coupled in this instance with an assiduous misinterpretation of warning signals from Washington and amiable dedication to the task of mutual reassurance regarding their invulnerability, Kimmel and his circle of naval and military advisers achieved a state of such supine complacency that they brought upon themselves 'the worst disaster in American history'.
>
> *(pp. 398–399)*

We are not suggesting that all beliefs in invulnerability arise only from feeling happy, but the study of the effects of happiness demonstrate that even in healthy individuals there is a bucketload of biases and problems that can accompany the emotion. The most common affliction is that of passionate love or infatuation, a state that artists, writers and philosophers have long considered as taking the sufferer close to madness. Indeed, we reported the results from Eleanor Sutton's empirical study that love and mania share many similarities to the extent that love without an appropriate attachment figure might perhaps provide a basis for understanding mania.

We emphasise again that the pursuit of happiness can lead to a superficial or insecure positivity that may be underlain by an extreme anxiety and insecurity. The apparent rise in the US of self-esteem, together with increased anxiety and depression, suggests a cultural encouragement of such splits in the self-concept with all the attendant risks for psychological and physical ill-health. An extreme version of such a split is exemplified by the repressor, a person who scores high on social desirability, defensiveness and self-reported happiness, but who physiologically shows high levels of anxiety and arousal. A culture that promotes the illusion that everyone can be president, that everyone can be famous, that everyone can be wealthy and that everyone can live happily ever after, needs to stop and examine the facts about poverty, homelessness, crime and illness, as Wilkinson and Pickett (2010) have so ably summarised. We must note, though, that the recent financial crisis is not just an American phenomenon; European bankers also demonstrated levels of short-term greed and long-term myopia in which the pursuit of personal wealth at the expense of everything else showed that if you have developed a pathological gambling problem, then casino banking is the best place to indulge your disorder. As we will examine in detail in the next chapter, the failure of people such as pathological gamblers, bankers and drug-addicted individuals to respond to negative emotions such as fear, guilt and shame suggests that such people have significant emotion-regulation problems, whilst they leave the rest of us feeling righteously angry.

3

THE POWER OF NEGATIVE EMOTIONS

There is nothing either good or bad but thinking makes it so.

(William Shakespeare)

Introduction

The H.G. Wells short story *The Country of the Blind* tells the adventure of a mountaineer in the Andes who stumbles across a lost Inca tribe. Because of illness, all the people in the tribe have been blind for hundreds of years. At first, the mountaineer thinks that he can be king amongst the blind because of his additional power of sight, but it soon becomes clear that his supposed ability leads him to be treated as a deluded imbecile, because his claims about the world conflict with the established beliefs of his blind captors. The story ends with a stark choice: in order to stay with the tribe he must allow them to remove the source of his delusions, his eyes, so that he will 'see' the world as they do; alternatively, he must risk death by trying to escape through snow and the impossible high Andean mountain passes.

A second and even more directly relevant science fiction story is the Ira Levin novel *The Stepford Wives* (1972), which was made into a film by Bryan Forbes in 1975, with a further remake starring Nicole Kidman in 2004. The story is set in the fictional town of Stepford, Connecticut, in which the eponymous wives are in a state of perfect docile happiness. The story centres on the arrival of a new wife, a talented photographer from New York, who becomes increasingly disturbed by the zombie-like nature of the other wives. Eventually, she tries to run away but she is caught by the men and is then herself turned into a happy, zombie-like Stepford wife.

Reading some of the early books on positive psychology reminds one of these powerful science fiction stories, which leave strong feelings that are a mixture of physical and moral disgust. In our own fictional remake of these two classics, which we will call *The Country of the Positive*, you must give up your delusional beliefs about fear, anger, envy and shame, and convert them all into positives. Negative is bad, positive is good. Make lemonade from lemons. Of course, John Stuart Mill's famous statement – better to be an unhappy Socrates than a happy pig – provides an elegant response to this happiness delusion, and in the remainder of this chapter we will examine so-called 'unhappiness' in all its many forms with the argument that the negative or 'unhappy emotions', such as fear, anger, sadness and disgust all have important functions in our lives. Fortunately, some of the more recent books on positive psychology have recognised the important role of negative emotions and negative events in terms of how they shape our lives, such as in Sonja Lyubomirsky's excellent *The Myths of Happiness* (2013) and Kashdan and Biswas-Diener's (2014) *The Upside of Your Dark Side*. These more recent books recognise that negative emotions are just as necessary and just as important as happiness, to the extent that their avoidance leads, for example, to reduced longevity and increased risk of a variety of illnesses, as we will summarise later.

The functional approach to emotion can be highlighted with a direct comparison between the role of the negative emotions and the role of physical pain. We would all agree that pain is an unpleasant and aversive experience. When we are experiencing it we normally do everything we can to make it go away, whilst wishing that we never experienced pain in the first place. However, pain plays a crucial function in our lives in terms of warning us about further risk or danger to our physical well-being. For example, if you place your hand into water that is too hot, then the instant experience of pain leads us to withdraw our hand before further risk or injury occurs. Patrick Wall in his book *Pain: The Science of Suffering* (1999) also reminds us that this immediate acute reaction may then be followed by a long recovery phase if damage has actually occurred. During this phase, pain (or the threat of pain) helps to protect the damaged area of the body until recovery occurs. Both the acute pain of the hot water and the deep pain in the recovery phase are extremely unpleasant, but, in both phases, pain functions to make us take immediate protective action where possible.

In fact, and just to highlight how necessary the pain response is, there is a rare genetic condition called congenital analgesia, in which children are born without a pain response. Wall (1999) states that the problem with this disorder is not only the lack of acute pain to provide the initial protection from danger, but also the lack of the recovery phase pain, which means that injuries may fail to heal and thereby lead to longer term physical problems in such children. A website (www.thefactsofpainless-people.com) that has been set up by two sufferers from congenital analgesia provides some startling accounts of the risks of the disorder. One of the sufferers, Paul, states:

I spent most of my childhood life in a wheelchair due to the damage I inflicted upon myself as a result of not feeling pain. . . . I would do things like jump down stairs and sometimes I would purposely injure myself by doing things like break my own fingers just to get my own way. . . . I now live with arthritis due to the amount of times I broke my bones as a child.

As much as we might sometimes wish for a life without pain, the tragic stories of children who suffer from congenital analgesia, most of whom die very young, emphasise that pain is necessary for health and survival. We will show in this chapter that our negative emotions are equally as functional as pain, and that without them life would be equally short and equally brutish. Unhappy Socrates is definitely the better choice than the happy pig.

The function of negative emotions

The basic emotions that have been most widely agreed upon and that have been included in almost all modern lists of basic emotions are the five shown in Table 3.1. That is, almost all commentators would agree that the emotions of anger, sadness, fear, disgust and happiness are 'basic' according to a range of criteria, though we have drawn the list from the seminal work of Oatley and Johnson-Laird (1987). As an aside, we might note that the number '5' for basic emotions has interesting precedents. Sun-Tzu, some 2,500 years ago in his classic *The Art of War*, notes in passing:

There are but five notes, and yet their permutations are more than can ever be heard.

There are but five colours, and yet their permutations are more than ever can be seen.

There are but five flavours, and yet their permutations are more than can ever be tasted.

(Sun-Tzu, 2002, pp. 25–26)

Indeed, the importance of five types in Chinese extends not only to the notes, colours and flavours commented on by Sun-Tzu, but, more importantly to the five

TABLE 3.1 Appraisals for five basic emotions

Basic emotion	Appraisal
Sadness	Loss or failure (actual or possible) of valued role or goal
Happiness	Successful move towards or completion of a valued role or goal
Anger	Blocking or frustration of a role or goal through perceived agent
Fear	Physical or social threat to self or valued role or goal
Disgust	A person, object or idea repulsive to the self, and to valued roles and goals

elements or phases (wood, fire, earth, metal, water) that form the basis of Chinese medicine and Chinese martial arts, and that are taken into account in the practice of Feng Shui, which considers the energy flows between the five elements.

Paul Ekman (e.g. 1999) has done most to summarise the criteria of 'basicness'. These include the universality of the emotion, its association with specific signals (e.g. particular facial expressions), its presumed innateness, its early appearance during child development, its fast and automatic generation, and a typically fast pattern of recovery. These characteristics do, of course, begin to change during development with the pressures of culture and family that shape the regulation and expression of different emotions according to cultural and familial 'display rules'. In addition, more complex emotions develop with time, some of which may be unique to a culture, but whose starting point is one of the basic emotions from which they are therefore derivable.

We have argued elsewhere (see Power and Dalgleish, 2015) that the essential defining aspect that differentiates one emotion from another is its core appraisal or evaluative situation, and we have offered in Table 3.1 a set of core appraisals or evaluations that lead to the generation of the emotion. These core appraisals are based on a set of relevant goals and plans for the individual. We will consider briefly each of the five basic emotions and will include a brief consideration of the basic emotion of happiness, even though this chapter is primarily about the negative emotions. Each appraisal or evaluation refers to a goal-based juncture in which the goals are personally relevant, whether in an immediate and direct manner or in a more indirect and abstract way.

Sadness is a consequence of the appraisal that there is an actual or possible loss of a valued role or goal. Thus, losses of significant others involve the loss of that relationship together with a whole range of subsidiary goals and plans that are entailed in such key relationships. Equally, sadness could result from the loss of a favourite pen, or the memory of the loss of childhood, or the imagined loss of a job, or that someone important to us such as a child or our favourite team failed to achieve something that we had hoped for. At another level, sadness could result from our favourite team losing, or our country performing badly in international sports. A whole country can go into mourning with the loss of a significant figure, such as the death of Princess Diana in 1997, when the UK went into a state of national mourning. The losses, therefore, can be real or imagined; they can affect us directly or indirectly because they happen to other people who are important to us, which, in the modern age, includes celebrity figures, and they can be recalled from our own past, or can be experienced empathically when losses happen in a film or a novel to someone that we have identified with.

In contrast to sadness, happiness refers to the appraisal of movement towards or completion of a valued role or goal. In this definition, we restrict 'happiness' to brief states such as joy or elation, rather than the state of 'life satisfaction' or Aristotle's notion of eudaimonia, to which the highly overworked English word 'happiness' also refers, as we have emphasised in the previous two chapters. These brief states of happiness occur when we complete something, or win something, or do a good day's work, or get to meet someone we like, or our child does well in her homework, or our football team wins a game, or the right person gets voted in as Prime Minister or we recall a success that we had at school. At this point, it is worth mentioning Ekman's (2003) confusion about positive emotion states in his claim that states such as amusement, gratitude and *Schadenfreude* should also be given the status of basic emotions. We would dispute such an approach and argue that each of these emotions is derivable from the basic emotion of happiness, as we have defined it here, as follows. Amusement is typically an aesthetic emotion – the equivalent of sadness or fear experienced at the movies – so let us use this as an excuse to tell a good joke and see why it might evoke amusement. The world of physics has been in the news with the announcement from CERN in Geneva that they have finally discovered proof of the existence of the Higgs boson, also known as the 'God particle', named after Professor Peter Higgs, who predicted its existence nearly 50 years ago. So here is a timely Higgs boson joke:

> The Higgs boson walks into a Catholic church and meets a priest. The priest says to the Higgs boson 'What are you doing here?' And the Higgs boson replies 'Father, you can't have mass without me'.

An amusing story typically creates a hypothetical scenario with a set of expectations that are not fulfilled because of an unexpected reason. Of course, one should not labour such analyses of humour, but the indirect or empathic involvement in such fictional scenarios provide a whole range of brief emotion states that the makers of soap operas rely on for their success.

The third basic emotion that is considered in Table 3.1 is anger. The key appraisal that has been proposed for the generation of anger is the blocking of a goal, plan or role through a perceived agent. For example, you are at work and are behind with a grant application deadline, you go to the photocopier and there are two people there chatting away and in no hurry to finish with the photocopier. You feel your irritation increasing and eventually feel quite angry. By their actions, they are blocking the completion of a goal, and, even though they are unaware of your goal, by their agency they are preventing your goal completion. This example highlights why even inanimate objects can be appraised as agents which are deliberately blocking goal completion. The next time you go to the photocopier with only minutes to the grant application deadline, you find that the photocopier is broken and you kick out at it in anger and frustration. We know that inanimate objects like photocopiers, computers and that cupboard at home that will never open properly all deliberately set out to make our lives problematic!

At this point, it is also worth noting some issues raised by the earlier non-appraisal theories of anger (see Power and Dalgleish, 2015). One of the most influential of these theories has been Leonard Berkowitz's (e.g. 1999) frustration–aggression hypothesis. Berkowitz argued that there are a number of drives or states that make people more aggressive. For example, if people are too hot, if they are in pain, if they are thirsty or in some other state of discomfort, Berkowitz and others have amassed a considerable body of evidence to show that anger, frustration and aggression are much more likely to occur. However, as DiGiuseppe and Tafrate (2007) have argued, this body of data can also be taken as evidence for the automatic route to emotion generation within the SPAARS model that will be presented in detail later in the chapter. Just as we can get angry with photocopiers and recalcitrant cupboards, so too can we get angry with states of the personal environment (too hot, too windy, or whatever) and states of our bodies (too hot, too sweaty, or whatever). There is no question that such reactions can occur without deliberate conscious appraisal via the automatic route, but even here these reactions are modifiable because of conscious appraisals. For example, if you have paid thousands of dollars to travel to a hot beach for your summer vacation, you are more likely to feel pleasure whilst lying on the beach even though you are feeling hot and sweaty, rather than feeling angry and frustrated. The context and meaning of the situation is crucially important, not simply the temperature of the body.

The fourth basic emotion in Table 3.1 is fear or anxiety. The primary level at which fear is generated is at the appraisal of physical threat to the physical body. Thus, the bear charging at you through the woods makes you so terrified that you climb a tree faster than you ever thought you could. Unfortunately, though, it turns out to be that rare species of tree-climbing bear that was chasing you. Alternatively, your boss has asked to see you. You know that you have been under-performing at work and rumours have been going round that the company has not been doing well and that cuts are going to be made. In this case, your physical self is not in any direct danger, but your social self and your valued work roles and goals are under threat. The night before your meeting you cannot sleep at all because of anxiety about the meeting in the morning. Another example of anxiety is when someone important to you, rather than you yourself, is the source of the anxiety. Your child has just been taken into hospital for emergency investigations because of abdominal pains of unknown origin. You feel so anxious and worried that you are unable to work or think about anything other than your son's well-being and what the outcome might be. In fact, this example relates to recent classifications of the aetiological trauma for the development of posttraumatic stress disorder (PTSD); thus, *DSM-5* (American Psychiatric Association, 2013) includes traumatic events that happen to people who are significant to us such as parents, partners and children – not just traumatic events that happen to ourselves.

These examples of the appraisal of anxiety all have in common a threat to something that is important or valuable to us, whether it is our physical existence, our social standing or our key relationships. The function of anxiety in these different circumstances is to motivate us to change something in order to protect what is valuable to us. These protective or defensive actions can be of the matter of milliseconds as we jump away from the speeding car, or they can be of a much more long-term nature when we give our children vitamin supplements because we are worried about their future health, or we switch to unleaded petrol because of our worries about the environment.

The fifth and final basic emotion listed in Table 3.1 is disgust. The origins of disgust in food-based and body-product reactions have been commented on since at least the time of Darwin (Rozin and Fallon, 1987). This primarily food-related focus led some earlier theorists to define the key appraisal for disgust around gustatory goals (Oatley and Johnson-Laird, 1987), but we have argued against this narrow view of disgust, given that, even in relation to body products, there are many non-food-related products that can evoke disgust, including phlegm, sweat, blood and sexual body products (Power and Dalgleish, 2015). Interestingly, the only body products that do not seem to evoke disgust are tears, which is probably because tears are uniquely human. No other animal sheds tears as part of emotion expression and therefore tears are perceived to be the least 'animal-like' of all body products (Power, 1999). Whilst we acknowledge the importance of disgust in food and food-waste products, we nevertheless prefer to consider the relevant appraisal in terms of a more general repulsion towards any object, person or idea that is seen as distasteful to the self and to significant others.

The disgust-based reactions seen in some eating disorders, in which both food or certain foodstuffs and aspects of body shape and size become repulsive, seem relatively straightforward and do not need to be discussed at this point. We will return to these disorders in Chapter 6 when we consider health and illness. Perhaps less obvious is the role that disgust plays in depression, and in some types of phobias, obsessive–compulsive disorders (OCDs) and PTSDs. In all of these examples, there is some aspect of the self or the world that is seen as unwanted and contaminating. Thus, in OCD, it may be certain aspects of the world that are seen as dirty or contaminating, whereas in depression it is part of the self that becomes unwanted and loathsome and that the person tries to get rid of.

In summary, we believe that these five basic emotions provide the building blocks for our emotional lives and therefore for the full range of emotional disorders that are encountered. Before we look at these disorders in more detail, however, it is necessary to consider two further aspects of this approach to emotion: first, the idea that all other emotions are derived from one or more basic emotions; and second, the related proposal that emotions can become 'coupled' with each other in ways that can be detrimental and form the basis of some of the emotional disorders.

Complex emotions

One of the central tenets of the basic emotions approach is that all complex emotions are derived from the set of five basic emotions. The proposal is analogous to the effect of mixing primary colours to produce distinct new colours, such as when blue and yellow are mixed together to produce green. In the case of emotions, these derivations can occur either through additional cognitive elaboration of an emotion, or through the blending of different emotions together, or through the process of coupling, mentioned earlier. Examples of cognitive elaboration shown in Table 3.2 would include worry as an elaboration of fear, in which there is rumination about the future, and guilt as a form of disgust that is directed towards an action carried out by the self. Examples of emotion blends include contempt and nostalgia. Thus, contempt, although listed under anger in Table 3.2, typically includes a measure of disgust combined with anger directed towards the person or object of contempt. Similarly, nostalgia, although listed under happiness, also includes a measure of sadness directed towards the person or situation that is the object of the nostalgia. Table 3.2 also illustrates another feature of the complexity of emotions, which is that the same emotion term in everyday usage can come to represent different emotion states. Thus, in the table, one form of embarrassment is primarily derived from fear (e.g. a negative social evaluation anxiety) and a second is derivable from disgust (e.g. a mild version of shame). There is at least one further version (not shown) which is a positive version (e.g. when being complimented in public). Another example of the multiple uses of the same word in everyday language is the word 'disgust' itself, which, in addition to referring in everyday language to a state of repulsion, is also used to refer to being angry as in 'I am disgusted with you for turning up late' (Power, 2006). The third process, that of coupling, follows along similar lines to the ideas of cognitive elaboration and blending, but we will consider it separately in the next section because of its putative role in psychopathology.

Another feature that should be noted about this approach to basic emotions and derived complex emotions can be illustrated by analogy to language. Language is based on a limited number of symbols, such as letters, words or ideographs, but from this limited number, an infinite number of different combinations can be generated. Similarly, as we noted above, a limited number of primary colours can be combined to give an infinite number of hues, tones and blends. So, although five might not sound like a large number to begin with, once you have allowed for the range of subtle personal, interpersonal and cultural elaborations, and the infinite number of potential blends of two or more basic emotions, then the emotion system has the

TABLE 3.2 Complex emotions derived from basic emotions

Basic emotion	Examples of complex emotions
Fear	Embarrassment (1)
	Worry
Sadness	Grief
Anger	Envy
	Jealousy
	Contempt
Happiness	Joy
	Love
	Nostalgia
Disgust	Guilt
	Shame
	Embarrassment (2)

potential to generate a myriad of unique as well as universal emotion states. There is no question that, both historically and cross-culturally, certain unique emotions have been apparent. Classic examples of these unique emotions include the medieval state of 'awe', a religious emotion felt in the presence of god, and the state of 'accidie' which was experienced as a type of spiritual fatigue (Oatley, 2005). There are also a number of 'culture-bound syndromes' that clearly incorporate some unique emotion and belief states. For example, *koro* is a condition specific to men in South East Asia in which they experience their penises as if they had shrunken back into their body, an experience that is typically accompanied by considerable anxiety and distress.

Emotion coupling

One of the proposals that we originally made in developing the SPAARS approach to emotion was that certain emotion modules might become 'coupled' with each other in ways that might lead to psychopathology (Power and Dalgleish, 1997, 2015). There have been one or two related ideas in the psychopathology literature, such as in the influential ideas of 'fear of fear' (e.g. Goldstein and Chambless, 1978) and similar ideas about 'depression about depression'. The 'fear of fear' idea is especially relevant to understanding how someone who has experienced an extremely aversive state such as a panic attack might go to considerable efforts to avoid such an experience in the future; that is, they might successfully avoid having a further panic attack through continued avoidance, but nevertheless live in a state of anxiety. We believe that similar couplings occur not just within emotion categories such as in these examples but between emotion categories also, and that these couplings are often linked to psychopathology.

Examples of 'coupled' emotions include: happiness–anxiety and happiness–anger, sometimes seen in manic states; anxiety–disgust seen in some phobias, OCDs and types of PTSD; sadness–disgust seen in depression; and sadness–anger seen in grief (see Power and Dalgleish, 2015). Each of the examples in any individual case is more complex than merely consisting of coupling, as we have shown with case studies elsewhere (Power, 2010). Nevertheless, these provide examples of different types of coupling mechanisms. For example, in PTSD, the victim may evaluate their experience of anxiety in a rejecting self-disgust fashion. This can happen to some male victims of assault who had seen themselves as tough and invulnerable prior to the assault. They now appraise their feelings of panic and anxiety as weak and pathetic, which leads them to feelings of self-disgust as well as anxiety (see Power and Fyvie, 2013). In this PTSD example, the coupling is caused by the appraisal of one emotion as weak and unacceptable, thereby leading to a second emotion.

Again, in depression, the coupling of self-disgust can occur directly to the feelings of sadness, especially in some male depressions, but, more typically, the feelings of self-disgust are directed at the self in addition to any specific emotions. For example, following the break-up of a love relationship, a woman might feel sadness because of the loss, but also feels anxious about how she will survive alone, whilst at the same time despising herself for needing a relationship and not being completely self-sufficient. In such cases, the coupling may be both direct and indirect, in that it is more the cause of the sadness (that of needing a relationship) than perhaps the sadness itself that becomes the focus of the self-disgust (Power and Tarsia, 2007).

The proposal for the coupling of emotions as suggested in the SPAARS model has primarily been supported by clinical and anecdotal evidence. Recently, however, one of my PhD students John Fox, tested a group of bulimic students using a so-called priming paradigm in order to test the prediction that anger and disgust could be coupled in bulimia. A group of female students who met clinical criteria for bulimia, together with a matched control group of healthy controls, were given an anger induction task. Their levels of anger and disgust were tested immediately before and immediately after the anger induction procedure. The results showed that both groups showed similar levels of disgust and anger before the priming procedure, and that afterwards both showed significant increases in anger (though somewhat more in the bulimia group). Most interesting, however, was the finding of a significant increase in the disgust levels in the bulimia group but no change in disgust levels in the control group (Fox and Harrison, 2008). John later replicated these findings with a clinical group (Fox et al., 2013). Such results show some support for the proposed coupling of anger and disgust in bulimia, and also show how the priming methodology can be used to test predicted couplings in other disorders, in addition to the self-report methods that we have used (Power and Tarsia, 2007).

Emotion regulation

The publication of the book *Emotional Intelligence* by Daniel Goleman in 1995 led to the sudden popularisation of the earlier proposal of 'emotional intelligence' put forward by Salovey and Meyer (1990), which, in turn, was based on earlier proposals such as Gardner's (1983) concept of social intelligence. The popularisation has led to the assessment and teaching of emotional skills in the workplace and in schools, though academically it has remained surrounded by controversy. The main arguments against the proposal (e.g. Davies et al., 1998; Roberts et al., 2001) are that it offers nothing unique that is not already covered by existing personality theory and existing approaches to intelligence. Our own view is that the term 'emotional intelligence' is one that is best avoided because of its value-laden and elitist implications, but that nevertheless there are important variations in emotional skills that should not be ignored.

The development of emotional skills is clearly evident throughout childhood (e.g. Izard, 2001), and there are developmental disorders such as autism that have been linked to deficits in theory of mind (e.g. Frith, 2003), and which therefore are, by definition, accompanied by deficits in emotional skills (e.g. Hobson, 1995). However, we prefer to refer to such skills as meta-emotional skills and associated meta-emotional representations, in parallel to the use of the term metacognition in cognition and development first proposed by Flavell (1979). These meta-emotional skills are likely to show a different pattern of population distribution than cognitive intelligence, which approximates the normal distribution curve, because of threshold effects consequent on problems and deficits that affect disorders such as autism and psychopathy. We acknowledge, though, that the term 'meta-emotional skill' may never have the same popular appeal and ring to it as 'emotional intelligence' and that Daniel Goleman is unlikely to write a book with this new title.

The key areas that are important in meta-emotional skills and representations include the perception and understanding of emotion in self and others, and the regulation of emotion, again both in self and in others. The deficits seen in the autistic spectrum disorders lead to clear problems with the recognition of emotions in self and others, together with the additional complexity that such disorders occur in far greater numbers in males than females (e.g. Baron-Cohen, 2004). Such gender differences do not imply, though, that all men are deficient in meta-emotional skills, contrary perhaps to some popular views, especially with the powerful cultural pressures on the gender-related expression of different emotions and that can be seen in the reported experience of different emotions (e.g. Scherer *et al.*, 2001).

One of the most important areas of meta-emotional skills is that of emotion regulation. There have been a number of conceptualisations of emotion regulation (e.g. Carver and Scheier, 1990; Gross, 1998; Larsen, 2000; Philippot & Feldman, 2004). In a recent summary of his own approach, Gross (2007) has drawn together work showing how different regulation strategies can be applied at different points during the course of an emotional reaction. Even before an emotion begins, you can avoid a situation because you know it will be emotional, or you can try to stop the emotion once it starts through inhibiting yourself from expressing the emotion, or you can change the consequences of having expressed (or not expressed) an emotion. In Gross's influential approach, the emotion is broken down into a series of temporal stages with the possibility of different strategies being applied at each stage.

In contrast to Gross's approach, we take a more holistic approach to the regulation of emotion and believe that people tend to regulate all aspects of an emotion in a similar way. For example, if you have intense exam anxiety, you will avoid exams if at all possible, and you may do things to avoid the actual experience of the anxiety itself, such as taking medication if you do have to take an exam. The common feature here is the attempted avoidance of the situation and the emotional experience. Our own approach (Phillips and Power, 2007) has been to consider first the fact that most emotions are primarily generated and experienced in an interpersonal context, therefore many emotion regulation strategies are interpersonal in addition to the perhaps more familiar intrapersonal strategies. Examples of interpersonal strategies would include talking to a friend or getting advice, but there are also other external strategies that are not inherently interpersonal, such as doing something pleasant like shopping or sports. Examples of internal emotion regulation strategies include inhibiting the experience of the emotion or ruminating about the emotion so that it continues for longer than it otherwise would. We believe, therefore, that one important dimension along which emotion regulation should be considered is whether the regulation strategies are internal or external. As an interesting aside, the internal–external dimension also maps very well to the distinction between internalising (e.g. depression) and externalising (e.g. conduct disorders) problems in children and adolescents (Casey, 1996), which has also been found to relate to early temperamental differences in children when followed up into their teenage years (Caspi *et al.*, 1995).

A second dimension along which emotion regulation strategies can be grouped is, we propose, whether the strategies are functional or dysfunctional. Writers such as Gross (2007) argue against using categorisations that evaluate some strategies as more negative than others on the grounds that what may be seen as dysfunctional in one culture, subgroup, family or individual, could be functional in another. However, we believe that there is a strong and well-supported tradition that goes back to both Sigmund Freud (e.g. 1926) and his daughter Anna (1937) in which the habitual use of certain defence mechanisms is seen to have problematic consequences for the individual, both physically and psychologically. Some of these defence mechanisms, such as regression and dissociation, are more likely to be dysfunctional, whereas other defences, such as sublimation and suppression, are more likely to be functional. Moreover, there is now a wide range of research from diverse areas in support of this categorisation. To cite but one example, George Vaillant's classic work (1990) on the lifetime follow-up of a group of Harvard students dramatically demonstrated how health and even premature death were predicted by the typical defence mechanisms that they used as undergraduates. However, and perhaps as Pierre Philippot (2007) has emphasised, it is also about the flexibility with which emotion regulation strategies are used (see also Chapter 6). For example, avoidance may be appropriate in some situations or contexts, but it becomes problematic if used excessively and inflexibly. Our meta-emotional skills can therefore help us to switch between regulation strategies as appropriate.

In summary, we have proposed that emotion regulation strategies can be usefully grouped along dimensions of internal–external and functional–dysfunctional. We acknowledge, of course, that under certain circumstances even the most apparently dysfunctional strategy can be functional. For example, dissociation during the experience of a traumatic event may permit the individual to function without being overwhelmed by anxiety and panic, similar to numbing during excessive physical pain. However, the habitual use of dissociation is clearly dysfunctional, as Vaillant's (1990) longitudinal follow-up of the Harvard students demonstrated. The combination of these two emotion regulation dimensions leads to the 2 × 2 classification system illustrated in Table 3.3.

We have given examples so far of the combinations of functional internal and external strategies, and of dysfunctional internal strategies, but Table 3.3 also shows a fourth combination: dysfunctional external strategies. Again, given the fact that most emotions are generated and experienced in interpersonal situations, there is no reason why the use of external interpersonal strategies should always be functional. Indeed, aggression towards others can be used by individuals to

TABLE 3.3 A 2 × 2 organisation of emotion regulation strategies with examples

	Internal	*External*
Dysfunctional	Reject emotion	Bullying
	Denial	Hitting
	Depersonalisation	Shouting
		Vandalism
Functional	Learn from emotion	Talking to others
	Reappraisal	Share feelings
		Writing blogs?

regulate a range of emotion states (see DiGiuseppe and Tafrate, 2007), which may be dysfunctional for all concerned. We therefore consider that there are a number of external interpersonal (e.g. bullying, physical and verbal aggression) and other external strategies (e.g. aggression against inanimate objects) that are also potentially dysfunctional, especially when used habitually (Phillips and Power, 2007).

Let us consider some of the specific emotion regulation strategies, especially in relation to their use with negative emotions. For example, expressive inhibition is an emotion regulation strategy that seems to be associated with the tendency to experience depressive symptoms (Joorman and Gotlib, 2010). People with anxiety and mood disorders spontaneously inhibit their negative emotions more than healthy controls do (Campbell-Sills et al., 2006). This tendency persists during remission, which seems to suggest a trait-like tendency in people who are emotionally vulnerable (Ehring et al., 2010). As we respond to and shape our interpersonal interactions, understanding the individual's tendency to inhibit expression of negative emotions requires an understanding of the interpersonal context, for example, as can occur in conflict in a romantic relationship (Richards et al., 2003). The emotionally flat response of one partner can distance the other, which can then generate an interpersonal tension that starts a vicious cycle that can further worsen mood.

Expressive inhibition has been studied primarily at the level of the individual, with emerging studies bringing increased attention to brain and culture. As we have noted for all the regulation strategies, inhibition is not intrinsically dysfunctional, but its chronic and context-insensitive engagement may leave one vulnerable to distress. Over time, ineffective self-regulation, attention to negative stimuli and increased levels of negative emotions are likely to further tune brain activation, forming, in SPAARS terms, an automatisation of the process.

Another classic example of problems of expression and inhibition of emotion comes from the work begun in the 1950s on personality and cardiac problems. We will return to this issue in more detail in Chapter 6, but the 'Type A' personality has entered common parlance as someone who is uptight, ambitious, competitive and hostile and who is prone to coronary heart disease (CHD). A study by Friedman and Rosenman (1959) in which they followed a group of healthy adult males for 10 years suggested that the Type A men were more prone to CHD. However, subsequent studies have not replicated the original findings and have given inconsistent results. Nevertheless, there is some indication from later research that the problem is not simply too much anger, but that too little anger (i.e. the over-inhibition of anger) is also a risk for CHD (e.g. Bleil et al., 2004). Other more recent types of proposed vulnerable personalities include the Type C cancer-prone and the Type D personality, which is also thought to be cardiac-risk prone, but all of these vulnerable personalities are characterised by dysfunctional emotion regulation strategies.

Some researchers have argued that Western cultural contexts are depressogenic (e.g. Eckersley, 2006). These individualistic and materialistic contexts may cause vulnerability to depression by broadening discrepancies between realistic personal outcomes and cultural ideals. Although moderately sized discrepancies may serve as motivational fuel, larger or irreconcilable ones lead to negative self-evaluation, resulting in profound distress. North American cultural contexts foster ideals of personal achievement, self-importance and happiness – the 'everyone can be president' mentality. Over time, these cultural ideals have become increasingly unrealistic and disconnected from the individual's past performance. As cultural ideals become more extreme, for example, based on celebrity lifestyles, the number of people who fail to attain these ideals increases. Moreover, as we emphasised in Chapter 1, the increasing discrepancy between rich and poor in Western countries such as the United States and the UK compounds further the sense of dissatisfaction for increasing numbers of the population (Wilkinson and Pickett, 2010). For example, between 1976 and 2000, American high school students increasingly developed unrealistic expectations for educational and professional attainment (Reynolds et al., 2006), leading many to fail to realise these goals. Reminders of such unfulfilled ideals may trigger unfavourable self-evaluation and distress. Indeed, endorsement of materialistic values, a failure to achieve a desired lifestyle, and exposure to more successful lifestyles combine to predict depression (see Kasser and Ahuvia, 2002). This line of research identifies a set of cultural characteristics that are linked to problematic individual-level outcomes, such as sickness and suicide.

Cultural scripts regarding emotion regulation are activated so frequently that they become automatic and rapid, shaping emotional behaviour within the first second after an event (Power and Dalgleish, 2015). For example, the costs of suppression disappear when it is engaged automatically, circumventing deliberate efforts to suppress (Mauss et al., 2007). In addition, the impact of suppression depends on the fit with cultural scripts of experiencing and expressing emotions. The impact within a cultural context that places value on moderating expression of emotions would be expected to differ from that in a cultural context that values expression of emotions. Indeed, recent studies suggest that the association between self-reported suppression and depressed mood observed in European American cultural contexts disappears in East Asian cultural contexts (Cheung and Park, 2010). The pattern of inhibited emotional reactivity displayed by depressed European Americans (Bylsma et al., 2008) does not hold for depressed Asian Americans, who tend to show unchanged or even exaggerated emotional reactivity in the laboratory (Chentsova-Dutton *et al.*, 2007, 2010). These studies suggest that expressive suppression can be either functional or dysfunctional, because its association with major depression may be determined by the extent to which it deviates from culturally normative ways of experiencing and expressing emotion. Similarly, submissive emotions are unrelated to happiness in the US but are highly associated with it in Japan (Kitayama, Markus, & Kurokawa, 2000).

Indeed, submissiveness is associated with depressive symptoms in Western contexts (O'Connor *et al.*, 2002), an association considered so self-evident that submissive behaviour is incorporated into animal models of depression (e.g. Malatynska and Knapp, 2005). The proposal is that neither psychological mechanisms of submissiveness nor cultural values regarding hierarchy are inherently dysfunctional, but that, in combination, the two may lead to vulnerability to depression, in which the conflict between submissive social position and cultural values make such a position undesirable. In summary, vulnerability can best be understood as an interaction between culture and psychology, which we must be aware of when we consider functional and dysfunctional aspects of emotion regulation. Nevertheless, once cultural context is taken into account, different regulation strategies become functional or dysfunctional, especially when they are used inflexibly by the individual.

Positive negative emotions

So far in this chapter we have argued that negative emotions are, just like the experience of pain, extremely functional in our lives, notwithstanding the fact that too much or too little of them, as with happiness, can lead to types of psychopathology. However, although we have been happy to use the phrase 'negative emotions' to group the four basic emotions of anger, sadness, fear and disgust together, in this section we want to turn the phrase on its head and illustrate some of its shortcomings through a consideration of what we will call the 'positive negative emotions'. These are complex emotions derived from the basic emotions, but which signify strong functionality and often strong motivational and moral imperatives in their experience and expression. We will give at least one example from each of the basic emotions in illustration.

Anger

> For the day of vengeance is in mine heart, and the year of my redeemed is come.
>
> *(Isaiah 63:4)*

The Bible is replete with examples of God's anger or wrath meted out to us lowly sinners, who have brought it upon ourselves through our sinful and deceitful actions. If God, therefore, can be justifiably angry, then anger is presented not as a negative emotion but as a positive emotion which serves the function of justice. Notwithstanding its use in the Bible, there is a strong tradition of the use of moral or righteous anger, whether used in order to bring justice or to motivate actions of revenge that can last over generations, as in some of the 'honour cultures'. For example, violations of the honour code in Albanian rural areas can see deaths and killings between families over many generations. In these blood feuds, the original violation might no longer be remembered, only the most recent perpetration of the inter-family violence. Indeed, such acts of moral anger or outrage can motivate whole-scale wars, as we will examine in Chapter 4.

Jonathan Haidt (2003) neatly summarises our viewpoint on anger in that anger is normally considered to be an immoral rather than a moral emotion, yet the notion of standing up for one's rights captures the everyday sense in which anger is as much of a moral emotion as an immoral one. Again, as Haidt notes, although the action tendency accompanying anger typically seems to be selfish and antisocial, he provides numerous examples such as racism, oppression, exploitation and genocide in which those who hand out justice against the transgressors may have had no personal involvement in the original incidents. Social outrage can motivate many such political actions, for the grapes of wrath have their own sweet righteousness.

In clinical work with couples, one of the frequent problems encountered is that the couple only use destructive anger in their relationship, and do not know how to use constructive anger (Power, 2010). In such cases, anger may be expressed infrequently and may be avoided under normal circumstances because the couple are aware of its destructive power when it is expressed. Part of the emotion-focused intervention with such a couple is to begin to teach them the skills of the constructive use of anger, such as avoiding physical and verbal aggression, listening to the other person, making clear statements of experienced injustice, and developing the capacities for apology and forgiveness. The fact that so many skills are necessary for the constructive use of anger in relationships means that most couples have to develop and enhance these skills over time, because they rarely will start a relationship with such skills already finely attuned.

Anxiety

The positive function of anxiety can be illustrated with an important motivating function which can lead the individual to postpone other concerns or pleasures and focus on the upcoming event that is leading to anxiety or worry. For example, if you have your state exams on which your future career depends in the next couple of months, your normal wish to socialise and party at weekends may be postponed whilst you work and revise for your exams in order to do well. The worry that you might not do well enough to progress appropriately for the next steps in your career provides a powerful motivation to postpone other activities and focus on those activities that increase the likelihood of success and decrease the likelihood of failure.

A different function of anxiety was highlighted by Freud (1926) in his concept of signal anxiety. In this case, the conscious experience of anxiety serves as a warning that the person may be avoiding something important, such as in their work, or in their close relationships, or perhaps denying the significance of a physical symptom that may be indicative of disease. The anxiety acts as a signal to which the person needs to attend so that its significance can be decoded. A related anxiety function is that of vigilance, which increases the level of attention being paid to possible sources of external or internal threat. This can be a life-saving function in times of imminent danger.

An interesting clinical observations that has been made by Adrian Wells (e.g. 1997) and others is that many clients who suffer from excessive worry, such as in generalised anxiety disorder, actually have positive beliefs about the function of their worry and, consequently, are reluctant to let go of their perceived function of worry. For example, an individual may believe that if he or she continues to worry about the possibility of being hit by a meteorite, the worrying will superstitiously prevent the unlikely event from happening. Thus, the 'proof' of the positive function of worry is that the event has not happened, which reinforces the belief through the non-occurrence of the feared outcome. Therapists who work with chronic worry, as with many other chronic disorders, need, therefore, to assess not only negative aspects of the problem, but also the positive functions which may be serving to maintain the problem.

Sadness

We will begin with the example of the aesthetic emotions for sadness, though we might have used it for any of the basic emotions we have considered. Works of art, fiction, film and music often depict strong and powerful emotions, indeed, such works are often judged by how well they engage our aesthetic emotions. For those of us susceptible to the pain of romance and what might have been, David Lean's film *Brief Encounter*, released in 1945 and based on a play by Noël Coward is a powerful emotional experience. In the film, Celia Johnson plays the part of the classic suburban repressed housewife surviving in a stagnated marriage. A chance encounter with the charming doctor played by Trevor Howard leads to a mutually passionate infatuation, which is only ever expressed in brief words and looks. In the end, they separate in order to preserve their marriages, but the penultimate scene in which Trevor Howard leaves on the train, knowing that he is going to go to South Africa and they will never meet again has to be one of the saddest scenes in cinema. Well, almost as sad as when Leonardo DiCaprio dies in *Titanic* and leaves Kate Winslet alone on her life raft, or when Ingmar Bergman flies off and leaves Humphrey Bogart in *Casablanca*. The important point about these romantic tragedies is that we love them because they make us weep, because they make us feel intensely sad. If sadness were simply a negative emotion, it would be avoided and we certainly would not pay good money to end up in tears. *Titanic* is the second highest grossing film of all time, making nearly US$2.2 billion to date, which is a lot of money to spend on making ourselves sad. Sadness is functional, and in its aesthetic form it can serve as an existential reminder that both our own lives and the lives of the people we love may be short and unpredictable and we may lose them at any time in the future.

Sadness helps to remind us of our priorities in life, and it helps to readjust them if they should get out of order. For example, let us consider the study of so-called posttraumatic growth, which, again, is an area about complex emotional reactions to trauma rather than just sadness, but we will list it under sadness because sadness and posttraumatic growth can have overlapping functions. Tedeshi and Calhoun (2004) have summarised data to show that some people after the experience of severe trauma, such as threat to their life or loss of a significant other, through the grieving process come to experience a new sense of meaning in life such as valuing of relationships more, investment in caring roles and increased contribution to community welfare. This combination of resetting and revaluing roles and relationships in life whilst turning more to others seems to be a key function of extreme sadness such as that following grief (Power and Dalgleish, 2015).

A related issue to grief and shared loss is the function of sadness in anniversaries, reunions and remembrance. Whether at an individual, a familial or a societal level, the rituals that accompany events such as anniversaries and remembrance provide important social structures that increase the social cohesion of the group whilst providing catharsis and reassurance for those who are still grieving (Power, 2012). It has been well known in the psychotherapy literature that anniversaries of events such as the deaths of significant others are typically accompanied by strong emotional reactions such as intense feelings of sadness and distress. Large-scale natural and man-made disasters have become the focus of research attention in order to track the progress of people affected by such disasters. For example, Assanangkornchai and colleagues (2007) followed up a group of Thai residents affected by extreme floods in the year 2000. Assessment of the victims over the following year showed that there was a gradual reduction in stress, except on the anniversary of the flood where the scores for distress increased, especially in those who were most affected and still living in the most flood-threatened areas.

Disgust

Similar to the discussion of the role of positive anger in morality and justice, so too does the emotion of disgust have an important function in the development of morality and in the foundations of our beliefs about systems of justice. Disgust is the basic emotion that underlies the complex emotions of guilt and shame. In Christian mythology, the fall of Adam and Eve was considered to lead to a state of original sin for all newborn children (the one exception being Mary, she of the Immaculate Conception), babies therefore being born in a state of guilt and shame, which can be removed by baptism. A simple scientific test of the effectiveness of baptism, therefore, would be to take matched groups of respondents who have or have not been baptised and then compare them on their scores for criminal activity, antisocial behaviour and sinfulness to see if baptism led to lower scores. Although we have not carried out this analysis, we suspect that baptism probably is not the crucial factor here.

To return to the moral emotions derived from disgust and their moral functions, there are numerous cultural variations on socio-moral aspects of disgust. For example, Rozin and colleagues (Rozin *et al.*, 1999) consider the example of the Hindu caste system in which the bodily activities (e.g. eating, bathing, drinking) of the different castes had to be kept separate in case the lower caste 'contaminated' the higher caste. Rozin *et al.* argue that, in Western cultures, it is typically when people 'degrade' themselves in some way that they evoke disgust reactions. These reactions therefore serve to define the limits of what is acceptable and unacceptable behaviour that defines in-group and out-group membership.

The positive functions of guilt and shame include reparation. A study by Barrett and colleagues (Barrett *et al.*, 1993) with young boys and girls demonstrated that, even by 3 or 4 years of age, young girls may be more prone to shame and show avoidance, whereas boys were found to be more likely to show guilt in the same circumstances and therefore make reparation. In the actual study, the child is allowed to play with a special toy that belongs to someone else, but the toy then apparently collapses because of the child's actions. Even for these young children, the guilt reaction was more constructive because it led to attempts to fix the toy and to apologise to the toy's owner. Guilt-proneness also seems to be associated with higher levels of empathy towards others than is shame-proneness (Tangney, 1999). However, although such studies show that shame is a more difficult emotion to cope with than guilt, and its role in psychopathology may have been considerably underestimated (e.g. Power and Tarsia, 2007), we can also ask what the adaptive role of such an acutely painful emotion might be. Paul Gilbert (e.g. 1998) has argued that shame may play an important social function when the self has lost status and feels devalued. That is, a display of shame in a social situation may serve to subordinate the self and appease one or more powerful others who might otherwise inflict further social or physical damage. Gilbert notes that typical shame signals, such as head and gaze down, gaze avoidance and hiding, are signals that display submissiveness interpersonally, in which a dominant other is appeased as a damage-limitation strategy.

Creativity and negative emotions

In addition to the argument that our so-called negative emotions have important functionality, we can go further and state that they are also fundamental to our creativity in the sciences and the arts, that their diversity of experience has been part of the adaptive success of the human species and that, without our negative emotions, we would still be just happy pigs wallowing in the mud (see e.g. Simonton's chapter in the *Oxford Handbook of Positive Psychology*, 2009). In evidence of this creative function, there have been numerous artists, writers and musicians who seem to have disproportionately suffered from mood disorders, including Edgar Allan Poe, Lord Byron, Robert Burns, Virginia Woolf, Sergei Rachmaninoff, Winston Churchill and Vincent van Gogh.

Of course, simply providing a list of famous people who have suffered with mood and other disorders is merely an anecdotal approach to whether or not creativity and madness somehow go together. The book by Kay Redfield Jamison, *Touched with Fire* (1993), provides a moving account of such biographies, and is written by a well-known clinical psychologist who herself suffers from a bipolar disorder. Together with her colleague Frederick Goodwin, Jamison later reviewed a wide range of studies of psychopathology that show a clear and significant elevation of rates of depression, suicide and mania in poets, writers and artists when compared to the expected rates in the general population (Goodwin and Jamison, 2007). Jamison emphasises that the majority of writers and artists do not have such psychopathology and that, equally, not all sufferers from mood disorders show high levels of creativity. The point she makes is that there is some clear association, which may hinge on a creative cycle in which low mood can provide insights into reality that then fuel the creative associations likely to occur with high mood. The point is that the 'negative' part of the creative cycle is just as important as the 'positive' part and that one would fail without the other. In order to illustrate this process, we will consider the work and life of Sylvia Plath, one of the greatest poets of the twentieth century.

Sylvia Plath

Sylvia Plath was born in Boston, USA, in 1932. Her father was German and taught both German and biology at Boston University, her mother having been one of his postgraduate students and 21 years his junior. Her father Otto died when she was 8 years old following surgery. In the semi-autobiographical novel *The Bell Jar* (1963), she describes a suicide attempt in which she took her mother's sleeping pills and crawled under their house where she remained undiscovered for three days.

On a Fulbright Scholarship to Cambridge, UK, in 1955 she met, and later married, fellow-poet Ted Hughes. They eventually settled in Primrose Hill, London, where she had two children. Sylvia discovered that her husband had been having an affair and separated from him in July 1962. Following the depression of separation, she experienced a high burst of creativity from October 1962 onwards, in which she wrote the majority of her great poems; these were published posthumously in *Ariel* (1965). However, by February 1963 she was again deeply depressed and she committed suicide through carbon monoxide poisoning. Robert Lowell, the famous American poet, described the poems in *Ariel* as 'playing Russian roulette with six cartridges in the cylinder'.

The issue that we return to when we consider great poets and writers like Sylvia Plath is how much of their greatness depends on the black abyss into which they descend and from which is hewn such brilliant and insightful poetry. In Sylvia Plath's case one might speculate that the loss of a distant but loved father left her with an unresolved grief, in which the suicide attempts were, in part, a wish to be reunited with him. The unfaithfulness of Ted Hughes, whose second wife also killed herself, left a trail, even after Sylvia's death, of hatred and accusation towards him, especially from feminist writers, who never forgave him for his treatment of Sylvia. However, her greatest works were written after his unfaithfulness and their separation, so part of her great skill as a poet was her capacity to turn pain into something starkly beautiful. Unfortunately, however, she succumbed to the abyss and her writing was not sufficient to combat its bleak allure. The question then remains: Would we prefer a bland monochrome world without diversity and pain? Or should we kneel in gratitude before those who have had the courage to fly into the eye of the cauldron?

Conclusion

In this chapter we have argued that our fictional land, *The Country of the Positive*, would be an artificial one-dimensional nightmare with as much connection to reality as *The Stepford Wives*. Negative emotions, like pain, have a deep and significant functionality in our lives. And, like pain, if we did not have these negative emotions, life would be brutish and short; our negative emotions play a crucial role in our lives. For example, without fear we would fall to our death from high places, drown in lakes and rivers when we did not know how to swim, or drive through traffic lights on red just for the fun of it. Similarly, with the emotions of anger, sadness and disgust, and all the complex emotions derived from them, there are crucial social and physical survival functions connected with each. Indeed, there are clear positive variants of each of the so-called negative emotions, for which we considered examples such as righteous anger, compassionate sadness and moral emotions based on guilt and shame. Our lives are enriched by our negative emotions to the extent that many of our greatest artists, poets and writers have suffered with severe mood disorders that seem to have been part of the rich creativity that has provided some of the greatest achievements of the human race. Even for those of us not blessed with such talents, our everyday experience of mood changes can be used in a creative way and, equally, we can use creativity to help us cope with our day-to-day mood changes, be it through gardening, sketching, writing poetry, photography, woodwork or whatever hobbies and interests we enjoy. Unfortunately, however, the positive psychology movement, certainly in its first strong statements, encouraged an unnecessary negativity towards negative emotions in our culture, as part of what might now be called the 'happiness industry'. It is to this industry that we turn next.

4

THE HAPPINESS INDUSTRY

The Way of War is a Way of Deception.

(Sun-Tzu)

Introduction

The world is full of groups, organisations and governments who tell us that their aim is to improve our happiness if we sign up to them. Clearly impressed by the politics of Bhutan, the British Prime Minister, David Cameron, announced his intention to measure the Gross National Happiness of the British people. Cameron's aim is presumably to show that under his Conservative government the happiness of the British people has improved because of his fine management. Now, if you are a member of the Conservative Party, earning over £150,000 per year, have just had a tax reduction and are living in the Home Counties around London, then you are a member of a group whose happiness level most likely has increased because of David Cameron's policies. However, if you are disabled, unemployed and Scottish, then David Cameron's actions are most likely to be making you more miserable, so he would be best off not attempting to measure your level of 'happiness'.

What these opposing reactions tell us is that, at the social level, one of the key factors that determines how well or how badly we respond to the actions of groups, organisations and governments is whether or not we are members of those groups that support those organisations or whether we are members of opposing groups. In this chapter, therefore, we will examine a diverse range of groups and organisations that constitute what might be labelled the 'happiness industry', but we will consider their impact in the light of social identity theory and the more general social identity approach within social psychology. This diverse range will include the impact of the organisations we work for, groups that we support, the pharmaceutical and related industries that attempt to bottle happiness, religious and political groups, and, ultimately, how our membership and definitions of ingroups and outgroups can fuel hatred, prejudice, conflict and war.

First, however, we will start with an outline of the social identity approach within psychology and how this can offer us a starting point for understanding the plusses and minuses of the wide range of ingroup and outgroup phenomena.

Identity and group membership

Social identity theory was developed in the 1970s by social psychologists such as Tajfel and Turner, and has continued to be developed and expanded in the decades since in what is known as the social identity approach. The original theory considered interactions of both an interpersonal and intergroup nature in which interactions can be understood through a combination of both individual and group characteristics (e.g. Tajfel and Turner, 1979). These proposals were further developed in self-categorisation theory, in which it is assumed that we aim to develop a positive social identity based on a positive self-concept and in which, therefore, there are important definitions of what, to the person, is an ingroup and what is an outgroup.

Factors that determine behaviour in intergroup relations are based on the perceived intergroup relationship; these include the permeability of the groups, the relative status of the groups and degree of competitiveness between the groups. If the boundaries between groups are seen to be permeable, for example, in a socially mobile country in which it is possible to pass from, say, working class to middle class, then people may work to move from the lower perceived group in order to become a member of the higher perceived group and to enhance their own self-esteem and social identity. However, where the groups are impermeable and movement between groups is impossible, because of caste in the Hindu caste system or because of ethnicity, for example, then the relatively devalued group may attempt to redefine the values on which the groups are compared, with Tajfel considering the 'black is beautiful' movement to have been one example of such a process. Where the groups are impermeable but the status relations are more unstable, there is likely to be greater competitiveness between the groups. Later in the chapter we will examine how these factors influence conflict and prejudice between groups, in addition to how the ultimate conflict, that of war, can be fuelled by such intergroup processes.

The combination of the social identity approach, together with the appraisal-based emotion theory that we have outlined in earlier chapters, provides a powerful tool with which to understand our reactions to groups, organisations and governments. This approach provides a framework with which to understand why one type of club membership, a type of work organisation or whatever can lead to a positive self-concept and positive social identity for one person, yet have quite the opposite effect for another person. Up to this point, we have been considering social identity and group membership in a very abstract form, so now we can examine concrete examples and how they impact on the individual's experience and behaviour.

Membership and support of specific football clubs provides an interesting forum in which to study ingroup and outgroup relations, with both psychologists and sociologists carrying out research on how football club support links to physical and verbal aggression and how it can spill over into football hooliganism. Supporters of clubs are often supporters of a club for life, with issues of status and competitiveness varying according to which outgroup is being considered. For example, the city of Glasgow has two famous football clubs, Glasgow Rangers and Glasgow Celtic, that provide classic examples of ingroup outgroup friction and rivalry. Just to add spice to the mix, the two clubs also divide on religious lines, with Glasgow Rangers being largely a Protestant club that attracts Protestant supporters and Glasgow Celtic being largely a Catholic club with Catholic supporters. An example of the extremes of this group definition through religion concerns the football player Mo Johnston. He was a Catholic who initially played for Celtic, where he was a prolific striker and scored numerous goals for the club. After a spell at Nantes in France, he then returned to Glasgow in 1989, but this time to play for Glasgow Rangers rather than Celtic. To this day, supporters of each club still argue over the rights and wrongs of Mo Johnston (*Guardian*, 10 July 2009), with one group of Rangers fanatics even providing 'corrected' statistics for the club's history that exclude all goals scored by him.

Of course, such conflict is mild in comparison to the fact that at least one war has resulted from a football game. The so-called *La Guerra Del Futbol* was fought for four days in 1969 between Honduras and El Salvador in Central America. A series of three matches in the World Cup qualifying rounds between the two countries highlighted existing border tensions that led to the four-day war in which thousands of troops and civilians died. Lucky that football is just a game.

Psychologists have now begun to study the presumed social identity processes that are thought to lie behind the violence and hooliganism associated with football. Hooliganism is not new to football but was apparent even during its origins in the nineteenth century, with deaths, injuries and damage to property being inflicted by one group of team supporters against another (Russell, 2004). Most significant football matches are now heavily policed such that groups of supporters may sometimes target the police rather than the other team's supporters in their attacks. Different research traditions on violence have either investigated individual personality differences with pro-violence attitudes, or the social identity and situational perspectives, which have included an examination of deindividuation involving loss of self-awareness from early work in sociology on group violence. In Reicher's (e.g. 2001) adaptation of the social identity approach for violent group behaviour, the proposal is not that people lose their identity as earlier models suggested, but rather that increased group salience, anonymity and adherence to the norms of the group may increase the likelihood of violence.

In a test of these different models, van Hiel *et al.* (2007) interviewed football fans in Ghent in Belgium and collected data from 109 participants. The results showed that individual attitude variables contributed to hooliganism, with pro-violence attitudes making a strong contribution. Equally, however, a strong sense of social identity towards the football club, combined with the pro-violent attitudes, provided the best prediction of participation in aggressive group behaviour. Part of this process involves the reduction in self-awareness that can occur in group situations.

The social identity approach also helps us to understand many ingroup and outgroup phenomena in relation to religion and religious identity. We will discuss religion in detail in Chapter 5, so at this point we simply want to show how the concept of social identity can help us to understand membership of religious groups. One interesting difference between religions is that some religions only allow membership through a person's parents, and so one cannot choose to be a member of that religion, whereas other religions actively invite non-members to join, sometimes with missionary zeal. Religions therefore differ on *essentialism*, the degree to which there is choice or no choice in membership. For example, Judaism is a highly essentialist religion, in contrast to the other two main Abrahamic religions of Christianity and Islam, which are generally pro-conversion and choice. It is possible to speculate that perhaps some of the 3,000 years of conflict and aggression towards the Jewish people has been fuelled by attempts to disprove Judaism's belief that they are God's 'chosen people', an elite club that no one can join except through birthright. Of course, later Abrahamic religions have responded tit-for-tat, such as in the Catholic claim that only Catholics can go to heaven, but such ingroup versus outgroup beliefs have contributed much to aggression and violence perpetrated by religious groups against each other.

A study by Fischer and colleagues (2007) examined attitudes of different Christian and Muslim groups towards themselves and each other on factors such as religious identity, aggression and attitudes towards terrorism. A sample of Christians and Muslims in the Ukraine and Azerbaijan completed questionnaires that measured each of these factors. The results showed that religious identity was more important to Muslim than to Christian respondents, but attitudes towards aggression and terrorism did not differ between the two groups. In contrast, a further survey of non-Muslim German respondents rated Muslims as having a more supportive attitude towards aggression and terrorism, results that ran counter to the study of Muslims themselves. These types of studies point to the increasing value of the social identity approach in our understanding of ingroup and outgroup relations, whether it be in terms of religion or other forms of social group membership. How we define our own ingroups versus how we define and contrast outgroups has important significance for intergroup relations in terms of prejudice, aggression and conflict. We will return to examine these ingroup–outgroup biases and how they impact on our search for happiness later in the chapter. First, however, we will turn to an aspect of the happiness industry that impacts both on those who work within it and those of us on the outside of it who are daily in receipt of its attempts to sell us happiness.

Work and emotional labour

The rise of the 'service economy' has led to an increased interest in the concept of emotional labour, in which an employee is required to express a publicly and organisationally acceptable feeling which may be in contrast to how the employee actually feels. The great sociologist, Max Weber, stated that, in the perfect bureaucracy, 'there is no place for love, hatred and all purely personal, irrational and emotional elements' (Weber, 1978), in the tradition of twentieth-century rationalist sociological models of organisations. However, the post-rationalist critical theories have provided a richer analysis of organisations that find value in the role of emotions within organisations.

The concept of emotional labour was first introduced by the sociologist Arlie Hochschild in *The Managed Heart* (1983). One of the groups that Hochschild was particularly interested in was that of airline flight attendants, who are typically expected to wear a smile and be polite and positive with airline passengers no matter how they are feeling themselves (though she had probably never flown on a Russian airline when she wrote the book). A contrasting group would be undertakers who attend funerals and who are meant to look sad whatever they might actually be feeling. In all cases, the worker is required to have face-to-face or voice-to-voice contact with members of the public in which the worker is meant to evoke or empathise with a particular emotion state during the interaction.

A further distinction that has been made is that between 'surface acting' and 'deep acting'. In surface acting, the employee is clearly faking the emotion, for example, with use of the 'false smile', which involves muscles around the mouth but not those around the eye that are present in the 'genuine' or 'Duchenne smile' (e.g. Ekman, 2003). With such false smiles, there is a faster return to the facial neutral state than with the genuine smile, which fades more slowly. In deep acting, employees may be expected to manage their inner feelings to match those expected in the interaction situation; thus, the employee is expected to become an expert actor who manages his or her inner feelings to be appropriate to the situation, such that a smile is expected to be a genuine smile and thereby recruit the muscles around the eyes as well as those around the lips. Some employers in the service industry train their employees in deep acting and how to manage emotion displays so that they seem authentic rather than false. There is some evidence to suggest that surface acting may be more stressful than deep acting because it may be more linked to feelings of inauthenticity and even depersonalisation and depression, which can lead to burnout. Within the SPAARS model presented earlier (Power and Dalgleish, 2015), surface acting could map onto the conscious and effortful generation of action, whereas deep acting would be the automatisation of the relevant skills so that the actions become more associative route based.

Although Hochschild originally focused on the airline industry, there are a large number of occupations in which demands of emotional labour are made, including restaurant workers, nurses, fashion models, care assistants, teachers, hotel workers, shop workers and telephone salespeople. One of the predictions that can be made on the basis of social identity theory is that, in organisations with which employees identify and which therefore provide part of their social identity, it should be easier for employees to provide more authentic emotional labour and thereby experience the work as less demanding and stressful than if they are working for an organisation with which they do not identify, and which therefore should be more stressful or demanding in the longer term. Philipp and Schupbach (2010) carried out a longitudinal study of 102 teachers over a period of a year, in which they were assessed on a variety of measures that included role identity, exhaustion and emotional labour. After one year, those teachers who showed authentic management of emotions, or deep acting, were significantly less exhausted than those teachers who used surface acting. Moreover, there seemed to be a negative cycle in which, as teachers became more stressed and exhausted, they attempted to use more surface acting strategies, which had an increasingly exhausting effect. The researchers also reported that teachers who were more dedicated, in that they identified closely with the role, that is, in support of the social identity prediction we made above, were less likely to use any surface or deep acting strategies and reported less exhaustion in their work.

One of the additional predictions from the emotional labour literature is that so-called emotional dissonance should also add to the stress of managing emotions in the service industry. Emotional dissonance, drawn from Leon Festinger's proposals in the 1950s for cognitive dissonance, is the situation in which the expressed or displayed emotion is discrepant from inner felt emotions. For example, in the SPAARS model (Power and Dalgleish, 2015), when the schematic model emotions differ from the low-level associative emotions because, for example, the situational demands force the employee to display a positive emotion in contrast to a negative mood state, this demand on resources is likely to prove exhausting, especially if the demands recur repeatedly over a long period of time. A study by van Dijk and Kirk (2007) demonstrated that both emotional labour and emotional dissonance could have separate effects on employees. In their study, they examined a group of employees working in heritage museum sites who were interviewed about their roles. Qualitative analyses suggested that emotional labour is demanding in itself, but especially so when they were experiencing emotional dissonance, such that both factors are important in describing work experience and demands in the service sector.

The other side of the equation for emotional labour research is whether or not an employee in the service economy who expresses appropriate affect actually has the desired effect on the client or customer. It is known from work on so-called emotional contagion (e.g. Hatfield *et al.*, 1994) that these interpersonal effects are commonly observed, such that the emotion expressed by one person is empathically experienced by an observer. Recent work on 'mirror neurons' showing that certain neurons can respond to social signals from others by mirroring their affect provides a neuronal basis for such effects (e.g. Rizzolatti and Craighero, 2004). Studies of emotional labour in general support the use of such strategies in that clients and customers are more likely to report satisfaction with the experience, are more likely to recommend a particular organisation to others and are more likely to return to such a business in the future. However, anyone who has ever flown on a Russian airline (as noted above) and then stayed in a Soviet-style, Soviet-era hotel will immediately experience a contrast to an American-style one, because the grim-faced hotel employees can seem more like out-of-work KGB interrogators than workers in the service industry. The difference, of course, is that the ex-KGB receptionist is at least giving you his or her genuine feelings with no acting whatsoever, an interaction that, at least in principle, should be appreciated by an emotion researcher. Of course, the fact that they are having to work in a different line of employment to that in which they were trained could lead to other personal problems that even their authentic displays of contempt and disdain might not be sufficient to counteract!

The oldest profession

The final area of work that we will mention in relation to emotional labour is that of the supposedly oldest profession, the sex industry, which must be near the pinnacle of the happiness industry. The Wikipedia entry for 'Pornography' (accessed 17 March 2015 in the name of science) states that the US pornography business is concentrated primarily in a single valley in California, San Fernando ('Silicone Valley' being one of its alternative names), in which there are approximately 200 production companies that employ 1,500 pornography stars. Wikipedia estimates that, in 2014, there was an income of US$13 billion from approximately 11,000 films that were produced. That is a lot of films per porn star! Other figures show that there are now over 4,000 striptease clubs in the US, almost a 100 per cent increase in the last decade, with an estimated income of US$3.1 billion. The sex industry is, therefore, one of the biggest industries not just in the US, but now worldwide.

The requirements for emotional labour and the experience of emotional dissonance must be higher for sex workers than for any other form of work. We will focus primarily on research carried out with female prostitutes, but note that male prostitution is an increasingly important area in need of research. The emotional management strategies that are involved in protecting oneself emotionally (and sometimes physically) whilst running a financially successful business, and which, typically, may have a regular set of clients, are likely to require some extreme and novel forms of emotional labour. As Pateman (1988) emphasised, many of the strategies used by prostitutes are designed to protect the woman's sense of self through a process of distancing in order to manage boundaries and feelings. Hoigard and Finstad (1992) reported that prostitutes carefully retained certain physical boundaries, keep strictly to time, disguise their own physical appearance and avoid emotional relationships with their longer term clients. Most prostitutes report limits on the type of activities they will perform, retaining certain body exclusion zones:

> If I have done the same client a million times, they still get the same *spiel*: don't kiss, don't do anal and you can only kiss and touch on top part of body.
>
> (*Krystal, quoted in Sanders, 2005*)

That is, many prostitutes reserve certain intimate sexual acts, including mouth-to-mouth kissing, for their personal romantic sexual relationships in order to maintain the boundaries between work and personal pleasure. Additional barriers include the use of the condom as a 'psychological barrier', which prevents the intimacy associated with romantic sex; thus, the condom is used not just for disease and pregnancy prevention but also as a barrier to psychological intimacy. O'Neill (2001) also noted that many of her interviewees prefer to offer domination services, not simply because these are better remunerated, but also because there may actually be less body contact and less likelihood of penetration. The client's fantasies involving caning, whipping or bondage typically include a set of routinised speeches and comments that are not part of the prostitute's own fantasy world, though the domination can offer a strong sense of increased power.

Teela Sanders (2005) carried out interviews with 50 female prostitutes working in Birmingham, UK. The participants were indoor sex workers, because, as Sanders notes, street workers are more characterised by drug use and abuse and exploitative 'pimping' relationships, whereas women who work in saunas, brothels and escort agencies represent the more typical majority form of sex work. She found that indoor sex workers tend to enter prostitution at a later age than street workers, at an average age of 23 years. More than half of the participants reported the preference for bondage and domination services, as noted above:

> The domination ones, they are not actually touching your body – it is all caning them or finishing off with the hand. They are the best ones. You are giving them abuse which you can't do in actual life to a man can ya?!
>
> *(Laura, quoted in Sanders, 2005)*

Many of the women in Sanders' study reported that there were no real emotions involved in their sex work, but they experienced the sex work as clinical and sterile:

> It is personal at home, in here it is clinical. At home it is for my pleasure. I swear to god sex work is like something you hate doing but it comes to me like washing up, like, it has got to be done.
>
> *(Astrid, quoted in Sanders, 2005)*

One of the most significant observations from Sanders' interviews was what she termed the 'manufactured identity' that many of the sex workers used specifically for their work. This manufactured identity typically includes the use of a pseudonym, which is widespread in the sex industry, an imaginary life story, with an imaginary family and childhood history, some of which can be extremely inventive:

> I come from a public school background and at 18 my father, who was a group captain in the Air Force, sent me to the States to university. Now I am spending time here and in New York. Daddy is a retired Marshall and worth three and a half million and I am now waiting for his inheritance.
>
> *(Natasha, quoted in Sanders, 2005)*

Sanders' notes that this participant, Natasha, has had breast implants, wears a gorgeous wig and the expensive clothes of a seductress, and rents a penthouse for her work which she claims to own. In reality, Natasha observes:

> I have a very normal background. Nothing like what I portray. But you get into role and you kind of believe it yourself, but of course I do this for the money. They believe it and it works for me . . . . At home I am completely different. I even look totally different and when women from the agency see me outside of here they don't recognize me.

The pseudonym and manufactured identity used by many sex workers allows the women, in emotional labour terms, to deep act and provide a more authentic and convincing performance for their clients. At the same time, the acted role protects the true self identity, in part to prevent clients discovering any personal details about them, but also, because many sex workers work in the sex industry without the knowledge of their family and friends, they thereby avoid moral condemnation and stereotyping through their assumed identities.

In summary, there is now an increasingly widespread service economy that makes high demands on employees who are required to perform emotional labour in their interactions with clients or customers. This service economy is just one part of what can be labelled the happiness industry in which the aim is to manufacture and sell happiness. Although the business is to some extent successful in that, sure enough, clients may report increased satisfaction with their 'have a nice day' sweet smiling attendants, especially when the roles are deep acted with authenticity, there can be a considerable cost to employees from this emotional labour. This leaves one increasingly concerned about the expectations of both employers and clients of the happiness industry. In the end, my heart is with the stern, Soviet-era, ex-KGB hotel attendants who give it to you straight. As Nixon (2009) noted in a study of 35 unemployed low-skilled men, there is a considerable antipathy in the masculine working-class identity to engage in these forms of emotional labour and to appearing deferential in the service sector, which excludes the service sector as a source of employment for them: 'I can't put a smiley face on'. Perhaps they need a strong dose of Prozac to set them to rights? The 'bottled happiness industry' will be considered next.

Bottled happiness

The possible intolerance and avoidance of negative emotions in our culture (see Chapter 3), especially as promoted early on in positive psychology, creates a social context in which people believe that they should rid themselves of negative emotions. The request of 'please take away my anxiety' or 'remove my depression' or whatever is heard regularly when new clients attend their initial appointments with psychiatrists or psychologists. The problem is that there is a major multi-national industry out there, which, in collusion with medicine, does attempt to take away our negative feelings and leave us living happily ever after, or such are the claims (cf. Frances, 2013).

The pharmaceutical industry is one of the major developments of the current era. Although all cultures throughout history have made use of naturally occurring plants and the alcohol that results from fermentation of sugars in fruit and other plants, the modern scale of the pharmaceutical industry has no comparison, apart from with the current drug, alcohol and tobacco industries. For now, we will concentrate on the pharmaceutical industry, but will further examine drugs and alcohol in Chapter 6 when we consider health and illness.

The scale of the pharmaceutical industry is immense. Figures on industry revenues (e.g. see VFA, 2015) showed that over US$962 billion were spent globally on prescription drugs in 2012, with the US accounting for the highest proportion at 36 per cent of this market. There has been a continuing increase in profits as other industries were going into financial downturn such that the pharmaceutical industries are the most profitable in the US. The major drugs sold worldwide include Pfizer's anti-cholesterol Lipitor with nearly US$13 billion global sales at its peak in 2006, followed by Plavix, an anticoagulant from Bristol Myers Squibb, and Nexium, an anti-heartburn pill from AstraZeneca. In terms of total revenue, Novartis lead the pack with US$50.8 billion in 2012, followed by Pfizer with US$46.9 billion, Merck and Co. at US$40.1 billion and Sanofi at US$37.8 billion. To put these figures in context, the estimated GDP for Mali, one of the world's poorest countries, was estimated at US$10.3 billion in 2012. Our pursuit of health and happiness is very big business indeed and it exists on a scale that puts many of the world's poorest countries into the shade.

It would be possible to examine the evidence for each of the pharmaceutical industry's major drugs and ask to what extent it improves the world's health and happiness. For example, on the basis of the record consumption of prescription medicines in the US, if the equations were that simple, then the US should have the best longevity and happiness of any nation by a long way. In fact, it is the opposite, as some of the figures that we examined in Chapter 1 demonstrate, for example from the work summarised by Wilkinson and Pickett (2010). The longevity figures alone show that the US trails most of Europe and Japan by a distance, so their heavy consumption of pharmaceuticals is not having the desired effect. However, rather than examine all prescription medicines with all their exaggerated claims and flaws, we will focus on mental health pharmaceuticals because they are explicitly marketed for the replacement of misery with happiness. And no pharmaceutical has gained as much notoriety as Prozac in this realm, so we will briefly consider the Prozac story.

Prozac

The story of Prozac begins in the Eli Lilly laboratories in the early 1970s when it was recognised that one of their antihistamines, diphenhydramine, seemed to show some antidepressant properties. One of the Eli Lilly scientists, David Wong, developed a substance with the intention of inhibiting uptake of the neurotransmitter serotonin, and then published the first article on the newly named fluoxetine in 1974, subsequently to be given the trade name Prozac in 1975. The drug was eventually given US Food and Drug Administration (FDA) approval in 1987, following which Eli Lilly began selling the drug, with sales in the US reaching US$350 million within one year. However, Eli Lilly's claim that they had developed the first selective serotonin reuptake inhibitor (SSRI) had to be corrected because an earlier SSRI, zimelidine, had been developed previously.

The controversy that has surrounded Prozac has not, however, been limited to whether or not it was the first SSRI, but has also included a range of critical clinical issues, some of which have not been fully resolved. The first clinical issue relates to the evidence base for the use of Prozac for depression in adults. Current National Institute for Health and Care Excellence (NICE) guidelines in the UK only recommend pharmacological treatment such as Prozac as a first-line treatment for severe depression (NICE, 2009). This recommendation is supported by a recent meta-analysis, which did not demonstrate the efficacy of antidepressants in minor to moderate depression (Barbui et al., 2011). However, the recommendations also state that treatment should be continued for six months following remission of symptoms. Continuing treatment with antidepressants reduces the odds of relapse by 70 per cent compared with treatment discontinuation (Geddes et al. 2003). Choosing among the different antidepressants available has not previously been evidence-based, but a meta-analysis in 2009 has offered some guidance. Cipriani et al. (2009) investigated the acute treatment of unipolar major depression with 12 new-generation antidepressants. Mirtazapine, escitalopram, venlafaxine and sertraline were found to be significantly more efficacious than Prozac and a number of other antidepressants. Escitalopram and sertraline were the best accepted, and hence less discontinued than antidepressants such as Prozac because of the side-effects from the medication.

There is also continued debate over the role of antidepressants in the long-term management of bipolar disorder. Earlier concern over their use resulted from a small maintenance study (Prien et al., 1984) that suggested that bipolar patients on imipramine alone experienced an unacceptably large number of manic relapses. Subsequently, most guidelines have reflected a more cautious approach to recommending treatment with an antidepressant such as Prozac. Long-term treatment of bipolar patients with antidepressants is very common in clinical practice, but evidence to confirm their role in the prevention of depressive episodes is lacking (Power, 2013b). Although almost all of the antidepressants used in the treatment of unipolar depression can have some efficacy in the treatment of bipolar depression, the response rates are even lower and there is a risk of precipitating a manic episode or inducing and accelerating rapid cycling between extreme mood states (Compton and Nemeroff, 2000). Evidence is scarce, but recent studies have suggested that SSRIs may be better tolerated, work more quickly and have lower potential of inducing mania or rapid cycling compared to the earlier tricyclic antidepressants (Nemeroff et al., 2001). In general, the choice depends on issues such as previous beneficial response, side-effects and tolerability. A randomised placebo controlled trial of cognitive behaviour therapy and Prozac found that pharmacotherapy alone reduced depression by only 18–21 per cent compared to placebo, but that combined treatment did not reduce the risk of relapse of moderate depressive disorder, which again points to the use of antidepressants such as Prozac only in severe cases of depression (Petersen *et al.* 2004).

The second clinical controversy surrounding Prozac is whether or not it increases the risk of suicide and homicide in adults. A famous case in 1989 led to a protracted law suit against Eli Lilly that was not settled until 1994. The case involved Joseph Wesbecker in Louisville Kentucky, who had been taking Prozac for four weeks, when he went to his place of work, a printing company named Standard Gravure, and opened fire with a semi-automatic rifle and a number of pistols at the staff working in the plant. Standard Gravure had not long before been in the news because it had been bought out by Michael Shea, who had used US$11 million from the employees' pension fund to enable the purchase of the printing works. Wesbecker, during a 30-minute shooting spree, killed 7 and injured 12 of the workers in the plant and then shot himself. As part of the legal proceedings against Eli Lilly and Prozac, Eli Lilly were forced to release internal company documents that had begun to chart the risks of suicide, homicide and increased violence linked with Prozac, which were then used as evidence in further legal cases against Eli Lilly.

The Prozac Survivors Group documented hundreds of such cases in the 1990s: people who had suffered from increased violence against self and others, increased suicidal ideation and increased suicide attempts. More recent summaries of the evidence suggest that, in adults, the net effect seems to be neutral on suicidal behaviour but possibly protective for suicidal ideation (Stone *et al.*, 2009; Gibbons *et al.*, 2012). In a large Finish cohort study, Tiihonen *et al.* (2006) found a substantially lower mortality during SSRI use, however, among subjects who had ever used an antidepressant, there was an increased risk of attempted suicide (39 per cent) even if completed suicide was reduced.

The third clinical controversy has been about the use of Prozac with children and adolescents. The risk of suicidality associated with use of antidepressants appears to be strongly age dependent, with adolescents at particular risk. In the early 2000s, claims that SSRIs increased suicidal behaviour threatened their reputation as 'safer' antidepressants. The US FDA issued a so-called 'black box' warning for antidepressants in relation to the risk of suicidal thoughts and behaviour in children and young adults following these concerns. Paroxetine and fluoxetine were particularly implicated, with their short half-life and significant withdrawal symptoms, which can be problematic where there is some erratic use of the medication in which the child or adolescent can be regularly going into a state of withdrawal. In children aged 10–19 years there was also a reported increased risk of death with paroxetine use (with an increased risk ratio of over 5.4). The UK NICE guidelines for treatment of depression in children and young people (NICE, 2005) state that antidepressant medication should not be used for the initial treatment of children and adolescents with mild depression, and that if they have moderate to severe depression the treatment offered should be a psychological therapy such as cognitive behaviour therapy, interpersonal psychotherapy or family therapy.

In summary, therefore, medical prescriptions for happiness are big business and one that the pharmaceutical industry thrives on. The dramatic increases in prescription rates for psychotropic medication in recent years is a testament to how medicine and the pharmaceutical industry collude together and make their fortunes from other people's misery. There are, however, an increasing number of critics of this aspect of the happiness industry (e.g. Healy, 2002; Frances, 2013), and it is reassuring that a number of national agencies have begun to protect the most vulnerable in society, such as children and adolescents, from the over-prescription of psychotropic medication. Nevertheless, we live in an age that encourages the intolerance of negative affect and the replacement of any form of psychic pain with the temporary anaesthesia produced by bottled happiness. As we have emphasised throughout this book, social and emotional development is about learning about all of our emotions and their functions, together with learning how to regulate them appropriately in a way that builds on our own development and brings us into healthy relationships with others. In the same way that, in previous decades, the over-prescription of antibiotics to children retarded their normal immune system development, the inappropriate over-protection of children and adolescents from negative emotions through pharmaceutical means will retard their socio-emotional development.

Conflict and prejudice

The majority of fair-minded liberal individuals would like to think of themselves as free of prejudice and believe that they support non-racist, non-sexist and non-ageist views and policies. That is, their stated or *explicit* attitudes demonstrate what fair-minded and liberal individuals they are. However, the truth tends to be less straightforward and more complex than this simple scenario would suggest. When it comes to measures of behaviour, automatic perceptual processes, reaction time measures and psychophysiology, indicators of prejudice and bias can often appear that the individual would consciously reject. They may even feel disgust that someone would suggest otherwise (Chaiken and Trope, 1999). In other words, people's *implicit* attitudes may sometimes conflict with their explicit attitudes. Such a system that leads to conflicting attitudes occurring in parallel with each other cannot be readily accommodated in the considerable number of single-process models that exist in psychology, such as in the cognitive therapy models that we have considered elsewhere (Power, 2010), because the models do not allow for parallel processes that potentially conflict with each other and produce different outcomes. However, in order to understand areas such as conflict and prejudice fully, we need to move away from these single-process models in psychology to dual-process and multi-process models (Power and Dalgleish, 2015).

To digress briefly before we return to the issue of conflict and prejudice, there is, of course, a considerable history within other areas of psychology for the idea of processes running in parallel with each other that are potentially in conflict. Hermann von Helmholtz, the great German nineteenth-century scientist, had, long before Freud, argued for the need for unconscious or automatic processes in visual perception and demonstrated conditions under which apparently integrated processes disintegrated or produced errors such as in visual illusions (Power, 1997). The psychoanalytic approach developed by Freud includes preconscious, conscious and unconscious systems that are typically in conflict with each other. Thus, the unconscious system is not considered to hold information in a consistent and logical manner, but contains contradictory and illogical material (e.g. Freud, 1915). The SPAARS model that we have presented does not owe its allegiance to psychoanalysis but is squarely based in modern cognitive approaches to emotion. Nevertheless, there are many insights within the psychoanalytic approach that inform both theory and practice in therapy that we will acknowledge as we proceed.

Our main point of departure, therefore, from extant single-process models in psychology is in the need for two distinct sets of conscious and unconscious or automatic processes that sometimes act in a synergistic manner, but at other times produce conflicting outputs. In addition to the evidence for two such routes or sets of processes that we have briefly cited from areas such as social cognition and psychoanalysis, there is also increasing evidence from research in neuroscience that two such separate routes exist. For example, Joseph LeDoux's (e.g. 1996) work on the acquisition and maintenance of fear in rats clearly shows the need for a fast fear-based system that operates through the amygdala in the mid-brain (or what used to be known as the limbic system) and a higher route through the cortex. These two routes can operate in tandem and synergistically or can produce conflicting outputs depending on the exact conditions and circumstances. LeDoux's work in animals together with similar work in human neuroscience points to the need for more complex multi-level systems in order to understand emotion reactions in humans. We argue therefore that our own SPAARS model of emotion can provide such an understanding and demonstrate the need for more complex models that do justice to the phenomena under consideration and provide a richer basis for the therapeutic endeavours needed to work with a range of emotional disorders.

Having taken this digression into dual- and multi-process models, we will now launch directly into some of the evidence in psychology and elsewhere that can help us to understand how conflict and prejudice operate even in apparently well-intentioned people.

The Stanford prison experiment

One of the most shocking and surprising studies ever carried out in psychology, and certainly one that no ethics committee would provide approval for nowadays, was the Stanford prison experiment. The study was headed by Stanford University professor of psychology, Philip Zimbardo, between 14 and 20 August 1971, though it had been planned to run the study for over a week longer. The study had such a devastating effect on Zimbardo and his colleagues that he did not write it up in full until 2007, when he published the full details in his astonishing book *The Lucifer Effect: Understanding How Good People Turn Evil*.

In the prison study, Zimbardo selected 24 healthy young men, mostly students, who were then randomly assigned to being either prison guards or prisoners. A makeshift prison was set up in the basement of the psychology department, in which prisoners were confined two to three in each cell and forced to wear tunics that reached only as far as their knees and without underwear. Many of the activities led to the prisoners' genitalia being on view, which encouraged some of the sexual humiliation handed out by the guards. The guards wore khaki uniforms and reflecting sunglasses so that prisoners were unable to see their eyes, which added to the sense of distance and detachment from the prisoners. The guards also carried wooden batons, which, although they had been instructed not to use in any form of physical violence, were actually used by some guards to that effect.

Zimbardo's (2007) gruelling account of the prison study begins with how, in order to add to the authenticity of the study, the prisoners were initially arrested by the Palo Alto police department and put though normal police procedures in which they were charged with a range of offences, including armed robbery, penal code violation and burglary. On the first day of the arrest, a Sunday, the prisoners were blindfolded, put in ankle chains and led into their basement cells. The guards had already agreed a set of 17 basic rules, which were read out to the prisoners. These included:

- Rule 7. Prisoners must address each other by number only
- Rule 10. Prisoners will be allowed 5 minutes in the lavatory. No prisoner will be allowed to return to the lavatory within 1 hour after scheduled lavatory period. Lavatory visitations are controlled by guards
- Rule 15. Prisoners must obey all orders issued by guards at all times
- Rule 17. Failure to obey any of the rules may result in punishment.

In fact, because of the punitive, humiliating, authoritarian and idiosyncratic nature of the tasks and treatment demanded by the guards, most of the prisoners were deemed to have broken at least one of the rules most of the time. By Monday, there was already a prisoner rebellion that was brewing because of the guards' punitive actions. By Monday evening, Prisoner 8612 was already close to breakdown and had to be released into the care of his girlfriend. However, by Tuesday, rumours circulated that the prison was going to be attacked by ex-Prisoner 8612 and his buddies, who were going to trash the prison and release the inmates. Zimbardo himself had by this stage become too immersed in his role as prison superintendent and completely believed the rumours to the extent that he tried to persuade the Palo Alto police to let him use one of their station prisons instead of the psychology department basement, so as to protect his experiment. Over the next couple of days, a further two prisoners had to be released because of concerns about their mental health, and Zimbardo's attempt to 'plant' an informant as a prisoner failed because the informant turned rebellion leader when he saw just how badly the prisoners were being treated by the guards. The prison was then closed one week earlier than planned on Friday 20 August because of the degree of distress being caused to the five remaining prisoners, in which many of the guards were inventing newer and more evil ways of torturing them.

One of the main precipitants for the closure seems to have been a powerful emotional outburst from Christina Maslach, Zimbardo's girlfriend and a psychologist, who, interestingly, became famous for her later work on 'occupational burnout'. Maslach is reported in Zimbardo's book, *The Lucifer Effect*, to have had a stand-up argument with Zimbardo on the steps of the psychology department in which she told him that what he was doing was wrong, that students were suffering and that he was personally responsible as the principal investigator: 'What you are doing to these boys is a terrible thing!' (Zimbardo, 2007, p. 171). Up until that point, Zimbardo seems to have been totally transfixed by the power of the prison experiment, and it took a metaphorical slap in the face from his girlfriend to wake him up. Before the study was wound up on the Friday, however, there was still time for further sexual degradation of the prisoners when half the prisoners were instructed by the guards to bend over and pretend to be camels, whilst the other half were instructed to 'hump them'. This degradation occurred at 1 a.m. when the prisoners were woken up in the middle of the night for one of their innumerable headcounts.

Zimbardo (2007) interprets the findings from the Stanford prison experiment to demonstrate that situational factors can be extremely powerful in making people become prejudiced and act in evil ways. His argument is that the prisoners and the guards were completely randomly assigned to roles from among an apparently healthy group of young male students. This 'situationism' runs contrary to many theories that assume that dispositional traits within individuals make them more or less prone to 'evil'. For example, the concept of psychopathy argues that some individuals, through a lack of empathy and appreciation of others, are capable of inflicting pain on others, but that the majority of us should not be so capable (Blair *et al.*, 2005). Whatever the explanation for the small percentage of such psychopathic individuals in the population, we believe that a more complex dual-processing account needs to be taken in order to understand the possibility for prejudice, conflict and evil in the majority of non-psychopathic individuals, but not in terms of the extreme situationism described by Zimbardo.

In a dual-processing or multi-processing model such as SPAARS, the balance between the high-level controlled processes and the low-level automatic processes will vary according to both conditions external to the individual and to internal conditions (Power and Dalgleish, 2015). Under conditions of stress, tiredness, illness, social pressures, and so on, the balance of psychological control is more likely to shift towards low-level automatic processes, which, in turn, are more likely to display prejudice, conflict and bias (cf. Kahneman, 2011). In the Zimbardo experiment, some of the guards under the social pressure from Zimbardo and his colleagues clearly went beyond normal moral limits in their treatment of the prisoners, but this mistreatment was exacerbated by a range of factors, including working nightshifts, wanting to do the study 'well' and opposition from the prisoners, which meant there was an ongoing level of explicit conflict between the two groups throughout the study. However, some of the guards at least some of the time distanced themselves from the maltreatment and tried to preserve some humanity in their relationship with the prisoners. Ultimately, the best way to understand these internal and external forces is in the form of an interaction between the two, an 'interactionism' that many in psychology would argue for. Subsequent attempts to replicate the Stanford study have not even partially led to the same conclusions. The BBC prison study *The Experiment*, for example, which was overseen by two psychologists, Steve Reicher and Alex Haslam, reached very different conclusions to Zimbardo.

In relation to prejudice and conflict, studies of intrusive thoughts and imagery in normal healthy adults show that approximately 80 per cent of people report experiencing intrusive sexist, aggressive, ageist or racist thoughts (e.g. Rachman, 2003), which we then work hard to inhibit or even counteract by being even more careful not to act in such a way, because we believe sexist, ageist and racist attitudes to be wrong. However, these consciously unwanted products of automatic implicit processes can be used as a healthy warning against inappropriate behaviour rather than lead us to worry about our unconscious attitudes.

War and happiness

It may seem odd to conjoin the words 'war' and 'happiness' into a single phrase that links them together, but the proposal is that everything that we have been considering in this chapter in relation to the relentless pursuit of happiness, social identity with ingroups and outgroups, prejudice and conflict reaches a terrible and disastrous climax in the human species propensity for war. Indeed, we will begin with a consideration of what at some levels have to be the most paradoxical and contradictory forms of war, the religious wars. Religious wars have to be the most contradictory, given that most religions teach some forms of love, tolerance, acceptance and meaning in life, as we will explore in Chapter 5 (see also Power, 2012).

In the Middle Ages, the Crusades provided the classic examples of religious wars that, many would say, have been re-enacted recently in the George Bush and Tony Blair invasions of Iraq and Afghanistan. The Crusades were religious wars between Christianity and Islam over the control of Jerusalem and the Holy Land. They were launched under papal initiative, with the First Crusade being launched by Pope Urban II in 1095. Over the following 200 years various campaigns were launched with differing degrees of success, but they eventually failed to liberate the Holy Land from Muslim control. Occasionally, the Crusades even turned against their own at the whim of the papacy if he felt his authority was threatened. The Fourth Crusade ended up in Constantinople rather than in Jerusalem, where they outrageously attacked and sacked the city even though, at that time, Constantinople was Christian. A similar fate befell the Albigensians, or Cathars, when a crusade was launched against them by the appropriately named Pope Innocent III because of their opposition to the Pope and their apparently heretical Christian views. Many of the Cathar priests were famously burned alive at the foot of their last refuge, Montsegur, in the Pyrenees. The commander of the crusader army is reported to have been asked before the siege of Béziers in the south of France how to tell apart the Cathars from the Catholics, to which he gave the reply that has gone down in history: 'Kill them all, the Lord will recognise His own'.

The theme of Christian against Christian makes good reading for understanding many of the wars in the past two millennia. The 'Wars of Religion' involved most European powers over a period of nearly 130 years (approximately 1524–1648). The wars that can be placed in this category took place in France, Germany, Austria, Bohemia, the Netherlands, England, Scotland, Ireland, Switzerland and Denmark. The cause of the wars was the Protestant Reformation, beginning with the Augustinian monk Martin Luther's statement against the Catholic Church in Wittenberg in 1517, for which he was subsequently excommunicated from the Church in 1521. Protestantism spread rapidly throughout Germany, which was then part of the Holy Roman Empire, with the first conflicts occurring in 1524 with the German Peasants' War, in which there were an estimated 100,000 deaths.

It is clear that, although religions teach love, they also teach war. There is no major religion that has not fought a war with another religion, and just as many wars have been fought within religions as splits have occurred. To the naive outsider, these holy wars, or jihads or whatever, in which each side believes that God is on only their side, seem in complete contradiction to the supposedly high moral principles and the claim that morality would fall apart if we all became atheists (Power, 2012). Current and recent religious-based conflicts include Sudan (Islamic–Christian), Northern Ireland (Christian–Christian), Pakistan–India (Islam–Hindu), Afghanistan (Islam–Islam, with Christian interference), Iraq (Islam–Islam, with Christian interference), the Balkans (Islam–Christian) and Sri-Lanka (anti-Buddhist). Of course, we are not claiming that wars are fought *only* on religious grounds. Even the two Marxist–atheist states of the USSR and China fought battles along the disputed 2,738-mile border between the two countries in 1968 and 1969, with many at the time worried that the conflict would lead to a nuclear world war because the Soviets came close to a nuclear strike against the Chinese nuclear test site at Lop Nur. The point is that whilst all religions take the high moral ground, at the same time they seem to consider that the initiation of war and the forced imposition of religious belief on conquered peoples is perfectly acceptable.

The world's major axis of conflict is no longer the cold war of capitalism versus communism, but it is now the holy war of Christianity versus Islam. In their histories, both Christian and Muslims have been guilty of unspeakable atrocities and of war-based expansion into peaceful territories. Add to this mix the continuing conflict in the Middle East between Islam and the third Abrahamic religion, Judaism, and you have to wish that Abraham and his religions had never been born. If one were to estimate the number of deaths due to conflicts within the Bible-based religions, it would be an unbelievable number and one that the war-mongering God of the Old Testament would have been proud.

Of the current religions with their propensity for war, the Islamic jihad ranks high in beliefs that can lead to a destabilisation of our planet. According to the *Dictionary of Islam*, a jihad is defined as: 'A religious war with those who are unbelievers in the mission of Muhammad . . . enjoined especially for the purpose of advancing Islam and repelling evil from Muslims'. Part of the problem for Islam is that the founder of the religion, Muhammad, spent much of his life fighting in wars; thus, even the most holy city of Mecca was not converted to Islam until Muhammad returned from exile in Medina with an army and took over the city. Up until that time, the holy site of the Kaaba in Mecca, which is now the primary pilgrimage destination for the Muslim *hajj*, is reported to have been a polytheistic religious centre with representations of over 360 gods that included statues of Jesus and his mother, Mary. Indeed, our term 'assassin' comes from a militant Islamic group that was established in Syria and Iran in the eleventh and twelfth centuries and that used political murder as a means of gaining control, a tradition that has continued in many militant Islamic groups to this day.

The role of dictators

It would be a mistake solely to focus on religion and religious wars as the only source of conflict in recent history. In terms of one of the themes of this chapter, we also need to consider the psychology of authoritarian dictators who have typically manipulated the ingroup versus outgroup stereotypes and have thereby led their nations both to internal conflict and genocide, as well as to wars with other nations.

The twentieth century has to be close to the top of the league for centuries with great dictators. Stalin, Hitler and Mao Zedong rank up there with any of the great dictators in history for their degree of ruthlessness and capacity to manipulate and control the masses. All were involved in either major national or international conflicts that led to the loss of millions of their citizens. All three of them had networks of spies and informants in which even husbands and wives could not trust each other, with millions of people imprisoned, tortured or murdered because they were perceived as threats. Each of these dictators also disposed of their own closest colleagues and allies who had assisted them and their parties to rise into positions of power. For example, Stalin, who was born in Georgia as Iosif Dzhugashvili, but adopted the name 'Stalin' from the Russian word for steel, prevented Leon Trotsky from succeeding Lenin as Head of the Soviet Union. Eventually, after Stalin had thrown him out of the communist party and out of the Soviet Union, Trotsky was assassinated in Mexico City in August 1940 by an NKVD agent (Stalin's predecessor to the KGB), who struck Trotsky with an ice axe. Mao Zedong used the brutality of the ironically labelled 'Cultural Revolution' in which young red guards were encouraged to brutalise and torture their seniors, also as a cover to rid the country of many senior members of the Chinese Communist Party. The first to be killed was the Minister of Coal, whom Mao hated (see Jung Chang and Jon Halliday's revealing biography *Mao: The Unknown Story* published in 2005). Ernst Rohm, who was head of the Nazi Stormtroopers and who had helped bring Hitler to power, was reputedly the only Nazi on personal terms with Adolf Hitler and who was allowed to call Hitler by his first name. However, that did not save Rohm from being arrested and then shot on Hitler's orders in the infamous 'Night of the Long Knives' in 1934, when Rohm and many other senior Stormtroopers and politicians were murdered because Hitler saw them as threats to his own power.

The point is that dictators such as Stalin, Hitler and Mao Zedong were all perfectly capable of murdering their closest colleagues and allies in order to remove threats to their power and to enhance their dominance. It is no surprise, therefore, that they were equally capable of murdering millions of anonymous people who were unknown to them, but who were typically members of stereotyped out-groups, who were blamed for their countries' ills.

The other side of the great dictators such as Stalin, Hitler and Mao Zedong was that they were also capable of convincing millions of others, their own loyal supporters, that what they were doing would lead them to happiness and to a utopian future. Hitler promised that the Third Reich was a new Roman Empire and that it would last a thousand years. Hitler's pure Aryan race would rule this empire and rid itself of the Semitic peoples who were long-described as an opposing race to the Aryans. The purity and superiority of the Aryan race was maintained through compulsory sterilisation of mentally ill and intellectually disabled people, and through the forced euthanasia of institutionalised individuals. The Final Solution was the programme of the Holocaust that was implemented by Heinrich Himmler under Hitler's orders. Himmler is reported to have always carried a copy of the religious text the *Bhagavad Gita*, because it was an ancient Aryan text that helped to relieve him of any guilt. The Nazi concentration camps were opened in Germany in 1933 when they were primarily used to detain Hitler's political opponents. However, by 1942 there were over 300 concentration camps in Germany alone, which held and then murdered Jews, political prisoners, gypsies, homosexuals and the mentally ill. An estimated 6 million Jewish people were murdered as part of the Final Solution, mostly in the main extermination camps, with over a million being killed in the Auschwitz-Birkenau camp alone. The total loss of over 60 million military and civilian casualties makes World War II the deadliest in history.

The challenges laid down by dictators and their authoritarian regimes are immense and require an understanding that is partly based on psychology, but where the solutions rest in social systems and politics. In order to understand evil on a mass scale, we need to understand not only each individual's varying capacity for evil, but also how group phenomena operate on the medium and large scale, otherwise psychology will never address the main issues that threaten our existence. In the next section, therefore, we will point to some of the first steps that are helping us to tackle some of these major issues.

A note of optimism

The problem with writing a book which, among many other things, is critical of some of the premises underlying positive psychology, is that people think not only that I am something of a party pooper who is raining on the happiness parade, but also that I must be one of those dour pessimists for whom nothing ever seems right – like some grim Scottish Calvinist from the Hebridean Islands who had positive emotions socialised out of him at an early age. Interestingly, Scottish Calvinism is not my background, but rather Irish Catholicism (now turned atheist), which allows for plenty of hedonism – just go to any Irish wake to see what I mean. In comparison, therefore, to some of my friends, I would be described as towards the more optimistic end of the scale, though I would like to think that I can move flexibly between optimism, pessimism and realism as appropriate to different goals and situations. OK, so you may have already spotted some aggrandisement tendencies as well . . . . Anyway, the point about this digression into my own personal psychology is to state that, despite the direction taken in this chapter, which has moved from ingroups and outgroups, to emotional labour, to conflict and prison studies, and ultimately to dictators and war, there is some room for optimism. Although the twentieth century, with the horrors of two world wars plus the holocaust and other genocidal atrocities, appears to point to the Armageddon end of days that many extreme religious sects seem to welcome, a full historical analysis of trends in violence from prehistory to the current day suggests a continuing decline in deaths from war and other types of violence. Steven Pinker, in *The Better Angels of Our Nature* (2011), has recently attempted to quantify this process across the past few million years or so.

Pinker argues that there have been several significant change processes that have led to the reduction in violence. First, a pacification process, in which between about 10,000 and 5,000 years ago hunter-gatherers began to settle and form the basis of the first agricultural civilizations (see, for example, Toby Wilkinson's excellent account of the formation of the Egyptian civilization in *The Rise and Fall of Ancient Egypt,* 2010). Second, a civilizing process, in which feudal territories of the Middle Ages gradually became the larger states with centralised power and governments of the nineteenth and twentieth centuries. Third, Pinker points to a humanitarian revolution that began in the Renaissance and continued in the Enlightenment, and in which there developed social movements against violence, slavery and despotism. Finally, Pinker points to developments following World War II in which the world's major powers have realised that peace is better than war and so have not gone to war with each other.

Pinker points to the importance of the human rights movements that have come to predominate in this period of peace. However, we would also add as a significant contribution to this major development the formation of the various agencies of the United Nations, which includes the UN itself, the World Health Organization and UNICEF. These agencies provide the highest levels of international cooperation, whose remit includes an oversight of war and conflict anywhere in the world, as in the example of the recent UN intervention (implemented by NATO) in the Arab Spring uprisings, which helped to overthrow the Libyan dictator Colonel Gadaffi. As Pinker has summarised, in the twenty-first century the chances of dying from any form of violence is the smallest that it has been at any time throughout humankind's history. However, this process can only continue if national and international political systems include democratic processes which can countermand the Stalins, Hitlers and Mao Zedongs among us, whose narcissistic psychopathy leads them to seek brutal domination of all those around them.

Conclusion

This chapter has ranged far and wide over a superficially diverse set of topics that has included social identity theory, the pharmaceutical industry, emotional labour, prostitution, conflict, prejudice and war. Whilst at first one might wonder what these diverse topics could have in common, there are a number of crucial themes that link them together. In our existence as a social species, our identities are formed in part through the groups of which we are members and equally, through the *non-membership* of groups that we reject. A basic study like the Stanford prison experiment, albeit flawed in many ways, nevertheless, demonstrates dramatically how stepping into one role and becoming a member of one particular group can influence our thinking and behaviour in substantial ways. Membership and non-membership of groups typically leads to a variety of attitude, bias and prejudice problems that are expressed towards outgroups. Our membership of these groups, however, has to be viewed in the context of the modern happiness industry, in which we are promised happiness by taking the right drug, by visiting the right sauna, by voting for the right political party or by waging a war against people who get blamed for our own failings and inadequacies, in which these failings are projected onto a hated outgroup. But in all of these cases, we allow ourselves to be led by simplistic and ultimately incorrect promises that happiness lies at the end of whichever rainbow we are pursuing at that time. We need to learn to step back and think for ourselves and not simply allow ourselves to fall into the happy pig trap, which allows others to do our thinking for us, and in which we might have the luxury of being well-fattened, but ultimately we end up being well-roasted.

5

A TIMESHARE IN PARADISE

Of gods and the afterlife

The easy confidence with which I know another man's religion is folly teaches
me to suspect that my own is also.

(Mark Twain)

Introduction

We live our lives in the pursuit of many delusions, but there are few delusions
as preoccupying, and as simply wrong as those that come under the heading of
religion. And one of these self-serving religious delusions, the ultimate delusion
amongst religious delusions, has to be the belief in an afterlife. This chapter will
start, therefore, with a review of where the various beliefs in an afterlife come
from, beginning with the Ancient Egyptians and reviewing more recent views
in Christianity and other current religions. The chapter will then consider some
of the benefits that accrue from religious belief and religious participation, such
as offering a sense of meaning in life, offering support and community, and even
impacting on lifestyle and increasing the likelihood of certain positive health
behaviours. However, we will then briefly consider modern science's challenge
to religion and religious belief, in particular, in relation to how psychology now
offers a profound challenge. These points will be summarised to illustrate how
the atheist should live in order to get the same benefits that many religious
believers obtain from their belief systems, but without the disadvantages that are
a consequence of following such belief systems, no matter how impressive they
may seem. The reason that we can be so certain that religions are wrong is, as
Mark Twain advised us, through the application of a very simple logic: namely,
every religion believes that it is right, but every religion disagrees with every

other religion in one or more fundamental ways, therefore none of them can be right (see Power, 2012). And where better to start than with beliefs about the afterlife to demonstrate this simple logic.

The afterlife: happily never after

We choose to begin this chapter on religion with the seductive promise of eternal happiness in paradise that most religions offer their believers, whilst at the same time offering the equally appealing promise of eternal hell and damnation for all one's enemies and for non-believers. How could you refuse such an offer! An eternity in paradise surrounded by your friends and family, whilst enjoying the eternal *Schadenfreude* of that hated boss, the malicious manager, the awful head of college, the pickpocket who stole your wallet in Prague, and Adolf Hitler roasting together in the fires of hell. The psychological appeal of such promises, along with Santa Claus, the Tooth Fairy, and winning the jackpot on the National Lottery, is so obvious and so transparent that, again, it has to be wrong. As we have presented in detail elsewhere (Power, 2012), there are a number of important psychological phenomena that we will examine throughout this chapter that seem to lead us into these delusional religious beliefs. The first phenomenon has to be that of consciousness and related altered states of consciousness, which many religions use as evidence of supernatural phenomena. We will return to these psychological phenomena, but first it is worth briefly reviewing the various beliefs about the afterlife, beginning with the Ancient Egyptians.

The Ancient Egyptians

It is worth spending a little time considering the afterlife beliefs of the Ancient Egyptians because, like many of their other religious beliefs, these have often been incorporated in one form or another into later religious belief systems such as the three main Abrahamic religions of Judaism, Christianity and Islam. There are few ancient civilisations that retain the fascination of the Ancient Egyptians; thus, the pyramids at Giza are one of the most visited tourist sites on Earth with an estimated 3 million visitors each year. Rosalie David's book, *The Ancient Egyptians* (1998), provides one amongst many overviews of the growth of religious beliefs in Ancient Egypt through its Predynastic, Old Kingdom, Middle Kingdom and New Kingdom phases. The Predynastic period began around 5000 BCE with Neolithic farming communities beginning to settle along the banks of the Nile, whose annual cycle of inundation and retreat provided a rich source of fertile land along its banks in a country that otherwise had too low a rainfall to sustain farming communities. The dependence on the cycle of the Nile became central, therefore, to Egyptian myth and religious belief.

These Neolithic communities seem to have been organised in the form of the chiefdoms, typical of agricultural communities, until around 3100 BCE following a new group of arrivals, the so-called 'Dynastic Race', into Egypt, probably from

Mesopotamia. From this period on there is a flourishing of art, architecture and writing within Egypt. The Upper (southern) and Lower (northern) areas eventually came to be unified initially under the Upper Egyptian king, Scorpion, then completed by his successor, Narmer (also known as King Menes). The first dynasty of the Old Kingdom therefore begins with Narmer. As part of the unification, Narmer moved his capital from the city of This in Upper Egypt to Memphis in Lower Egypt, though the city of This continued as an important religious centre.

The Predynastic and Early Dynastic Egyptian burial practices provide most information about the religious beliefs of this period. The fact that the dead were carefully buried with a variety of personal possessions, food and drink points to a belief in life after death. The inclusion of amulets for magical protection with the bodies became increasingly common, with these being shaped in the form of animals such as the crocodile, the snake and the falcon. The body was buried with the head facing south and looking to the west. Initially, the chieftains were given similar graves to their subjects, but, with the appearance of the Dynastic Race, more elaborate tombs came to be built for the ruling classes. The style that emerged for the noble burials in the early period continued with the burial below ground, but increasingly elaborate buildings were built above the ground in which the initial funerary practices were carried out. The careful burial of certain animals such as cows and jackals also indicates the development of animal cults in these early communities.

The Egyptian Old Kingdom saw the king become a near-divine being who is the son of a god but born to a human royal mother (here one already sees echoes of the 'virgin birth' in Christian mythology of Jesus as the son of a human mother and a divine archangel). This unique birth gave the king the central role as the intermediary between the gods and humans. However, in order to maintain the succession, the eldest daughter of the ruling king and queen normally became the wife of the next heir, which was usually her brother or half-brother. The king, as a divine being, owned all the land and the people of Egypt, and the successful passage of the dead to the afterlife came to be seen as dependent on the good will of the king. The Old Kingdom also saw the building of the pyramids, with the first step pyramid at Saqqara being designed by Imhotep, vizier to King Djoser. Imhotep was also known as a great healer (under his Greek name Asclepius he became the god of medicine, and he is the likely origin of the 'Great Architect of the Universe', which is the name given to the god of the Freemasons) and he became the only non-royal to be elevated to divine status in later Egyptian history.

The famous step pyramid at Saqqara was the first of the great pyramids. Sixty-two metres high, it is oriented east–west and consists of six giant steps, which are believed to permit the ascension of the king to join the sun-god Ra in the celestial barque as he makes his daily journey across the sky. Although the later pyramids at Giza did not have the step structure, King Cheops, the builder of the Great Pyramid, covered his pyramid in white limestone, which was believed to focus a ray of sunshine along which the king could travel back and forth between the heavens and his burial place. The original Egyptian name for pyramid ('pyramid' is the later Greek name that has come to be used) was 'Mer', which has been translated as a 'place of ascension' (again one can note resonances with the ascension of Jesus into heaven from the Mount of Olives near Jerusalem). Whilst on the subject of the etymology of well-known Egyptian words, subsequent kings of Egypt came to be known as 'pharaohs' because the royal residence in Memphis or 'Great House' was called the 'Per Wer' in Egyptian, a name that was eventually applied to the king himself.

The Egyptian Middle Kingdom and the preceding 'First Intermediate Period' ran from about 2181 to 1786 BCE. The decline of the power of the pharaohs at the end of the Old Kingdom changed religious beliefs and practice in that successful passage to the afterlife was no longer considered to be dependent on the gift of the pharaoh, but, instead, came to be considered as based on the actions of individuals themselves, such as in the observation of appropriate rituals and worship of the gods. Because of the significance of Osiris, in that he was murdered but then resurrected, his cult became of increasing importance in the Middle Kingdom period. Abydos, near to This in Upper Egypt, became a pilgrimage centre for the Osiris cult because Osiris' body was believed to have been buried there. Pilgrims who visited his cult centre thought that his resurrection there would increase the likelihood of their own resurrection. An annual cycle of mystery plays were enacted at Abydos by the priests, presenting the birth, death and resurrection of Osiris. The eternal paradise, which now became the dream of all, was known as the 'Field of Reeds', in which there was permanent springtime with lush and abundant harvests that never failed. It is remarkable how the conceptualisation of paradise simply represented an easier version of life on Earth.

In *The Rise and Fall of Ancient Egypt* (2010), Toby Wilkinson describes in detail the fascinating voyage and tribulations that passage into the afterlife involved and which explains the numerous grave goods that were buried with the dead in order to help them on that journey. Much Egyptian tomb decoration included:

> Scenes of busy bakers and brewers, potters, carpenters and metalworkers; of fishermen landing prodigious catches; of offering-bearers bringing joints of meat, poultry, fine furniture and luxury goods; all were designed to ensure a never-ending supply of food, drink and other provisions to sustain the tomb owner in an all too earthly afterlife.
>
> *(Wilkinson, 2010, p. 143)*

For the Egyptians, the soul or *ba* flew out of the coffin and joined the sun-god Ra on his daily journey across the skies. Although the *ba* returned to the body at night, its counterpart, the eternal spirit or *ka*, had to make its journey through the underworld, overcoming various obstacles and learning various spells in order to pass through each stage. Coffins were often painted on the inside so that the deceased could read the instructions that included a variety of maps and spells in order to pass safely through the underworld and into the domain of Osiris, the god in charge. Once there:

> I shall eat in it and I shall wander in it.
> I shall plough in it and I shall reap in it.
> I shall have sex in it and I shall be content in it.
>
> *(Wilkinson, 2010, p. 142)*

Of the various trials and tribulations that the deceased had to overcome, perhaps the one that most captures the imagination, and the one that influenced a number of religions, especially Christianity, is the idea of a last judgement. The early Egyptian text *The Book of Two Ways* describes the first stage of judgement as *The Island of Fire*, which only those who were good enough were allowed to pass through, whereas those who were evil were consumed in flames. There next occurred a 'calculation of differences', in which the person's good deeds were weighed against bad deeds. This took place on a giant set of scales, a symbol still used to this day in the form of the scales of justice. Maat, the goddess of truth, weighed the deceased's heart, in which the Egyptians believed that the mind, emotions and memories resided, against the feather of truth, a procedure later elaborated on in the *Book of the Dead* (e.g. Tyldesley, 2011). Because of the importance of the heart for the Egyptians, it was the only internal organ that was left inside the mummified body. In contrast, the brain was always removed because its function was not understood and therefore not thought to be needed in the afterlife. (It sounds like there must be some fairly numbskull pharaohs wandering around paradise not knowing where the hell they are.) Anyway, those who were judged to be sufficiently 'light-hearted' became the blessed dead and were allowed to pass into paradise, the Field of Reeds. In contrast, those who were 'heavy-hearted' were punished in the place of destruction, which, by the time of the New Kingdom had transformed into Ammit, the beast of destiny who fed on the damned.

Other religions

We have presented the development of Egyptian ideas about the afterlife in some detail because, as noted earlier, many of these ideas have reappeared syncretically in later religions, so let us now consider some of these later developments and their links to Egyptian beliefs. The word 'hell' derives from a Germanic word that denoted the abode of the dead, but which was incorporated into the Christian version. The division between heaven and hell, between good and evil, is present in most world religions. The last judgement condemns the unjust to hell in religions such as Zoroastrianism, and the Abrahamic religions of Judaism, Christianity and Islam. Like the Egyptians, Zoroastrians believe that the judgement process is a weighing of good deeds against evil deeds, but those souls who cannot cross the bridge into heaven fall into a hell that, in contrast to the Egyptian and Christian versions, is freezing rather than hot, perhaps because of the worship of fire within the Zoroastrian religion. The Christian view of hell developed from the earlier Jewish notion of Gehenna, derived from the Valley of Hinnom just outside Jerusalem where, according to the Bible, child sacrifice through burning was carried out for the Ammonite deity Moloch. In Islam, similar to Zoroastrianism, the soul must pass over a bridge into heaven, but those who are damned fall into a crater of fire and suffer. The concept of hell in Hinduism, Buddhism and Jainism is more similar to the Christian notion of purgatory, in that punishment is related to the amount of wrong-doing during life, but from which the soul is eventually liberated in order to continue on the wheel of karma.

The Roman Catholic notion of purgatory derives again from earlier Jewish views, though it was not until the Middle Ages that it was finally defined. In fact, an interesting and profitable sideline for the Catholic Church in the Middle Ages was that the prayer, almsgiving and indulgences of the living were considered to aid those in purgatory to pass through to heaven more quickly. However, other Christian churches such as the Protestant and the Eastern Orthodox deny the existence of purgatory, in part, as a reaction to the profit-oriented selling of indulgences by the Catholic Church against which the Protestant Reformation reacted so strongly.

The concept of limbo, developed by the Roman Catholic Church in the Middle Ages, offered solutions to at least two theological conundrums: namely, what happened to the saints of the Old Testament who, in theory, could not be admitted into the Catholic heaven because they were unbaptised; and what happened to unbaptised babies whose original sin had not been washed away, because it seemed too harsh in its judgement to condemn these innocents to damnation in hell for eternity. Unfortunately for such innocents, Pope Benedict XVI was reported in 2007 in the media to have abolished the concept of limbo, with headlines such as 'The Pope Closes Limbo' appearing in many newspapers. This caused panic amongst those who had assumed that their unbaptised children were peacefully residing there. As a note of hope, we might also point out that Father Gabriel Funes, the priest-astronomer in charge of the Vatican Space Observatory, has stated that there may be other planets where intelligent life-forms do not have original sin, in which case they could go straight to heaven without being baptised. It begins to make heaven sound like an episode of *Star Trek*.

In the best biblical tradition, we have, of course, saved the best until last as we briefly consider definitions of heaven in current religions. Originally regarded as the celestial space occupied by Yahweh, and emphasising the importance of the sky for the gods of earlier religions, in later Jewish beliefs, the righteous joined Yahweh in this heavenly sky abode above the clouds. This later view of heaven was incorporated into both the Christian and the Islamic traditions. An additional feature of psychological wish-fulfilment and the afterlife is that a person's earthly body is believed to be replaced by a new, pure and incorruptible body with no sickness and no death, a wish that must have been dreamed of by anyone who has ever suffered from a chronic disease or deformation or who suffered in pain before they died. Of course, there are plenty of alternative views of hell, such as the one suggested by George Bernard Shaw, in which hell is an eternal round of parties, which, in my case, would consist of spending eternity making small talk to telephone salespeople and hamburger sellers.

Psychology and the afterlife

In order to understand our psychological motivation for wanting to believe in the afterlife, there is no better place to start than in our experience of consciousness itself. Consciousness has to sit in prime place as the most important and most puzzling question that remains to be answered by psychological science. Consciousness puts the individual at the centre of a personal universe whose idiocentrism has clearly been the source of both confusion and extravagant beliefs, both from an individual and a social perspective. It is no surprise that our first human conceptions of the general universe were geocentric, given that consciousness provides an idiocentric or egocentric starting point for the personal universe that each of us inhabits. It also seems likely that the unique now-ness and personal ownership of consciousness has led many of the owners of consciousness to have made extravagant but mistaken claims about the properties of that consciousness. These imagined properties include omnipotence, omniscience, invulnerability and eternal existence, all properties that have also been offered as descriptors of possible monotheistic and polytheistic beings. We have called this problem of consciousness the 'immortality illusion' (Power, 2012). Such properties are not simply imagined from our historical past, but are evident in ordinary people, especially when they are pushed to their limits, such as in the experience of trauma, the experience of certain personality disorders (especially personality disorders of a more narcissistic type) and during normal stages of development in childhood and adolescence.

So what is the function or purpose of consciousness? Within the dualistic philosophies such as that of Descartes, the specialness of consciousness leads to either its equation with an eternal and supernatural soul, or at least that it is the location of such a soul or psyche. Most philosophers, psychologists and neuroscientists in modern times reject the so-called 'substance dualism' in which the mind/soul and the body are two completely different kinds of substances. At the other extreme, modern philosophers, such as Daniel Dennett in his misleadingly entitled book *Consciousness Explained* (1991), provide an eliminative reductionism, which ultimately dismisses consciousness as illusory. Dennett sees the distinction between the hardware and the software of the computer as providing a model of the distinction between the brain (hardware) and the mind (software). However, if consciousness were that simple, why do computers not display consciousness? When will my desktop on which I am writing this chapter turn around to me and say 'Look, I am having a bad day today, I feel like my world is falling to bits (or maybe even to bytes) and don't feel like typing words for you' or perhaps 'I have had enough of being a mere desktop. I want to be a mainframe! I want out!' There are clearly problems with both the dualistic consciousness as soul and the simple materialist computer model, otherwise Microsoft and Bill Gates would be the new gods of consciousness. Many cognitive scientists believe that computers could come to display consciousness (e.g. see Phil Johnson-Laird's *The Computer and the Mind*, 1988), but this seems unlikely because consciousness has arisen as a consequence of the evolution of neurological systems. Consciousness is located in the brain and it sleeps or dies when the brain sleeps or dies.

What is therefore clear from the little we know about consciousness is that it is an emergent property of our highly complex brains (see, for example, John Searle's *The Mystery of Consciousness*, 1997), features of which are present in lower animals and disorders of which can occur in humans. For example, splits in consciousness can occur in dissociative states and dissociative identity disorders (previously known as multiple personality disorders). Such states show that the sense of unity and continuity in consciousness is something of a cognitive illusion, in the same way that we see a continuous visual field despite the break caused by the optic nerve on the retina. Our brains are good at adding in information or 'joining the dots' at an automatic or unconscious level so that we experience continuities in consciousness. It is also clear that there are different states and varieties of consciousness, as emphasised in the Buddhist philosophies. Being conscious of objects in the external world allows us to move beyond their simple physical or perceptual properties and can clearly offer new perspectives that simple data-driven perception would not permit.

It is clear that consciousness has many psychological and social functions. Explanations in cognitive psychology tend to emphasise the role that consciousness plays in the assignment and re-assignment of goal priorities in the complex multi-goal systems that we are as humans (see, for example, our discussion in *Cognition and Emotion: From Order to Disorder*, Power and Dalgleish, 2015). Expressed more simply, at any point in time, consciousness acts as a central executive system that says, for example, the many things that you could or should be doing at the moment: you can watch football for the next half-hour, but then you will need to get back to the exams you are supposed to be marking, and in between you will need to go to the toilet, eat a sandwich, and remember to put on the washing machine. Again, whilst it is clear that complex multi-goal systems like ourselves require some form of overall executive system for setting and re-setting currently active goals, such a system is implementable on a multi-tasking computer, and therefore does not necessitate that the computer's central executive is also conscious. Consciousness achieves all of these computational functions, but it offers something else besides.

In the search for an understanding of consciousness, another interesting line of research has been the focus on the inter-individual functions of consciousness, not just its intra-individual functions. We might begin here with Robert Burns:

> O would some Power the gift to give us
> To see ourselves as others see us
>
> *(from 'To a Louse')*

Although Burns was clearly invoking the need for a *supernatural* power to help us, evolutionary psychologists such as Nick Humphrey (e.g. see *The Mind Made Flesh: Essays From The Frontiers of Psychology and Evolution*, 2008) have argued that, because we, like other higher primates, are fundamentally social animals, we have developed a capacity to understand other minds, and, thereby, the capacity to understand how other minds see us. For example, the capacity to lie is a highly evolved human capacity, though it is an example of deception that is used for individual advantage throughout nature. In *The Selfish Gene* (1976), Richard Dawkins goes as far as to speculate 'It is even possible that man's swollen brain . . . evolved as a mechanism of even more devious cheating, and ever more penetrating detection of cheating in others' (p. 188). But the capacity for lying requires awareness of your own true belief, the provision of false information to another, and, in skilled lying, the judgement that the false information has been believed, which then permits the liar to take full advantage of the successful lie.

This capacity was developed into perhaps its highest art form in Machiavelli's *The Prince* (1532/2003), which provided an insight into the politics of the Florentine court in the fifteenth and sixteenth centuries, and which has given politics a bad name ever since. Our purpose here is not to digress into endless, though illustrative, examples of famous lies in politics, or personal examples of how we have all suffered at the hands of skilled liars (though I have to confess that my own experience in academia is that many of my academic colleagues could outperform Machiavelli and Clinton any day of the week). The more general point is that consciousness allows us not only the capacity to reflect on ourselves, but also to construe other people's mental states, and thereby to construe how they construe us. In a social species, the possession of such a capacity provides a major advantage, though it can be used for both good and bad.

To return to the starting question, however, we began this section with the proposal that the experience of consciousness has, we believe, contributed to the dualism or split between body and soul, and that the 'immortality illusion' permeates religious belief and earlier philosophical approaches that have led to beliefs in an afterlife. The major religion that has been most clearly based on a projection of experienced varieties of consciousness onto a model of the universe is Buddhism. Indeed, Buddhist meditation practices encourage the training of skills in self-consciousness and reflectiveness as a route to spirituality. However, modern philosophy, psychology and neuroscience mostly reject 'substance dualism' accounts that are beloved of most religions. In place of dualism, consciousness and the mind more generally, as we have said, can be understood as emergent properties of a highly evolved complex neuronal system that are also evident in other social higher primates, but which have further evolved in humans because of the social and evolutionary advantage of such capacities. Of course, this line of explanation still does not answer fully the question of how consciousness can emerge from its complex neuronal underpinnings. Although science does not have the complete answer, it is not necessary to equate consciousness with something akin to an immortal soul that can exist separately from those neuronal underpinnings; the immortality illusion is, by definition, an illusion. Furthermore, work in psychology from von Helmholtz and Freud onwards (e.g. Power, 1997) has emphasised that consciousness is just the tip of a mental iceberg in which so much of our waking and sleeping activity occurs at an unconscious or automatic level that is outside of our awareness.

Unusual experiences

In addition to consciousness itself, there are some unusual experiences of consciousness that have also been taken as evidence for the existence of an afterlife (Power, 2012). Two such examples include out-of-body experiences (OBEs) and near-death experiences (NDEs). There is some overlap in the experience of NDEs and OBEs because the NDE is often accompanied by an OBE, so we will focus here on the NDE. In a study of 183 cases of NDE, Bruce Greyson (1990) reported, in the appropriately named *Journal of Near-Death Studies*, a number of common features that included the following:

- That time stopped and there was a sense of peace
- That there was bright illumination
- The experience was out-of-body
- 'Spiritual' beings were experienced, including dead friends and relatives
- There was a sense of joy on entering a mystical place.

Sometimes the experience is so powerful that the person feels a reluctance to return to join the living. These similarities have led Gregory Shushan, in his book *Conceptions of the Afterlife in Early Civilizations* (2009), to argue that there is a considerable uniformity amongst largely unconnected ancient cultures regarding belief in life after death and that the core elements of these religious beliefs are largely similar to the core elements of NDEs. In his book, he examines conceptions of the afterlife in Ancient Egypt, Mesopotamia, China (before the arrival of Buddhism), India (also before the arrival of Buddhism) and pre-Columbian Mesoamerica. Shushan compares the afterlife accounts in each of these five civilisations and concludes that the differences between the afterlife experiences in ancient texts and the NDE accounts are predominately at the symbolic, culture-specific level, but that 'the NDE itself appears to be a collection of subjectively experienced universal phenomena'.

Shushan summarises a number of key elements in the NDE forming the basis for afterlife conceptions in these early civilisations that include:

- The out-of-body experience
- Corpse encounters, for example, with dead relatives (ancestors)
- The experience of passing through darkness or a tunnel
- Passing into the presence of intense light
- An experience of union (oneness) and enlightenment
- The feeling of being in another realm or at the point of origin.

Shushan argues persuasively that NDEs were clearly part of the experience of these ancient cultures and that they provided key evidence for the nature of the afterlife in an otherwise diverse set of religious beliefs and practices. For example, he argues that, in contrast to conceptions of the afterlife, these same ancient cultures have extremely diverse accounts of creation or creation myths ('cosmogonies'), because there is no shared experiential basis from which to develop a culture's creation myths.

There is considerable modern interest in psychology and neuroscience in NDEs, similar to the increased interest in OBEs, because of their implications for the functioning of the brain. The development of cardiac resuscitation techniques has permitted researchers to study systematically the experiences of people who, clinically, have been close to death. The Dutch cardiologist Pim van Lommel and his colleagues studied a consecutive series of 344 cardiac patients who had been resuscitated after cardiac arrest (van Lommel *et al.*, 2001). They found that 62 patients (18 per cent) reported NDEs. Those patients who did have an NDE were significantly more likely to die within 30 days of the experience compared to those who did not have an NDE. Of those patients who experienced an NDE and who survived, follow-up at 2 and at 8 years showed, from an examination of life changes, that the NDE group were significantly more accepting, loving and empathic towards others, they were more spiritual and felt they had a deeper sense of purpose in life, and they were more likely to believe in an afterlife and had less fear of death. These findings are dramatic in the sense that it is not just the near-experience of death itself that is important, because all of the patients in van Lommel's study were close to death, but, when combined with an NDE, indeed, one can gain an insight into the origins of religious beliefs in the afterlife as Shushan has suggested.

More benefits of religion

The importance of social capital has been emphasised by sociologists such as Robert Putnam (2003) in his well-known book *Bowling Alone: The Collapse and Revival of American Community*. Community involvement and participation have been on the decline over the past 50 years in places such as the US, in part because of the impact of television on such activities. Yet it is clear that one of the benefits of religion is the sense of community and belongingness that active membership of a religious group bestows. Regular church attendance can enhance this sense of community, and it appears to offer benefits for health and longevity. The evangelical Protestant movements of the Southern US and of South Korea have sought to capitalise on community in their establishment of mega-churches. Similarly, many of the new religious movements have sought to establish their own religious communities that work along the lines of the earlier monastic movement established in religions such as Christianity and Buddhism.

Sociologists such as Putnam have also shown the importance of volunteering, that is, the value of engagement in activities that aim to help the disadvantaged in the community such as the young, the elderly and the disabled. These activities are often a normal or expected part of being a member of a religious community and they can bring benefits not only to the recipients of volunteering, but to the volunteers themselves.

Perhaps one of the most difficult challenges for atheists is to obtain a sense of community and participation that is equivalent to that obtained by many members of religious groups. There are no obvious equivalents to the sense of community that is obtained from regular church attendance, from the celebration of saint's and other feast days, and from the visiting of religious clergy amongst their communities. The proposal by the well-known atheist Alain de Botton in *Religion for Atheists* (2012) to build temples of atheism in London, or wherever, seems to miss the point completely. Of course, membership of political parties, of pressure groups such as Greenpeace and Amnesty International, and the celebration of family and cultural events can go some way to establishing some sense of community for atheists. Indeed, the increased importance of social network groups via the internet may be of particular benefit. However, there is still a real need for atheists to have a *local* sense of social involvement and participation, which may need to be structured around more mundane hobbies and interests rather than 'temples', but which require local participation, in order to capture something of the sense of community and belongingness that members of religious groups can obtain very readily.

At this point, however, we need also to remind ourselves that not everything is greener and better on the side of religion than of atheism. The claimed superiority of each of the monotheisms over everything else, the drive for expansion and conversion within Christianity and Islam, the feuding within the splits that have occurred within Christianity and Islam – all of these factors bring with them a risk to global stability. The global split between Christianity and Islam currently provides the highest risk of a next world war, especially if the tensions between Judaism and Islam are added into the equation. In sum, between them, the three great monotheisms, although they share beliefs and scriptures, could yet bring about their own great end of days. None of the individual and local benefits that accrue from the monotheisms are worth the exchange for the risk that these religions create for the rest of us. It is attendant on all atheists, who are not burdened with the prejudices of the religions, to step into the void between the religions and lead the way forward. So, even though our starting point in this section was to praise religion for the sense of community it offers its followers, in the end it must be damned because it views those outside that community as the heathen enemy, creating the ingroup and outgroup effects that we considered in Chapter 4. The simple splitting that the monotheisms offer as their view of good and evil, in which god and his followers are all good but those who do not follow are all bad, is a crucial part of the global risk of war and misery that they present and that atheism must strive hard to overcome.

So what does the general evidence on the relationship between religion and health look like? We will deal with the more general issues of positive psychology and health in Chapter 6, but it is worth summarising some of the findings specially related to religion here (see Power, 2012, for a fuller account). Fenix et al. (2006) reported a study in which they followed up 175 primary caregivers of cancer patients who subsequently died in a hospice in Connecticut. The caregivers were followed up for over a year after the deaths of their loved ones, and the research found that those with high religiousness were significantly less likely to suffer from major depression in comparison to those with low religiousness. Religiousness was therefore strongly protective for bereaved caregivers in the difficult period following the death of a family member.

Green and Elliott (2010) analysed data from the 2006 General Social Survey (GSS), a nationally representative survey of US adults that is carried out regularly and run from the University of Chicago. Earlier studies had established that church attendance seemed to be beneficial for both physical and mental health (e.g. Idler and Kasl, 1992), but Green and Elliott were interested to know whether or not other confounding factors, such as employment, financial status and family support, might account for these apparent benefits from church attendance. In multiple regression analyses that partialled out the effects of these variables, a positive effect of religiosity on both self-reported health and happiness was still found, which indicated that these particular variables did not explain away the health benefits from religiosity. Interestingly, the authors reported that, amongst the religious groups, those with more liberal views tended to report better health, whereas those with more fundamentalist views reported more happiness.

A summary of studies on mortality by Hummer *et al.* (2004) concluded that whilst there is good evidence that church attendance is linked to increased longevity, there are many other factors and mechanisms that need to be explored in order to understand the links better. Koenig (2009) reviews both the positive and negative effects of religious belief on mental health, noting that for some vulnerable individuals in some religions there may be increased risk. For example, in a re-analysis of the US Epidemiologic Catchment Area (ECA) survey, Levav *et al.* (1997) reported that Jewish men had significantly higher rates of depression in comparison to men from all other religious and non-religious groups, such that the 2:1 ratio for adult female to male rates of depression that is normally found is not present in the Jewish population, where the ratio is 1:1. Kate Loewenthal (2008) has summarised research that suggests the higher rates of depression in Jewish men may be linked to factors such as low use of alcohol in the Jewish community.

In an attempt to disentangle religion from other confounding factors, Baetz and Toews (2009) examined a range of social, psychological and biological factors that must be taken into account. As Baetz and Toews point out, the social domain has probably been best explored in order to understand the possible mediation of the religion–health links. In the social domain, religions often proscribe against the use of alcohol and drugs, proscriptions which can therefore impact on health behaviours in a positive way. Equally, church attendance can provide an important source of social support and group membership. On the psychological level, the Allport and Ross (1967) distinction between intrinsic and extrinsic religious orientation has received wide consideration in research. Those people with intrinsic orientation obtain meaning and purpose from their religious beliefs, whereas those with an extrinsic orientation are considered simply to use religion for reasons such as sociability and security. There is evidence that intrinsic orientation is protective against depression, whereas extrinsic may increase depression risk (e.g. Smith *et al.*, 2003). The work of Pargament (1997) has further extended the earlier Allport and Ross work with findings that are largely consistent with the view that religion can be both positive and negative in its impact on health, though it depends on the approach that the person takes towards religion.

Baetz and Toews' third group of factors are biological, which includes an area of study that has been labelled 'neurotheology'. One of the questions for religious belief is whether, in times of stress following significant life events and other adversity, religious belief can help to buffer the effects of stress through, for example, enhanced immunological system functioning and better regulation of stress-related hormones such as cortisol. For example, Carrico et al. (2006) found that religiosity in HIV-positive men and women was related to lower urinary cortisol levels, findings that supported the possible stress-buffering role of religious belief.

This brief overview of the impact of religious belief on physical and mental health supports the general proposal that religious belief can have positive benefits on health and happiness. However, it is still early days in terms of understanding the social, psychological and biological mechanisms through which belief can have its beneficial effects. There are also problems with understanding what 'religiosity' actually is and how it should be defined. Earlier research which simply looked at church attendance has shown positive benefits on physical health, mental health and longevity, but church attendance can occur for many different internal or external reasons, not all of which appear to be beneficial. Recent research has taken a more complex approach to the understanding of religiosity, but, again, this work shows that there can be both positive and negative impacts of religious belief that depend on the type of religiosity and the type of outcome being measured. In the remainder of this chapter, therefore, we will try to further disentangle some of these positive and negative effects, beginning in the next section with studies of religion as a possible coping mechanism.

Religion, stress and purpose in life

We have touched on the role of religion as a coping mechanism in times of stress throughout this chapter. A number of studies have investigated whether or not religious belief can help people at times of stress, such as during illness to themselves and to loved ones, during times of financial hardship and during natural disasters such as earthquakes, floods and tsunamis (e.g. Baker, 2008). Johnson and Spilka (1991) studied women with breast cancer in the US and found that 85 per cent reported that religion helped them cope with the stress. However, when they looked at the effect of Allport's intrinsic–extrinsic classification, as mentioned above, the researchers found that the benefits of religion were primarily for those with an *intrinsic* orientation. Researchers such as Cohen and Hill (2007) and Loewenthal (2011) have further suggested that intrinsic religiosity may be of more benefit in individualistic cultures, especially predominantly Protestant ones, whereas extrinsic religiosity may give more health and well-being benefits in collectivistic cultures.

Ringdal (1996) further showed that in a group of cancer patients, there was a 14 per cent better survival rate in those with religious beliefs. Oxman et al. (1995) found that in a group of 232 cardiac patients, 5 per cent of those who regularly attended religious services died compared to 12 per cent of those who rarely or never attended religious services. A meta-analysis of 29 studies by McCullough et al. (2000) concluded that there was a significant benefit for religious belief for survival rates in a range of physical illnesses. Again, the benefits of religion include improved health behaviours such as less smoking and less alcohol intake, and increased social support. Drevenstadt (1998), in a study of 11,000 people in the US, found a positive correlation between church attendance and self-reported physical health, which for the middle-aged white population was primarily due to the social support that church-going offered. However, in this study the benefits of church-going were only found for young people if there was sufficient religious belief as well. The study shows that the benefits of church attendance on health may vary across the lifespan, with social support being a more major factor at some life stages than at others.

The buffering effect of religious belief is also clear from those coping with death of loved ones. McIntosh et al. (1993) followed up 124 people who had experienced the sudden death of a child. Those who attended church regularly reported being given more social support and finding more meaning in the loss, such that, by 18 months following the loss, they were less distressed. In a study reported by Loewenthal et al. (2000), a total of 126 participants from Protestant or Jewish backgrounds were interviewed. The participants had recently experienced stressful life events to do with finance and employment, illness and family problems, and were selected to be either high or low on religiosity, with those at intermediate religiosity not being interviewed. The results showed a possible causal model for both Jewish and Protestant participants in which religiosity leads to certain religious causal beliefs (e.g. God is in control), which leads to positive mood, which in turn lowers reports of distress. However, the authors did not run a simultaneous groups analysis to check if their stress-coping model fitted both the high and the low religiosity groups equally well; that is, it seems unlikely that the low religiosity group would show the same coping mechanisms as the high religiosity group.

A recent study by McGregor et al. (2010) studied the general observation that, under stress, people often become more superstitious in their beliefs and behaviour, which, when applied to religious ideals, may mean that people become more religious, an effect that had been noted earlier by William James in *The Varieties of Religious Experience* (1902). In their first study, they found that a mild academic threat to a group of undergraduate students significantly increased the students' ratings of their religious ideals. A replication in a second study further showed that such threats had more impact on those students with more monotheistic beliefs, especially for jingoistic items on superiority of one's own belief system and supporting war. In a third study, McGregor et al. tested the possible buffering effect of successful pursuit of worldly goals on religious idealism when under threat. As the authors note, more international aid is sometimes directed to parts of the world at risk for increased religious idealism in the hope that the support of everyday goals will ameliorate the tendency towards religious extremism under conditions of threat. In the third study, the authors used an interpersonal threat task in which the student participants were asked to think for 2 minutes about an important conflicted relationship in their lives. Again, as for the second study, the results showed that the monotheistic students had higher religious zeal, with the effects of goal engagement showing a significant impact of threat on religious zeal at low levels of engagement, but not at high levels of engagement. The authors argue that these results, albeit with students, provide tentative support for policies that enable basic needs and other goals to be pursued in regions of the world that are vulnerable to religious extremism.

The relationship between stress and religious belief is, of course, a double-edged sword, in that whilst some people may benefit from religious belief at times of stress, for others their religious beliefs may become weakened because of the stress. A study by Chen and Koenig (2006) found that, in a group of 745 elderly patients admitted to Duke University Medical Center and followed up over three months, increases in severity of illness led to decreases in church attendance and in religious belief at follow-up. Although the church attendance reduction was mediated by reductions in physical activity, the reduction in belief was not mediated by the reduced physical activity. A meta-analysis reported by Ano and Vasconcelles (2005) that included a total of 13,512 participants from 49 studies examined both the positive and the negative links between religious coping and stress. The authors found support, first, for positive religious coping being associated with positive psychological adjustment; second, for positive religious coping being associated with a reduction in negative psychological adjustment; and third, for negative religious coping being associated with negative psychological adjustment. However, negative religious coping did not seem to be associated with a reduction in positive psychological adjustment. Ano and Vasconcelles defined negative religious coping to include factors such as spiritual discontent, demonic reappraisal and belief in a punishing God. These findings highlight that the relationship between religion, coping and stress is a complex one, in particular when stress impacts negatively on the religious belief system, for example, if the person comes to believe that a physical or mental health problem is a punishment from God for previous wrong-doing (cf. Loewenthal, 2000).

One of the perennial complaints made by religious believers about atheism is that it leaves people lost in a meaningless world in which all morality breaks down and chaos results; their fantasy is something along the lines of a world full of Viking raiders run amok. Such fantasies probably say more about the repressive nature of some religions and the restrictions that they place on their followers, especially in relation to sex and aggression. We will return to this issue later in the chapter. For now, it is important to note, first, that there are plenty of atheists around the world who do not spend their time running amok, and second, there have also been, and still are, vast areas of the world governed by atheistic ideologies. Two examples of these have been the Soviet Union and China, in which the majority of people have been atheists. Now you might try to cite the Soviet Union as an atheistic system that collapsed, but you only need to read accounts such as Peter Kenez's *A History of the Soviet Union from the Beginning to the End* (2006) to understand that it was the wayward internal economics of the Soviet Union rather than the lack of religion that led to its collapse in 1991. In contrast, Chinese communism in the era after the death of Mao Zedong in 1976 reinvented itself so as to incorporate capitalist economics and is set to become the world's major economy. China's primarily atheist ideology has not produced a nation of wayward Vikings, though its political restrictions sometimes seem as excessive as the religious restrictions it has come to replace. Still, given the choice between a feudal theocracy such as existed in Tibet and Chinese capitalist communism, there is no doubt which way I would choose if those were the only two choices.

But there are humble beginnings that we must look to in order to understand our search for meaning and purpose in life. To begin with, we need to understand how and when the search for meaning and cause develops in childhood and, therefore, what types of causal explanations are preponderant at different developmental stages. One place to start such a quest is with the work of the famous Swiss child psychologist Jean Piaget who, despite never having any formal qualification in psychology, proved to be one of the most insightful observers ever of his own and other children's development. Piaget (see e.g. *The Construction of Reality in the Child,* 1954) proposed that there are four main developmental stages:

- The sensori-motor period (roughly 0–2 years)
- The pre-operational stage (roughly 2–7 years)
- The concrete operations period (roughly 7–11 years)
- The formal operations period (roughly 11 years upwards).

Piaget defined these stages in terms of the logical capacities of the child at the different stages, though more recent developmental psychologists would place less emphasis on logical development. The important point for our discussion is that a variety of different capacities develop across these developmental stages that impact on the child's ability to understand reality, including conservation (e.g. the famous study that when a liquid is poured into a taller glass the child reports that there is now more liquid), object permanence and egocentrism. Studies of the first 2–3 years show that babies already have a basic understanding of cause-and-effect outcomes in the physical world and display some basic understanding of human intentions. This capacity for causal reasoning develops considerably in later stages of development, but there is much use of animistic explanations of the form 'the rope is untwisting because it wants to' and magical thinking is seen to predominate up until about age 7 years and the start of the concrete operations stage. Similarly, normal children develop so-called 'theory of mind' at about 4 years of age as they move from the egocentrism of the sensori-motor period and begin to understand that other people also have thoughts and feelings that are separate from their own. Problems arise for children with autism in whom this developmental step is extremely delayed or even absent, and who therefore continue with the young child's egocentrism (see e.g. Leslie, 1994).

Piaget's developmental psychology emphasises, therefore, the preponderance of egocentric, animistic, magical thinking until about 7 years of age. Although after age 7 or thereabouts, thinking becomes more realistic, even in adulthood thinking can be animistic or magical; the difference is that the adult normally can easily distinguish between animistic and magical thinking, such as knowing that the computer has not 'deliberately' lost your morning's work even though you might shout and swear at it as if it had done it deliberately. Although mindful of Claude Levi-Strauss's warning in *The Savage Mind* (1962) that one must be careful when attributing child-like animistic thinking to early prehistoric human groups and to current nomadic tribes, a subtler version of the possibility arises from the observation that people with autism, schizophrenia and some types of personality disorder have poor theory of mind and display more egocentrism and greater amounts of animistic and magical thinking. Given, as we have argued elsewhere (Power, 2012) that priest-shamans were more likely to suffer from such disorders, there is good reason to suspect, as others have, that the persistence of animistic and magical thinking into adulthood has been a source of much religious inspiration and belief.

Science's challenge to religion

Science is both a process, or method, and an accumulation of facts and theories. The scientific process leads to an examination of religious beliefs and practices in a way that many religious individuals find contrary to statements of faith, which, they argue, are givens that cannot and should not be examined by such rationalist means. Perhaps, though, if the early scientific investigations had supported the idea that the Earth was flat, that it was at the centre of the universe, and that god had created the Earth and all creatures in 6 days in 4004 BCE (the date that in 1650 Archbishop Ussher declared to be the age of the universe based on the genealogies within the Old Testament), then religions might have been a lot happier with science. The problem is, however, that the Earth is round, that we are nowhere near the centre of the universe, and that your mother really was an ape. We will examine briefly how Christianity has tried to deny, has persecuted those that dared to suggest, and has now had to play catch-up with the extraordinary developments in science over the past few hundred years. Some, like Stephen Jay Gould, have claimed that religion and science are different domains and that science has no relevance for the domain of religion, but such claims are disingenuous nonsense because the claims of religion are testable with the methods of science, as we will summarise.

The climax of the scientific challenges to the Catholic Church from Galileo onwards came with Charles Darwin's publication of *On the Origin of Species* in 1859. However, Darwin's momentous work must be considered in the context of an accumulation of questions about the biblical timescales and creation story, such as the claim in 1650 by Archbishop Ussher that the Earth had been created at midday on Monday 23 October 4004 BCE. Prior to Darwin, the evidence from geology and palaeontology was already leading to widespread questioning of the biblical account. James Hutton (1726–97), known as the Father of Geology, had observed a range of 'uncomformities' in East Lothian near Edinburgh, including at Siccar Point, which necessitated geological cycles of seabed deposition, uplift and erosion in order to explain some of the geological structures that he observed. Hutton noted in 1795, in his famously unreadable *A Theory of the Earth with Proofs and Illustrations*, that 'we find no vestige of a beginning and no prospect of an end'. Charles Lyell (1797–1875) was the great Victorian geologist who became a close friend of Darwin. Indeed, the young Darwin did Lyell the honour of taking a copy of his *The Principles of Geology* with him on the voyage of the *Beagle*, and wrote that 'it altered the whole tone of one's mind . . . when seeing a thing never seen by Lyell, one yet saw it partially through his eyes'.

During the nineteenth century the estimated age of the Earth increased into the millions of years, with Lord Kelvin estimating it to be in the order of 20 million years old. Darwin himself had estimated the age of the area near his house at Down in Kent to have taken over 300 million years to form. More recent estimations from radio isotope dating put the Earth's age at over 4.5 *billion* years, which, to put it mildly, is just a little beyond the biblical estimate.

The impact of Darwin's work on the theory of evolution must therefore be understood in the context of the accumulation of geological and palaeontological evidence that was a direct challenge to the biblical account. Geological evidence had begun to accumulate to show that the Earth was at least millions of year old rather than the 6,000 or so proposed by biblical scholars; palaeontological evidence demonstrated that there were creatures such as the famous dinosaurs (the name first given to them in 1841 by the palaeontologist Richard Owen and that means 'terrible lizard') that were long extinct, and that therefore disproved biblical statements about the permanence of all species. Darwin's work was, therefore, the climax of the Victorian attack on the Bible because it demonstrated that, over sufficiently long periods of time, species evolved or died out through processes such as natural selection, and that all species did not exist from the beginning of creation, in contradiction to the statement in the Bible:

> And God created great whales, and every living creature that moveth . . . and the evening and the morning were the fifth day.
>
> *(Genesis 1:21–23)*

Although Darwin did not discuss the origin of mankind in 1859 in *On the Origin of Species*, the implications for the evolution of humans were soon apparent. It was not until *The Descent of Man*, first published in 1871, that Darwin clearly stated that humans had developed from earlier primates.

The reaction of different religious groups to Darwin's proposals have lain at the extreme in the past 150 years. It is well known that all biblical religions vehemently rejected evolution to begin with. Subsequently, during his tenure of the papacy from 1878 to 1903, Pope Leo XIII proposed a compromise with Darwinian evolution in the suggestion that the human *body* might have evolved from earlier animals, but that the human *soul* was created by God. However, the creationist movement in the USA has been far less compromising than a Roman Catholic Church that perhaps learned something from its medieval mistakes with the likes of Galileo. The infamous Scopes Trial in Dayton Tennessee in 1925 set the scene for the American creationists' attacks on the teaching of evolution in schools, when the teacher John T. Scopes was found 'guilty' of teaching evolutionary theory, a trial that was captured in the Stanley Kramer film *Inherit the Wind* in 1960 with Spencer Tracy and Fredric Marsh playing the combative lawyers. In 1961, the Americans Henry Morris and John Whitcomb published *The Genesis Flood* in which they claimed that the world really was created in six days and therefore that humans had lived concurrently with dinosaurs. Following from the Morris and Whitcomb book, there are now Intelligent Design and Creation institutes and museums all over the US. For example, take a look at the website for the Creation Museum in Petersburg, Kentucky (at www.creationmuseum.org) and you can see the museum with its displays of dinosaurs roaming around the Garden of Eden next to Adam and Eve. You might have thought that Genesis would have mentioned dinosaurs, instead of just highlighting whales, had they been known to be wandering around the Jurassic Park version of paradise.

The puzzle for psychology is how people maintain views of the world that are contrary to the evidence. Why, for example, is the US a powerhouse of science and scientific discovery, whilst, at the same time, it demonstrates a rapid growth in fundamentalist religious sects that deny or distort the very evidence that science presents? Elsewhere, we have examined the range of psychological mechanisms by which belief systems are maintained (Power, 2012) and how reasoning processes can be biased in support of false beliefs. Psychology demonstrates that distortions in memory, belief, reasoning and perception are commonplace. Whilst such distortions can be mildly amusing and entertaining when it comes to visual illusions such as the Müller-Lyer, recent debates and arguments over so-called repressed memories and false memories have led to bitter court cases in alleged child abuse cases. It can be seen that, even in the secular world, our psychological faculties place restrictions and limitations on us, some of the consequences of which we have examined in other chapters in this book.

Psychology's challenge to religion

In a previous book, *Adieu to God: Why Psychology Leads to Atheism* (2012), we examined in depth what it is about human psychology that has led to the invention of religion in all cultures. In this chapter we will concentrate on a few important issues that are worth picking up and that will set the scene for more detailed discussions later. The issues that we will consider briefly are what we will label 'man-as-god' and 'god-as-man', in order to illustrate the general approach that can be taken to religion and religious belief in a psychological analysis.

Two recent examples of the man-as-god phenomenon are the 14th Dalai Lama, Tenzin Gyatso, and Emperor Hirohito of Japan, both of whom serve as a reminder that we cannot simply dismiss the man-as-god phenomenon as a thing of the past. Nevertheless, it is worth reminding ourselves of previous divine humans because it has to be one of the best jobs around if you can get it. The catch is that whilst it may be relatively easy for some people to persuade themselves that they are gods (both in the metaphorical sense if you are a famous film star or pop star, or in the literal sense if you are suffering from a delusional psychological disorder), the catch is that you also have to persuade a large group of other people of your god-like status as well. Of course, if you have been lucky enough to have your ancestors establish these claims on your behalf, as with the Egyptian pharaohs and the medieval kings of Europe, then you are halfway there. Take for example, King Jayavarman II, who became king of the Khmer Empire with its capital at Angkor in Cambodia (see Higham, 2001). On his ascension to the throne in 802 CE, he declared himself 'king of the world' and 'god-king'. One of his many privileges as god-king was that any beautiful woman could be summoned to the royal court 'to serve the king at his whim'. Given that Angkor has been estimated from satellite mapping to have been the largest pre-industrial city in the world, with a population of upwards of a million people, that was some choice of women that the god-king had. Again, very nice work if you can get it.

We considered earlier how the impact of science in the West has led most Westerners to have at least some scepticism about anyone who claims to be 'a god'. Indeed, most people in the West would now expect modern-day gods to be referred to psychiatry where they would be likely to be diagnosed with a delusional disorder and treated with major tranquilisers. Nevertheless, the majority of Christians in the West, despite the advances of modern-day science, hold the belief that Jesus was the 'son of god', born of a union between the divine god and an earthly virgin mother (as we noted earlier, a claim that is identical in all details to the Egyptian pharaohs' accounts of their own divine births). The advances of science, therefore, as in the case of evolution and the rise of creationism in the US, are relatively superficial in their impact on the religious beliefs of the majority of people, hence, perhaps, the tolerance of people in the West of more recent claims of people in the East, such as Emperor Hirohito and the 14th Dalai Lama, that they are reincarnated gods. As Levi-Strauss emphasised, the primitive or savage mind is identical to the 'modern' mind in terms of the range of belief systems, the processes of reasoning and the capacity to distort or reject evidence that is contrary to these belief systems. In fact, Levi-Strauss despaired of the 'modern' mind with its capacity for denial and distortion, which led him to declare 'The world began without the human race and will certainly end without it'. His conclusion certainly does not equate man-with-god, but the opposite, in fact.

The Judaeo-Christian God has been pictured traditionally as a wise old man with white hair and a beard in a long white tunic, an image that has presumably been encouraged by old men with white hair and beards. No surprise then that he could even remind you of your local priest. And that is exactly the point. If there is a universal deity who is omniscient and omnipresent, who occupies the vast expanse of the universe(s), and who knows the past, present and future position of every atom in the universe(s), it would be physically impossible for such a being to be an old man sitting on a cloud just above planet Earth. This anthropomorphic view of the gods has a long and famous history; the animal, animal–human and human gods evident from Palaeolithic cave paintings onwards (see for example, David Lewis-Williams book *Conceiving God*, 2010, in which he analyses the cave paintings from France and Spain, approximately 50,000–12,000 BCE) demonstrate how our visualisation of the gods are remarkably limited to what we see around us, that is, animals and other humans. The Judaeo-Christian biblical literalist will, of course, quote the Bible as the only necessary evidence:

> And God said, Let us make man in our image, after our likeness. . . . So God created man in his own image, in the image of God created he him; male and female created he them.
>
> *(Genesis 1:26–27)*

The simple answer to the literalist is that the Bible was written by men with their own anthropomorphic view of what God would look like, to which the literal-ist would reply that the Bible is a scripture that was *revealed* to the writers and the prophets, therefore every word must be true. Although it would be possible to conclude that the debate has reached an impasse at this point, the problem for the literalist is that the Bible repeatedly contradicts itself, so it is therefore absolutely impossible for the Bible to be literally true (see for example Jason Long's *Biblical Nonsense*, 2005). Even the story of the creation of man is contradicted within Genesis; thus, according to Genesis Chapter 1 (cited above), males and females were both created at the same time on the sixth day of creation. However, by Chapter 2 of Genesis there is already the well-known alternative account:

> And the Lord God took the man, and put him into the Garden of Eden to dress it and to keep it. . . . And the Lord God said, It is not good that the man should be alone; I will make him an help meet for him. . . . And the Lord God caused a deep sleep to fall upon Adam, and he slept; and he took one of his ribs . . . and made he a woman, and brought her unto the man.
>
> *(Genesis 2:15–22)*

The best conclusion, therefore, is that *man* created god in his image and likeness, not the other way round.

We must also note that the other biblical religion, Islam, has a very differ-ent approach to the use of images to represent God or Muhammad, with such images being banned in mosques and many earlier images of Muhammad being defaced in more recent times because of Islamic iconophobia. A more positive view of the Islamic approach is that it suggests a more complex and less anthro-pomorphic view when it argues that its God cannot and should not be visualised.

An example of the negative consequences of this approach occurred when, in 2005, the Danish cartoonist Kurt Westergaard had his life threatened for drawing a cartoon of Muhammad. Apparently, amongst many other appalling consequences, this resulted in the Danish children's toy Lego being banned in Saudi Arabia. Yes, that needs to be said twice – Lego was banned in Saudi Arabia because of a cartoon in a Danish newspaper. The recent murder of the cartoonists and journalists who worked on the publication *Charlie Hebdo* on 7 January 2015 in Paris because they dared to represent the Prophet Muhammad in cartoons shows religious belief at its most extreme and its most dangerous, whatever the supposed benefits might be.

Healthy atheists

One of the clear benefits of religions is their promotion of positive health-related behaviours, though there is the occasional downside, as can be seen with the Catholic Church's confused and misogynistic views on sexuality that have contributed to the AIDS crisis in Africa and a worldwide sexual abuse of children scandal amongst its clergy. But let us leave these obvious negatives aside for a moment in order to focus on the positive contributions that religions make towards health behaviours amongst their followers. As we summarised earlier, religions generally discourage drug and alcohol abuse, smoking and gluttony, and encourage a balanced lifestyle with exercise and respect for oneself and one's body. From the studies that we reviewed, the least religious people seem to be most at risk for excesses or problems in one or more of these areas, though what is cause and what is effect is unclear. As we stated, we are not here to write a book about the details of what a healthy lifestyle should be, but we have tried to highlight what is, in the main, a positive contribution of religious belief to health and longevity, though which does not in itself explain away all the benefits of religion. The challenge for atheists, therefore, is to take what is good from religion whilst avoiding that which is bad, similar to the general approach that we have taken in this book towards the positive psychology movement.

To give an example, one interesting area of work in relation to religious practices concerns the examination of the possible benefits of meditation and prayer. The benefits of meditation have become so clear that now many Western psychotherapies have begun to include it in their practice for people with a range of psychological and physical problems. The practice of meditation encourages the development and use of a mode of consciousness in which the individual steps back from an immersion in experience in order to become an observer of the self that is experiencing that experience. Such a capacity provides a high-level emotion regulation strategy that may be particularly useful when the individual is in times of stress (Power, 2010). However, as we presented elsewhere (Power, 2012), the evidence to date on the claims for the benefit of prayer are much more mixed. Some of the research seems to have verged on the fraudulent, but then religions have always been vulnerable to fraudulent though charming psychopaths of the Joseph Smith and the origins of Mormonism variety. In the case of prayer, the best and most believable studies do not show that petitionary or intercessory prayer is of any proven benefit. However, that is not to doubt the claims of religious individuals that prayer is of personal benefit to them, only to assert that the mechanisms of that benefit are not from the intercession of the supernatural, but through a psychological process of emotion regulation and narrative construction. The practice of meditation does not, therefore, require the purchase of a lorry-load of religious beliefs, but can be part of the day-to-day lifestyle practices of any atheist.

Conclusions

In this chapter we have ranged across a variety of religions in order to give a sense of some of the outrageous claims that have been made about ourselves, the universe and all who boldly go through it. In terms of happiness-related delusions, perhaps the most obvious and psychologically transparent beliefs relate to the belief in an afterlife. Those poor Ancient Egyptian farmers, whose lives depended on the annual cycle of the flooding and receding of the river Nile for the growth of their crops, believed in an afterlife, the Field of Reeds, in which the crops grew high and in abundance. Moreover, the Egyptians then went on to create a harmonious paradise where your enemies had been burned or eaten up, so that you were surrounded only by those you loved, together in the eternal company of the gods. Of course, those of us in later civilisations who lived in cities and were removed from the toil of farmers in the fields no longer dreamed that paradise had anything to do with abundant supplies of wheat, though we did hang on to and elaborate on the sustaining belief that our enemies would burn in hell. But science and psychology have gradually eroded the certainties of religions, such that many religions have been playing an embarrassingly obvious catch-up whilst other religions become increasingly bizarre in their rejections of science and psychology.

Although religions clearly offer some benefits for some people some of the time – there is no doubt that benefits occur from improved health behaviours, a sense of meaning and purpose, and from the support of a like-minded community – these benefits are obtained through adherence to delusional systems which simply cannot be right. Religions represent an early developmental stage in the growth of humanity in which factors of egocentrism, magical thinking and narcissism are significant contributions, but some cultures have begun to move beyond such an early developmental stage into a later, more mature stage of civilisation which does not need such magical thinking to sustain it. The splits between the three great Abrahamic monotheisms of Islam, Christianity and Judaism threaten our future existence, so it is only by moving beyond the biblical God and his prophets of Armageddon that we have any chance of survival.

6

POSITIVE PSYCHOLOGY, HEALTH AND ILLNESS

Happy people don't get sick.

(Traditional saying)

Introduction

Barbara Ehrenreich received a diagnosis of breast cancer in the year 2000, an experience that provides the opening for her moving and insightful book *Smile or Die: How Positive Thinking Fooled America and the World* (2009) (published in the US under the title *Bright-Sided*). As she began to track through the hundreds of websites that are devoted to breast cancer, she states that she was left with a feeling of isolation. She knew that, contrary to most of what these websites recommended, she did not want to 'positively embrace her cancer' or see it as the 'gift' that many describe. Even the American Cancer Society offers a 'Look Good . . . Feel Better' programme in which 30,000 women a year participate. Instead of loving her cancer, Ehrenreich felt angry and repulsed by the 'think positive', 'pink ribbon' culture:

> As an experiment, I posted a statement on the Komen.org message board, under the subject line 'Angry', briefly listing my complaints about the debilitating effects of chemotherapy, recalcitrant insurance companies, environmental carcinogens, and, most daringly, 'sappy pink ribbons'. I received a few words of encouragement in my fight with the insurance company . . . but mostly a chorus of rebukes.
>
> *(Ehrenreich, 2009, p. 32)*

Ehrenreich set about examining the evidence of whether or not a 'positive attitude is supposedly essential to recovery' (p. 33), which she then extended to other areas of our culture in her challenging book. Her argument is that any simple 'think positive' message can contribute not just to the silent misery of many cancer sufferers pretending to love their cancer, but also to the financial and economic collapse that the banking industry has led us into. Whatever the truth of the think positive view leading to the financial collapse, in this chapter we will try to examine systematically the evidence for the claimed links between health, happiness and well-being to see if Ehrenreich is justified in her criticisms. We should note that Ehrenreich even provides an account of a humorous attempt to interview Martin Seligman about positive psychology, and, in frustration, she says that she felt like Dorothy trying to meet the Wizard of Oz (or she might instead have said Wizard of *Pos?*). As she states in her criticism of Seligman's happiness equation H = S + C + V:

> But clearly Seligman wanted an equation, because equations add a veneer of science, and he wanted it quickly, so he fell back on simple addition. No doubt equations make a book look weightier and full of mathematical rigor, but this one also makes Seligman look like the Wizard of Oz.
>
> *(p. 158)*

Happiness and health

In this section we will begin with a relatively uncritical review of the evidence in favour of the links between happiness, illness, health and well-being. Having provided an overview of what this evidence looks like, we will then provide a critique of the types of evidence that have been collected, the types of research design that have been used, together with their strengths and weaknesses, and the types of measures that have been used to draw conclusions. In later sections in the chapter, we will consider some specific but major health conditions, including an update on the issues raised by Barbara Ehrenreich in relation to cancer and the long-standing issues that have surrounded the links between personality, well-being and cardiac risk.

The evidence in favour

There is evidence that positive mood can be a protective factor for physical health and mental health, and that it may have a therapeutic effect (e.g. Lyubomirsky and Dickerhoof, 2005). Frequent experience of positive emotions is correlated with growth, resilience and flourishing, sometimes in adverse circumstances (e.g. Fredrickson, 1998). Happiness may reduce the impact of negative emotions at a number of levels including the psychological, cognitive and physiological level

(Fredrickson, 1998). The well-known emotion theorist Carroll Izard (1991) suggested that one of the possible functions of joy is 'recuperation from stress and strain'. Melnechuk (1988) found that positive emotions can help the immune system and thereby promote recovery.

Positive affect may increase longevity. In a fascinating book, *Aging With Grace*, David Snowdon (2001) presented a summary of the findings of a longitudinal study of old age in a group of American nuns (see www.nunstudy.org). The study began in 1986 with a group of 678 nuns from the School Sisters of Notre Dame, who are a group primarily devoted to teaching. At the beginning of the study, the nuns ranged in age from 75 to 102 years. Amongst a number of findings from the study, autobiographies written when the nuns started in the religious order, at average age 22 years, were found to predict morbidity and mortality approximately 60 years later. Positive emotional content and ideational complexity in these early autobiographical sketches were found to be significantly predictive of better outcomes in later life. Lower levels of smoking and alcohol use than in matched age and gender comparison groups were also associated with overall increased longevity, with the exception that the nuns were found to have higher rates of breast cancer and genital organ cancers because of nulliparity (absence of children). Higher educational qualifications, such as having a bachelor's degree or better, was also found to be associated with greater longevity (average 89.4 years) in comparison to those with the lowest educational attainment (average 82.0 years longevity). The Nun Study is fascinating on two counts: first, the nuns were found to live, on average, longer than women in the general population, and second, within the group it is possible to examine why some of the nuns live even longer than others.

Fredrickson *et al.* (2000) found that positive emotions managed 'to undo the [health-damaging] cardiovascular after effects of negative emotions'. Their study provided evidence that positive emotions do not just replace negative emotions, but actively undo them at the physiological level. These findings may mean that positive affect helps the body (e.g. the cardiovascular system) to return to homeostatic levels of arousal and to recover from physiological changes associated with negative emotions (Fredrickson *et al.*, 2000). This may provide a possible mechanism by which positive emotions can impact on health.

Another possible function of joy that Izard (1991) pointed to is the facilitation of social interaction. Fredrickson's (1998) broaden-and-build theory suggests that positive affect helps build lasting resources, such as social relationships. Positive emotions elicit 'broad thought–action repertoires', which means that they widen one's spectrum of responses and increase one's cognitive flexibility and creativity, which helps to build resources (Fredrickson, 1998). Positive emotions can encourage exploration, play and social interaction, which are useful for increasing social resources and strengthening relationships, which, as we saw in Chapter 5 on religion, can provide buffering against stress and adversity and improve health. Happiness can also be accompanied by an increase in self-confidence and self-esteem (Izard, 1991). Martin Seligman has argued that positive emotions also appear to be at the foundation of strengths and virtues, which he emphasises in his

Authentic Happiness (2002) approach. All of these factors suggest that joy and happiness are important for long-term health and well-being.

Several therapies that aim to increase positive affect and encourage personal growth have now been developed. Seligman has developed positive psychotherapy (PPT), which is based on the theory that increasing happiness and building meaning can be an effective treatment strategy for emotional disorders. Depression and anxiety disorders have a low mood component and generally show a lack of positive emotions, which suggests that positive psychotherapy can be a useful complement to other forms of therapy and may prevent relapse in such disorders.

Well-being therapy (WBT) is another new positive psychotherapy which has provided evidence that distress can be prevented and counteracted by positive emotion (Ruini and Fava, 2012). WBT aims to develop a habit of focusing on the positives in one's life and becoming more aware of emotions. This therapy is based on Ryff's model of well-being (e.g. 1989), which suggests that in order to experience psychological wellness, a person has to develop environmental mastery, purpose in life, autonomy, self-acceptance, positive relationships with others, and to strive for personal development. Development of these factors becomes the focus of WBT and it has been successfully implemented with adolescents. One of the interesting points made more recently both by Ryff (e.g. Ryff and Singer, 2008) and by Ruini and Fava (2012) is that optimum well-being is about balance rather than extremes of happiness, very much in the tradition of Aristotle's sense of eudaimonia that we discussed in Chapter 1. A strength, therefore, of this approach is that it acknowledges that too much positivity may be just as unrealistic and harmful to mental health as too much negativity, very much the approach that we have taken in this book.

Gratitude has become an important component of the positive psychotherapies and is defined by Seligman as 'being aware of and thankful for the good things that happen'. Gratitude has been varyingly conceptualised as an emotion, a general worldview, a virtue and a trait (Emmons, 2009, p. 442). According to Seligman (2002), in order to be happy one needs to be 'satisfied about the past, optimistic about the future and happy in the present'. Expressing gratitude, such as in writing, in thought, or person-to-person, achieves these objectives. Gratitude helps the individual to realise that positive things have happened to them in the past, which can help you feel happy in the present, and therefore optimistic about the future. Gratitude increases both eudaimonic and hedonic types of happiness (see Chapter 1) because, Seligman argues, it can heighten mood in the short term (hedonic happiness) and help to find meaning and contentment in the long term (eudaimonic happiness). Gratitude expression is associated with good psychological and physical health (Emmons and McCullough, 2003), as well as optimal social functioning, optimism, life satisfaction and well-being (Emmons and McCullough, 2003). In addition, gratitude enhances resilience in the face of adversity and can protect against emotional disorders such as depression and anxiety (Emmons and McCullough, 2003). It may also protect against cardiovascular dysfunction and strengthen the immune system, though we will consider this possibility in more detail later in this chapter in the section on cardiac functioning.

One of the most successful happiness-enhancing methods is the so-called 'counting one's blessings' exercise. This involves writing down several things for which one feels thankful, or writing a letter expressing gratitude to another person (Emmons and McCullough, 2003). The exercises seem to be effective in inducing sustained positive mood. Emmons and McCullough (2003) reported in two related studies that there was a 25 per cent increase in happiness in the group that did gratitude exercises once a week for 10 weeks, compared to control groups who carried out non-gratitude tasks. In addition, the gratitude group were more likely to engage in positive health behaviours such as exercise, and they reported more optimism about the future. However, we would note a measurement overlap issue in that the positive well-being terms included gratitude-related affect items such as 'thankful' and 'appreciative', which should therefore be more likely to be endorsed by the group who were told to write about things to be grateful for, as opposed to one of the control groups who wrote about hassles or another who wrote about day-to-day events.

Other studies of gratitude include those by Seligman *et al.* (2005), who recruited participants who visited Seligman's happiness website (www.authentichappiness.org). In the gratitude exercise, the participants were given one week to write a letter to someone to whom they were grateful but whom they had never properly thanked. In a control group, the participants were simply asked to write about their early memories once a day for one week. The participants were then followed up for up to six months. The results showed an initial benefit immediately after the one-week exercise with increased ratings of happiness and reduced levels of depression. However, these benefits had disappeared by the six-month follow-up. One of the other groups in this study who were asked to write about three good things that went well that day for one week did not show any significant benefit in terms of happiness at one week, but did show lower levels of depression. These benefits were still present at six months and there were also significantly higher levels of happiness at this point. Seligman and colleagues think that those people who continued the exercises beyond the one week (even though they were not asked to) may have received more benefit. We would note though a triple bias effect operating in this study: first, the study begins with a biased sample of only those people interested enough to visit the Authentic Happiness website; second, only those people who believed sufficiently in the positive interventions will have continued through to six months follow-up; and third, only those people who believed that the positive interventions were helpful to them would have continued practising them beyond the one-week intervention.

Lyubomirsky *et al.* (2006) found that doing the gratitude exercise once a week, as opposed to several times a week, may be the optimal frequency. This gratitude approach is similar to positive reappraisal because the individual is encouraged to re-interpret past and present stressful life experiences in a more positive manner. It seems, therefore, that expressing gratitude may be associated with increased well-being in both non-clinical and clinical samples. A meta-analysis reported by Sin and Lyubomirsky (2009) summarised data from 51 interventions that included 4,266 participants. The meta-analysis showed that positive psychology interventions increase well-being (mean effect size $r = 0.29$) and decrease levels of depression (mean effect size $r = 0.31$). However, the results from tests of moderator effects in the analyses suggested that self-selected participants showed greater benefits from the interventions that, interestingly, individual interventions were more effective than group interventions, that the outcomes from the interventions were extremely heterogeneous, and that longer term continued practice of the intervention seems to have the best effect. The authors also note that members of individualist cultures may show greater benefit from positive psychology interventions than do members of collectivist cultures.

A pilot study by Carson *et al.* (2010) looked at the impact of gratitude exercises on a small sample of nine service users with long-term mental disorders in a South London community health team. The service users were asked to write down three things that they were thankful for every day over a period of one month. The research showed that the gratitude intervention led to a significant increase in subjective well-being, in life satisfaction, in social feelings and in environmental mastery. In addition, the participants stated that they had enjoyed keeping their gratitude journals. However, Emmons and Shelton (2002) note that the practice of gratitude can be difficult for a variety of reasons for some participants, for example, because it is commonplace just to take things for granted and not express gratitude to the people around us.

Positive reminiscence, or replaying happy memories in one's head, in writing or talking, is another effective method for inducing positive mood (Bryant *et al.*, 2005). Happy memories can refer to the events of years ago or to the very recent past. Positive reminiscence is related to savouring, which is 'the capacity to attend to, appreciate and enhance the positive experiences of one's life' (Bryant *et al.*, 2005). Positive reminiscence has been tested less than the gratitude approach, though there is evidence for a positive influence of reminiscence on social functioning and well-being in older adults. According to Webster (2002), reliving and sharing happy memories can have a number of positive functions such as: (1) it may help to build identity, (2) it can strengthen identity continuity, (3) it can increase acceptance of one's mortality, (4) it can remind one of helpful coping strategies that have been used in the past, (5) it can combat boredom and (6) it can foster intimacy and connection with others. In addition, positive reminiscence has been consistently found to improve self-esteem in older adults (Westerhof *et al.*, 2010). Recent studies, however, suggest that the positive effects of reminiscence might not be age-specific and that younger people might also derive benefits from its use. For example, Bryant *et al.* (2005) found that a positive reminiscence exercise showed significant benefits in 98 per cent of cases. For the participants in the study, there was an increase in subjective well-being, the opportunity to review happier times, and even to gain new insight into past experiences.

The purpose of the positive reminiscence task is intended to help the participant to focus on good memories in order to elicit positive emotions. During the exercise, participants are asked to recall happy events or images from their past in as much detail as possible whilst avoiding over-analysis of the events, which can in fact result in negative, as opposed to positive mood (Lyubomirsky *et al.*, 2006). Positive reminiscence is used in WBT (Ruini and Fava, 2012). As mentioned above, in this therapy, individuals learn to identify their emotions and to pay attention to the positive events in the present, via working through positive events and the feelings associated with them. Increased self-awareness and feelings of well-being, as well as lower levels of dysphoric symptoms and psychosomatic complaints have been reported as some of the benefits of this approach. It must be noted, though, that the manner in which positive memories are recalled and analysed may be more important than has been considered in most of the positive psychology literature. As noted above, Lyubomirsky *et al.* (2006) found in one of their studies that participants who wrote about their happiest memories, which they were asked to analyse, reported lower life satisfaction and health over a short one-month follow-up period in comparison to a control group who had not performed such a task.

The evidence against

The evidence presented so far has been treated in a relatively positive way with only light criticism, so in this section we will take a more negative psychology stance in that we will offer a range of comments on various aspects of this positive psychology literature.

We can begin with some studies from within the positive psychology movement itself. On a superficial reading of some of the earlier literature in the area (e.g. Seligman, 2002), it would be possible for the reader to come away with the impression that one should aim to be positive all of the time and exclude any of the negative feelings that will merely rain on one's positive parade. We have argued in Chapter 3, however, that the negative emotions are equally as functional as the positive emotions. In addition, a study by Barbara Fredrickson herself, who is one of the most cited researchers in the positive psychology literature because of her broaden-and-build theory of positive emotions, actually provides some support for the need for negative emotions. Fredrickson and Losada (2005) asked 188 participants to provide diary reports of positive and negative emotions over a period of 28 days. Participants who were classified as 'flourishing' ($N = 45$) were found to report positive to negative emotion ratios above 2.9 (the 'Losada line'), whereas participants who were more 'languishing' reported ratios below 2.9. Fredrickson and Losada also found that *too much* positivity is bad for mental health, with no flourishing occurring at ratios above 11.6:

> [P]roblems can occur with too much positivity . . . appropriate negativity may play an important role within the complex dynamics of human flourishing. Without appropriate negativity, behavior patterns calcify.
>
> *(Fredrickson and Losada, 2005, pp. 684–685)*

Fredrickson and Losada (2005) summarised a number of additional studies of individuals, married couples and business teams in which ratios of positive to negative emotions of exactly 2.9013:1 or better (up to a maximum of 11.6346 apparently, after which things start disintegrating) leads to flourishing individuals, flourishing marriages and flourishing teams. The precise values of 2.9013–11.6346 came from Marcial Losada's use of fluid dynamics differential equation models applied to emotions. However, in a dramatic head-on onslaught rarely seen in psychology, Nicholas Brown, at the time an MSc student at the University of East London, and his colleagues tore apart the Fredrickson and Losada misuse of fluid dynamics (Brown *et al.*, 2013). In summary, Brown and colleagues showed that the fluid dynamics equations had been misunderstood and misapplied by Fredrickson and Losada to the extent that Fredrickson (2013) has now withdrawn the earlier positivity ratio claims whilst confessing that she does not understand fluid dynamics. Her colleague Marcial Losada has disappeared back to Chile and refused to comment, and the journal itself, *American Psychologist*, has also officially retracted the positivity claims made in the 2005 paper. Further exchanges about the problems with the claimed ratio have been published in *American Psychologist* in their September 2014 issue. Beware, therefore, of positive psychologists making claims about positivity ratios, including an earlier tradition based on the Golden Section or Phi of the presence of a balance of a higher ratio (of 1.6178:1) of positive to negative in healthy individuals (e.g. Schwartz, 1992).

The broaden-and-build theory has clearly identified an important role for positive emotions in the control of attentional and thinking processes, and in the development of resilience in the individual, despite the theory having recently hit the buffers. However, it remains to be seen if *all* positive emotions have a broaden-and-build function; thus, the positive emotion of amusement, for example, has been shown not to broaden attention (Finucane *et al.*, 2010). One is also reminded of the negative attitude to certain positive emotions such as pride, which, certainly in the Ifaluk and in traditional Christianity, are seen to lead to an increase in the individual's selfishness and to reduce social awareness (Lutz, 1988).

A study by Isaacowitz and Seligman (2002) reported on a group of 93 older adults aged 60–99 years of age. These participants were assessed on a range of measures, including positive explanatory style and dispositional optimism at Time 1, then followed up over six months. Contrary to positive psychology predictions, those older adults with a positive explanatory style developed *more* depressive symptoms over the six months than those with more negative explanatory styles. In fact, Isaacowitz and Seligman (2001) reported similar findings with a different group of 71 older adults aged 64–94 years who were followed up for 12 months. Those older adults who were optimists were found to have *increased* risk of depressive symptoms in comparison to those with a more pessimistic explanatory style. The general point we wish to make from these sorts of findings is not that all optimism is bad or that all pessimism is good, but rather that these styles and traits interact with life stage, with culture, and with the social and experiential context that the person is in. Thus, for these groups of older American adults, being overly or unrealistically optimistic and positive about events increases vulnerability rather than provides protection. These are issues that we will return to throughout this chapter.

A similar conclusion about the importance of interaction effects rather than main effects for the consequences of optimism and pessimism comes from a study of immune system functioning by Cohen *et al.* (1999). In this study, 39 healthy women were followed up over three months, during which time immune status and the experience of stressors was assessed at monthly intervals. The participants were also assessed on their dispositional optimism using the Life Orientation Test (Scheier and Carver, 1985). The study found that optimists showed better immune system functioning following *acute* stressors, but poorer immune system functioning in the face of chronic persistent stressors. These findings demonstrate, therefore, that, as we have suggested, whether optimism or pessimism is more protective in the face of stress depends on the type of stress being experienced. It is not the case that one style is inherently better than the other – it all depends!

In a very different sphere to immune system functioning, Gibson and Sanbonmatsu (2004) reported a study that used the Life Orientation Test measure of dispositional optimism in a group of 55 student gamblers who frequently attended a casino near to the university campus. In the first study, optimists were found to be more positive in their views about their likelihood of success at gambling, with particular endorsement of the item 'I gamble because I believe I can make money in the long run'. In a second study carried out in the laboratory, the participants played 20 hands of the card game blackjack. In the final blackjack game, participants were allowed to bet differing sums of money. Pessimists were found to be more likely to adjust their bets downwards following poor performance on the previous hands, whereas optimists were unaffected in their level of betting by prior poor performance. A third similar study that used a computerised slot machine game again showed that pessimists reduced their betting in the loss conditions, but optimists did not. Moreover, the optimists recalled higher numbers of 'near wins' than did the pessimists, a bias which may also help to sustain the belief that they would be more likely to win in the end.

Findings such as these again run counter to the overly positive conclusions reached about the value of optimism suggested by proponents such as Carver and colleagues (2010). Authors such as these argue for main effects of optimism over pessimism, but, as we have stated, these are the wrong analyses because one needs to examine interaction effects with a variety of other factors, as the next set of studies also demonstrates.

Cross-sectional studies of marriage have been cited frequently as evidence in favour of many of the tenets of positive psychology. Grateful, kind, forgiving partners who possess all the great positive virtues have the happiest and most successful marriages, or so the story goes. For example, McNulty and Karney (2004) reported on a study of 82 newly wed couples who were followed up over a period of 4 years. As predicted, initial marital satisfaction was higher, with initial optimism and positive expectancies of marital outcomes. However, as the couples were followed over time, a more complex pattern began to emerge; the initial optimism interacted with subsequent reality in that higher optimism coupled with greater unmet expectancies led to more marital problems and less satisfaction than that seen in couples with lower optimism initially. McNulty and Fincham (2012) summarise results from four such longitudinal studies of marriage which show that the basic traits of positive psychology, such as forgiveness, optimism, kindness and positive thinking, can either lead to good marital outcomes or bad marital outcomes depending on other factors.

Another example they cite from a study by McNulty and Russell (2010) showed that forgiveness interacted with agreeableness such that forgiving increased satisfaction and reduced aggression in agreeable partners, but, unfortunately, forgiveness exacerbated problems with aggression in partners low on agreeableness. What McNulty and Fincham (2012) summarise, therefore, from their review of studies of marital success and satisfaction, is entirely consistent with the present argument: namely, that the various positive traits can in fact turn into negative traits in the wrong sorts of relationships. There is an interaction between the trait and the situation in which that trait is expressed – an interactionism that has long been recognised in the criticisms of personality trait psychology (e.g. Mischel, 1993).

Cancer, personality and happiness

There has been a long-standing tradition from the time before positive psychology of investigating possible personality risk factors for serious physical illnesses such as cancer and cardiac problems. In this section, therefore, we will consider some of the evidence of putative personality links to cancer, and, in the next section, of links to cardiac disorders and, more generally, whether other psychosocial factors and the use of psychological therapies can impact on the course and outcome of cancer survival rates. The reason why we are discussing this earlier tradition of research in the context of positive psychology is the suspicion that should the findings point to positive versus negative personality factors, such research can be viewed from a slightly different perspective by positive psychologists as evidence for their proposals. In the spirit of Barbara Ehrenreich's *Smile or Die* (2009) and her own experience with cancer, this topic deserves full attention.

Early work on the cancer-prone Type C personality suggested that people who were poor at expressing emotion and who denied or repressed emotional experiences such as anger, resentment or hostility in particular were more likely to develop cancer. As Jennifer Barraclough summarised in her book *Cancer and Emotion* (1999), the inhibition of these socially unacceptable emotions meant that the Type C person came across as overly nice, too ready to please and uncomplaining, even in the face of difficulties and problems. In addition, and perhaps because of this repressive style, the Type C personality was also considered to be more at risk for depression and feelings of hopelessness about the future. These negative feelings are also contrary to the 'fighting spirit' coping style that is especially beloved of the self-help literature on coping with cancer, in which sufferers are encouraged to visualise healthy cells fighting with and defeating the enemy cancer cells. The Mental Adjustment to Cancer (MAC) Scale developed by Maggie Watson and colleagues (1988) contains five subscales labelled 'helpless', 'anxious preoccupation', 'fatalistic', 'avoidance', and 'fighting spirit'. The fighting spirit sub-scale contains items such as 'I believe that my positive attitude will benefit my health' and 'I see my illness as a challenge'. We will return to the issue of coping styles, therapy and cancer, but first let us consider the work on personality and cancer that has dominated the psycho-oncology literature for some time.

A study by Dattore *et al.* (1980) provided evidence for the possible role of personality in the onset of cancer. Whereas much previous research had collected personality data *after* the development of cancer, in which case it is possible that the experience of cancer could have impacted on aspects of personality, Dattore and colleagues had access to prior personality assessment from a male Veterans group. The Veterans had been previously tested using the Minnesota Multiphasic Personality Inventory (MMPI) as part of their military screening. These records were later assessed for a sample of 75 cancer and 125 non-cancer control patients at a Veterans Administration (VA) hospital. The results showed that the cancer group scored higher on the repression scale of the MMPI, though, interestingly, they also scored lower on the depression subscale.

An example of a study in which personality data were collected retrospectively after onset comes from a study of lung cancer onset reported by Augustine *et al.* (2008). These researchers found, in a study of 203 people with lung cancer who were all smokers, that higher levels of 'trait negative affect' were associated with earlier onset of lung cancer, even when controlling statistically for smoking behaviour. The trait negative affect was assessed using a variety of well-known measures, which showed higher levels of neuroticism, behavioural inhibition, anger, hostility, aggression, anxiety and depression. Although this study suffers from the limitation noted above that the measurement of personality was carried out after cancer onset, the authors make the interesting comment in relation to the mixed and inconsistent findings on personality and cancer that the relationship may be stronger in the case of smokers and lung cancer than in non-smokers and other types of cancer. Again, the important point is that interaction effects are more likely than main effects for the impact of personality on health, as we have noted throughout this chapter.

However, not all of the studies on cancer and personality have shown significant associations. A large-scale study was carried out of over 30,000 adults in northern Japan who were followed up for 7 years by Nakaya and colleagues (2003). They found 671 cases of cancer at baseline, with a further 986 cases that developed over the 7-year period. The researchers had included the Eysenck Personality Questionnaire (EPQ) in the initial assessment. The results showed that neuroticism from the EPQ showed a significant correlation with cancer status at baseline for those who already had cancer, but there was no significant correlation for those who developed cancer over the 7-year period. As the authors suggest, these results point to the hypothesis that so-called neuroticism may be a consequence of having developed cancer, but it is not a cause or risk factor for the development of cancer. A study by Ian Deary and his colleagues reached a similar conclusion (Shipley *et al.*, 2007). In their study, over 5,000 participants in an earlier Health and Lifestyle Survey were followed up after 21 years. Again, results from an earlier Eysenck

Personality Inventory (EPI) neuroticism assessment did not show any association with subsequent deaths from lung cancer or from other types of cancer.

A more recent development of the so-called Type D ('distressed') personality scale, which is similar in content and conceptualisation to the earlier MMPI repression scale, has also provided support for personality contributions. For example, Mols *et al.* (2012) reported on analyses of the Eindhoven Cancer Registry, which included a variety of cancer types, in which they found that the cancer sufferers with Type D personality were at greater risk of depression and other mental health problems and also reported lower quality of life than non-Type D personality types.

Studies have also begun to investigate the role of positive psychology traits such as dispositional optimism in coping with cancer and the various side-effects and consequences of cancer treatment. Kurtz *et al.* (2008) found in a study of 214 patients undergoing chemotherapy treatment for cancer that patients with higher levels of optimism showed better response to a pain control intervention programme and had lower fatigue scores at 16-week follow-up. Similarly, Friedman *et al.* (2006) showed, in a sample of 81 female patients with breast cancer, that outcomes such as self-reported quality of life and depression were influenced by levels of optimism, with greater optimism being related to higher levels of well-being and lower levels of depression. Luo and Isaacowitz (2007) showed in a study about the risk of skin cancer development that one of the effects of dispositional optimism may be to increase the number of positive health behaviours that people engaged in following information about skin cancer risk.

Finally, the fact that personality and other factors have been implicated in the cause and course of cancer has led to the development of a large number of self-help and other therapeutic interventions for people with cancer, as we noted earlier in our discussion of the 'fighting spirit' coping style. One of the most widely cited early studies was made by Spiegel *et al.* (1989), who reported that women with breast cancer who received group psychotherapy survived almost twice as long as women in a control condition who did not receive the group intervention. Their study consisted of 86 breast cancer patients with metastases (where the cancer has spread to other parts of the body as well), who are much less likely to survive than patients without metastases. By the 10-year follow-up only three of the women were still alive, but the authors had the records of the women who had died so were able to estimate their length of survival. On average, the therapy group survived 18 months longer than the control routine oncological care group.

Unfortunately, the promise of these early studies, such as that by Spiegel *et al.* (1989), has not always come to fruition. A systematic review by Coyne and colleagues (2007) concluded:

> No randomized clinical trial designed with survival as a primary endpoint and in which psychotherapy was not confounded with medical care has yielded a positive effect.

> *(p. 367)*

The authors note that some of the interventions may impact on quality of life or on levels of depression, but such benefits have to be considered in the context of little or no impact on the disease process itself.

As a tail note to the issue of cancer and personality, we should comment that there is some emerging research about coping with cancer in childhood that points to the possibility that a more repressive style of coping may lead to a better outcome in children. Phipps (2007) has summarised a number of studies of children that suggest that there may be a range of benefits for children who use a more repressive style in coping with cancer in relation to well-being and levels of psychological distress. However, again, we would add the Jim Coyne caution that such gains do not necessarily lead to improved survival rates in children with cancer. We would also note that the repressive coping style has been associated with *increased* risk in adults for a range of disorders, as we will consider in the next section (see also Chapter 2).

The Type A personality story

In the previous section, we presented accounts of the Type C and Type D personalities, so now in this section we will fill in for the missing Type A and Type B varieties. The Type A personality was described in the 1950s by two cardiologists, Meyer Friedman and Mike Jordan, who, from their clinical experience, recognised a coronary heart disease (CHD)-prone type of person that they described as Type A. The cardiac-prone Type A is in many ways the opposite of the perfect positive psychology personality, in contrast to the Type B person, who is described as relaxed, easy-going and with a positive outlook. In fact, the Type A sounds like the personality that Martin Seligman describes himself as before he transformed himself overnight into the positive Type B (see Seligman, 2002). The original descriptions of the Type A personality include time-pressured, aggressive, ambitious, easily irritated and overstretched workaholics. In a 10-year follow-up study of a group of healthy males aged between 35 and 59, Friedman and Rosenman (1959) concluded that the Type A personality had almost twice the risk of CHD in comparison to the Type B.

Matthews *et al.* (2003) reported on the first-wave cross-sectional study of a community sample of people aged 28–74 years living in Heidelberg in Germany. The study was designed to examine the correlations between a variety of personality scales and factors and a wide range of different physical disorders. The Type A personality variables were found to be correlated with a number of disorders, especially with CHD, but even more so in individuals with multiple disorders that included CHD. However, the comparisons between the single- and multiple-disorder groups only showed that the personality factor of emotional lability (the experiencing of too much emotion sometimes combined with over-inhibition of emotion at other times) rather than Type A distinguished these groups. Amelang *et al.* (2004) reported on a follow-up over 10 years of the Heidelberg cohort in which 257 participants were found to have died and 120 of the survivors had

CHD. Although Type A and the emotional lability personality factors both were associated with CHD, when the researchers controlled statistically for age, gender and smoking behaviour, only emotional lability remained as a significant predictor, Type A personality no longer did. Interestingly, and consistent with our conclusions in the earlier section on cancer, none of the personality variables (which included dispositional optimism) were found to have any predictive relationship.

Woodward *et al.* (2003) reported on a longitudinal study, the Scottish Heart Health Study (SHHS), of 11,619 Scottish adults aged 40–59 years who were followed up for an average of 7.7 years. The researchers were especially interested in factors that contribute to social inequality in the prevalence of CHD and other mortality risks, in which low social status increases the risk for diseases such as CHD (e.g. Marmot *et al.*, 2006). One useful indicator of social status is housing tenure: people who rent their accommodation are typically of lower social status than those who own their accommodation. When Woodward and colleagues examined CHD in rented versus owner groups, the men who rented were found to be 1.48 times more likely to have CHD in comparison to men who owned their accommodation, and women were 2.64 times more likely. The main factor that predicted the difference in CHD between the social status groups was smoking, which was much higher in the rental groups. Type A personality was found to make only a small contribution for the differences between the women in CHD, but not for the men, and, overall, it was not an important factor.

Subsequent research has therefore questioned the links that were proposed in the 1950s between Type A personality and CHD. However, more recent research has examined the complex of multiple attributes which were taken to characterise the Type A personality, which have been grouped into the three main factors of competitiveness, hostility and time pressure (e.g. O'Gorman, 2010). Even this deconstruction of the concept has led to mixed results in relation to CHD. One possibility is that the emotional lability, which can be reflected in too much and too little anger, aggression, hostility, etc., may show some worthwhile pointers for future research (Power and Dalgleish, 2015).

A second personality type that has been linked to CHD and other disorders is the repressor type. As we noted in the previous section on cancer, there may be some evidence that this personality type may help children cope with cancer (Phipps, 2007), even though the research with adults has considered it to be a risk factor rather than a positive protective factor. Thus, a meta-analysis by McKenna *et al.* (1999) found a significant effect size for denial/repression coping on the development of breast cancer. In Chapter 2 we considered the question of individuals who maintain their self-esteem or happiness by denying the existence of negative material in their lives. Researchers of this so-called 'repressive coping style' (e.g. Derakshan *et al.*, 2007) have conceptualised it as the avoidance of anxiety, but, as we noted, it is equally feasible to consider the motivation to be the maintenance of a state of positive affect though at a price. Thus, it is an as yet unanswered empirical question as to whether repressive coping only relates to anxiety avoidance or whether other aversive emotions, such as anger and disgust, are also avoided.

A recent meta-analysis of the links between repressive coping and a variety of somatic diseases was carried out by Mund and Mitte (2012). In 22 relevant studies that met their criteria, they found an association between repressive coping and cancer, and also with hypertension, though the relation with CHD was less clear. However, in longitudinal studies, Denollet *et al.* (2008) followed up 731 patients with CHD for between 5 and 10 years. Repressors were found to be at significantly increased risk of mortality and of further cardiac problems in comparison to the non-repressor group. A similar earlier study, the Montreal Heart Attack Readjustment Trial, followed up 1,376 cardiac patients for 5 years post discharge and found both male and female repressors to be at increased risk of mortality (Frasure-Smith *et al.*, 2002). The Montreal study also attempted a psychosocial intervention over the first 12 months, but the repressor group were found to make poorer use of this intervention and needed higher levels of benzodiazepine prescriptions in comparison to the non-repressors.

In her summary of the literature on repressive coping, Lynn Myers (2010) makes the important point that, as we have noted earlier in the chapter, there may be important interactions between repressive coping and the type of somatic disorder that repressors are suffering from. Thus, repressors may respond better to disorders that they perceive to be more within their control (e.g. asthma, diabetes) in comparison to disorders that they perceive to be outside of their control (e.g. cancer and CHD). Certainly, this more complex picture is consistent with the general conclusions that one can reach in relation to the positive psychology aspects of personality and issues about risk and protection from somatic disorders such as cancer and CHD. The findings in the literature often appear to be inconsistent, for example, when repressive coping appears to be positive for children but negative for adults, or that it appears to be protective for some diseases but a risk for others. Such findings point against simplistic models, in which simple main effects of factors such as dispositional optimism or other personality types have been claimed. As we will review in the next section on mental health, flexibility and adaptability may be more crucial for physical and mental health rather than always presenting with one style that is either positive or negative.

Back to the -isms: optimism, pessimism and realism

The positive psychology literature tells us that optimism is good, pessimism is bad, and, well, realism is what you make it – witness the likes of Martin Seligman's *Learned Optimism: How to Change Your Mind and Your Life* (1998). As Seligman's book cover says 'When you know how to choose the power of optimism, you'll gain an essential new freedom to build a life of rewards and lasting fulfilment'.

So, and to adapt the normal phrase, why do bad things happen to optimists, and why do good things happen to pessimists? One reason is that many of the things that happen to us are outside of our control, but many of us, especially optimists, suffer from illusions of control (e.g. Kahneman, 2011). For example, if you are told that you have a 10% chance of winning $100 in a raffle, optimists will believe that it will be themselves who will win, pessimists will believe that it will be someone else who will win, and realists will know that there is a 1-in-10 chance of winning. In practice, the pessimists will be more likely to be correct in this chance situation and the optimists will be more likely to be incorrect because their beliefs have no impact on the relatively low probability of winning. However, a subtler positive psychology argument might be, sure, you know that you only have a 1-in-10 chance of winning, but as an optimist you can enjoy the game of chance more than the pessimist would, so you can be happy and excited even if you do not win – the important thing is to be happy and optimistic and take part!.

There are, of course, at least some detractors from this early positive psychology bias that optimism is all good and that pessimism is all bad (e.g. Kashdan and Biswas-Diener, 2014). So far in this chapter, we have examined the impact of positive psychology factors on different aspects of physical health, mental health and well-being. Our basic approach has been to present some of the positive psychology evidence and then either to point to some weaknesses in aspects of the research or to quote other research that has come to different conclusions. The starting point for our discussion has been to take the positive psychology claim and then examine weaknesses and limitations, typically coming to the conclusion that so-called positive traits often interact with other aspects of a situation, context or person, and that these interactions can reduce or even nullify the supposed positive benefit. However, what if there is a different stance that can be taken; namely, that under some circumstances pessimism or realism actually outperforms or brings greater benefits for physical and mental health than optimism does? We will examine, therefore, some of these proposals before we come to a different conclusion and way forward for the '-isms'.

When pessimism is best

The proposal that pessimism is better than optimism does, of course, fall into the same trap that we have pointed out for positive psychology, in that the main effects of these factors cannot be predicted because of interactions with situation and other person variables. Evidence that we will present for the benefits of pessimism must be taken, therefore, with this caveat in mind.

In a book called *The Positive Power of Negative Thinking*, which might have benefitted from a better title, Julie Norem (2002) summarises a very important type of beneficial pessimism. She and others have given this variety of pessimism another unfortunate title, that of 'defensive pessimism', presumably on the mathematical basis that two negatives (i.e. both 'defensive' and 'pessimism' have negative connotations) when multiplied together produce a positive. Anyway, Norem has presented defensive pessimism as a particular style that some people use to their benefit. There seem to be at least two important components to this approach, the first of which consists of negative expectations about future events in which the person worries about possible problems, and the second of which is a reflectivity on those possible problems in which the person attempts to obviate the problems that they have thought of in the first step. In such cases, therefore, worry has a constructive function (see also Chapter 3 where we considered some of the functions of 'negative' emotions such as anxiety) in which the person imagines potential disasters and then does his or her best to plan ways around them. Norem (2002) offers a wide range of examples to illustrate how defensive pessimists can often come off best. For example, Norem likens the defensive pessimist's mental rehearsal to an imagery technique used in sports psychology in which athletes are encouraged to rehearse their routines mentally, including how mistakes might happen and how they would overcome the mistakes if they do happen. Norem points out that the dispositional optimist's strategy, in which the athlete simply assumes a perfect winning performance, may be less effective and more disruptive to performance following an actual mistake for which the optimist has not prepared.

Another important point that Norem makes is that defensive pessimists have learned better both to tolerate and work with their negative emotions, such as anxiety, than optimists often have, because many of the mental strategies used by optimists are designed to avoid negative emotions such as anxiety. In that way, the optimist may have poorer emotion regulation strategies than the pessimist, which, again, are likely to lead to problems in some circumstances, leading to the important concept of 'unrealistic optimism' (Weinstein, 1984). Unrealistic optimists are more likely to abandon exercise programmes, for example, because they are too confident about their current and future health status. Norem also notes that defensive pessimists tend to list more negative characteristics about themselves than do optimists, but she notes that these negative characteristics tend to be very specific, in contrast to dispositional pessimists who tend to refer to themselves in global negative terms. The defensive pessimists tend to use this self-critical knowledge in a more constructive manner under appropriate circumstances, because they use the awareness that they have of their faults to overcome them or compensate for them in those circumstances. For example, a defensive pessimist might be aware of a tendency not to compliment the people around him enough, but by making himself aware of this fault and carefully judging and reflecting on situations in which it is appropriate to make a compliment, he can compensate to some degree for this tendency – or at least offer an apology to his wife when he fails to compliment her on her new hairstyle! Newman *et al.* (2009) showed that defensive pessimists are the one group that do not show self–other recall biases in memory for positive and negative personality feedback, again because they are more likely to make use of the feedback even if it is negative.

In a study comparing dispositional pessimists, defensive pessimists and optimists in a laboratory anagram-solving task, del Valle and Mateos (2008) found that optimists and defensive pessimists were more similar to each other in their performance, in that they adjusted their performance under different conditions, whereas dispositional pessimists made no adjustment to their performance under different conditions and showed the most rigidity in their performance. Sweeny and Shepperd (2010) reported on a study in which optimistic and pessimistic students were asked to predict the outcome of their exams and were then followed up and assessed when they found out the actual outcome. The strongest effect was for optimists, who over-estimated their predicted performance, but then failed relative to their expectations and felt worst immediately after the exam outcomes. As this study illustrates, part of the function of pessimism, whether it is dispositional or defensive, can be a self-protective one in that, for example, the reduction of expectations in relation to uncertain outcomes in a wide range of domains can lessen the impact of failure or an undesired outcome.

Ntoumanis *et al.* (2010), in a study of physical education in British schoolchildren, found that defensive pessimism served this protective function especially where the pupils perceived themselves to be less competent and in competitive situations in which they experienced fear of failure. However, the self-protective benefits seem to be balanced out by less enjoyment of physical education and less likelihood of participation in future optional sports programmes.

Another beneficial category of pessimism has been labelled 'retroactive pessimism', a type, in fact, that is sometimes used by optimists and not just by pessimists. The failure of a desired goal, whether in a competition, an exam, a job interview or a date that goes wrong, often leads people to readjust their expectations of success and failure retroactively. It is a type of hindsight bias, as Kahneman (2011) would describe it, in which we downgrade our expectations once we know the actual outcome. Wann *et al.* (2008) studied the effects of retroactive pessimism in groups of supporters of US college basketball teams, with the additional assumption that the stronger the sense of group identity with their team, the stronger their sense of disappointment. The supporters were assessed just before and just after actual games, and the results supported the predicted group identity effect, in which expectations were more downgraded and the strength of the opposing team more upgraded the stronger the identity with the team.

Tycocinski and Steinberg (2005) further showed that the greater the sense of disappointment that results from a 'near miss', for example, if your team almost won, or if you failed the exam by just one mark, in comparison to missing by a long way, then the more likely the retroactive downgrading. They also found that 'near miss' individuals are more likely to inhibit upward counterfactuals, that is, the 'what if' and 'if only' type statements in which you think about what you might have done better in order to succeed. Similar to the function of defensive pessimism, therefore, retroactive pessimism plays a self-protective role that helps us cope with the disappointments that we all experience in life.

Cross-cultural issues

One of the questions that has to be asked about optimism and positive psychology in general is whether it is a culture-specific phenomenon that captures a time in American history when the American Dream and the 'everyone can be president' mentality has come to predominate. Do other cultures also promote the positive and show benefits from optimism and the like in terms of health and well-being? In answer to this question, in principle, there could be a culture in which happiness and optimism are socialised out, in which, for example, a sense of suffering, together with appropriate accompanying emotions, were socially sanctioned, and, because of this, people might benefit in terms of health and longevity by being more socially adherent to values such as pessimism and fatalism. Indeed, in Chapter 2, we briefly reviewed the work by Catherine Lutz (1988) with the Ifaluk Islanders in the South Pacific, who socialise out the emotion of happiness from an early age such that happiness is considered to be a negative selfish emotion that runs counter to the values of the group. We also noted that the Free Presbyterians in the Isles of Lewis and Harris in the Scottish Western Isles share a similar disdain for happiness and pleasure. However, we do not know how these cultures might or might not benefit from the proposals of positive psychology. They would probably laugh at them if they could, but their socialisation would not allow such a response.

There are some relevant studies that point to ethnic and cultural differences in optimism and pessimism. Spencer et al. (2009) studied a sample of 2,729 black and white US elders aged 70–79 years on health pessimism and objective physical functioning. Black elders were found to express lower self-rated health compared to white elders, especially at the highest levels of functioning, that is, independent of actual health status. Hardin and Leong (2005) compared European and Asian American groups of students on optimism, pessimism and depression and found that pessimism was a stronger predictor for the European Americans than for the Asian Americans, but self-discrepancies were more predictive of social anxiety in the Asian Americans.

The American approach to cross-cultural research typically consists of recruiting participants from different areas of Los Angeles or New York, so the American studies do need to be supplemented by some genuine cross-cultural work. Chang et al. (2003) compared South Korean to European American students on optimism, pessimism and psychological adjustment. One of the important characteristics of a collectivist culture such as Korea is that self-criticism is seen as important in order to maintain social harmony, in contrast to individualist cultures such as the US where self-enhancement seems to be more important in self-definition rather than harmony with others. Chang et al. found that the South Koreans had higher levels of negative affect, whereas the Americans had higher levels of positive affect (both measured on the Positive and Negative Affect Schedule [PANAS]). Furthermore, life satisfaction was linked to both optimism and pessimism for the Korean students, whereas positive affect was more important for life satisfaction in the American students. The results indicate that thinking positively seems to be more important and to have more impact on psychological adjustment for Americans compared to Koreans.

A similar conclusion can be reached from a study by Rose et al. (2008) who found that US participants showed higher levels of unrealistic optimism than their Japanese counterparts in a judgement task in which participants assessed the likelihood of positive and negative events happening to them in the future, especially if these judgements were made separately for self versus others.

In relation to defensive pessimism, a study of Singaporean participants reported by Chang and Sivam (2004) looked at defensive pessimism and health-related behaviour during the SARS (severe acute respiratory syndrome) crisis. Participants were assessed to examine the extent to which they endorsed traditional Chinese values of prudence, industry and civic harmony, which, they argued, should be more linked to defensive pessimism. The results showed that the traditional Chinese values were correlated with levels of defensive pessimism, and that these in turn were more likely to lead to beneficial health-related behaviours during the SARS crisis. The results again confirm the beneficial action function of worry in defensive pessimism, and at the same time show how such values may be more culturally attuned to Eastern collectivism than to American individualism.

Flexibility

So where do all these findings point to in relation to optimism, pessimism and realism? As an aside, whilst, in principle, one might wish to plump for realism in the midst of the clear biases that both optimism and pessimism are associated with, there is the philosophical problem noted by constructivists (e.g. see Ulric Neisser's overview in *Cognition and Reality*, 1976) that because we can only filter and distort reality through our own limited sensory and cognitive systems, these systems are inherently distorting, so realism may be both philosophically impossible and psychologically unattainable as a choice. Moreover, if we are simply talking about probabilistic events that have not yet occurred and that are outside of our control, the three choices of pessimism, optimism and realism by definition have no impact on the likelihood of the event occurring, so it is arguable that it does not matter what choice you make. However, where we can influence the likelihood of good and bad events occurring, there may be motivational consequences of these different options that need to be considered carefully. These motivational consequences are not necessarily obvious, as we have seen throughout this chapter, because sometimes optimism can be accompanied by over-confidence and too little effort, whereas pessimism may actually lead to greater effort and more careful planning in order to obviate possible difficulties. One suspects that sometimes optimism, sometimes pessimism, and sometimes realism might be preferable depending on other aspects of the person and the situation. If this conclusion is correct, then *flexibility* may ultimately be the most beneficial viewpoint, as we will consider next.

The concept of flexibility has begun to be of increasing importance in psychology. Kashdan and Rottenberg (2010) have summarised a wide range of relevant work that points to the importance of flexibility for benefits and improvements in health. They point to a diverse number of areas of psychology where, under one guise or another, the concept of psychological flexibility resides, including the concept of ego-resilience in psychotherapy, of executive control in neuropsychology, and, more generally, of self-regulation and emotion regulation in general psychology. In contrast, there are also a number of inflexible psychological processes that have been studied, including rumination, worry, perseveration, stress regulation and poor planning capacity. Taken together under the umbrella of psychological flexibility, these diverse areas point to a meta-level skill with clear all-round benefits. For example, one of the personality correlates of flexibility is the Big Five factor of openness to experience (e.g. McCrae and Costa, 1997). People who are more open to experience show more curiosity, they are more receptive to new knowledge and new experiences, and broaden their efforts and interests in order to maintain a flexible sense of self.

Burton *et al.* (2012) reported on a study of coping flexibility in recently bereaved adults in the US and in Hong Kong. In both cultures, increased coping flexibility was associated with a better outcome from the bereavement such that those who developed the most severe complicated grief reactions were less likely to show overall coping flexibility. A related concept of 'belief inflexibility' has been shown to be important in the development of delusional convictions. For example, So *et al.* (2012) reported that, in a large sample of 273 patients with delusions who attended for a treatment trial, upwards of 75 per cent of the sample showed belief inflexibility and 50 per cent showed a characteristic jumping-to-conclusions bias. These biases remained stable over the 12 months of the intervention. The importance of psychological flexibility has also been emphasised in acceptance and commitment therapy (ACT), developed by Steven Hayes and his colleagues (e.g. Hayes *et al.*, 1999), who have developed an Acceptance and Action Questionnaire (AAQ) designed to measure psychological flexibility. Another example is the Coping Flexibility Scale developed by Kato (2012).

Between them, these types of scales have begun to highlight the importance that psychological flexibility has across a wide variety of domains, be they health, social relationships, or goals and plans. The capacity to try one approach but then relinquish that approach in the face of feedback that it is not working and then try a new approach is a healthy sign of an advanced and mature psychological capacity that the simplistic analyses of the earlier positive thinking approaches fail to appreciate. The capacity for psychological flexibility is a capacity that we will return to in the next chapter.

Conclusions

There is evidence that optimism can be good for health and longevity, though if it becomes too unrealistic or too excessive then these beneficial effects begin to be negated. There is also evidence that pessimism can be good for health and longevity when it is of the defensive pessimism variety, because defensive pessimists are more likely to think ahead and plan for the specifics that might go wrong in a situation. There is also evidence cross-culturally that optimism may be of more benefit in some individualistic cultures, whereas pessimism may be of more benefit in some collectivistic cultures. At first sight, these apparently contradictory conclusions seem typical of psychology – just when you are looking for a simple and neat solution, somebody comes along and complicates it all. Well, perhaps there is a (relatively) simple solution to this contradictory complexity, at least at a meta-level. The benefits of optimism, pessimism and realism vary according to the person, the situation and the cultural context, but even within the one person in the one context different responses may be beneficial at different times.

Ultimately, psychological flexibility seems to win out against any main effect trait assumptions of the form 'always look on the bright side of life'. Such excesses of positivity may work in the short term for one-off acute and controllable stressors, but they may lead to a blindness and vulnerability in the face of more complex chronic adversity in which the individual's normal coping resources become overwhelmed. Whether it is in the face of major illnesses such as cancer and CHD or dealing with the health problems of old age, a flexibility in the approach to such disorders, together with a tolerance for the strong emotions that they evoke in oneself and in others, is more likely to improve overall coping whatever the eventual outcome.

7

TRANSFORMING THE SELF

The biggest risk in life is not to take any risks.

(BBC TV tennis commentator, 2012)

Introduction

On the roller-coaster of life there are only two things that we can be certain of: death and taxes, as Benjamin Franklin astutely observed. Most other things tend to have a degree of uncertainty. One simplistic approach to this uncertainty enshrined in pop psychology runs along the lines of 'always look on the bright side of life', because these other things might just go better for you if you take this optimistic view. Throughout this book we have tried to examine in a diverse set of areas that have included work, religion, sex and health, whether or not such simple optimism is always better than the alternatives. In statistical terms, the argument is that there should be 'main effects' of optimism, that optimists should have better outcomes for life, longevity, happiness and whatever, in comparison to the rest of us. Although some such main effects of optimism and more general positive traits have been observed in a number of areas of psychology, by and large, the research tends to point to more complex outcomes, which, again to put into statistical terms, are best described as 'interaction effects'. Indeed, these interaction effects do not simply amount to a thereby qualified support for traits such as optimism, but in fact point to times when optimism (or its positive variants) for some people under certain circumstances, may actually be *bad* for you, whereas for other people under other circumstances pessimism may actually be *good* for you.

The task lying ahead for psychology is to work out how to describe and understand these more complex interaction effects. As the American psychologist Jerome Kagan states in his book *Psychology's Ghosts: the Crisis in the Profession and the Way Back* (2012), many in psychology, and others besides, have failed to take account of the impact of the situation on psychological behaviour, for which we should also remember the broader socio-political context. As for the measurement of 'happiness' itself, Kagan is highly critical because every different version and personal definition of the term gets lumped under the one umbrella term, which, Kagan argues, thereby loses all meaning.

Although so far in this book we have mostly limited ourselves to modern work in psychology about the evidence for optimism, pessimism and their interactions with circumstances, in the next section we will consider some examples of survival under extreme circumstances as examples of how these factors can either be good or bad depending on what these extreme circumstances are. It is also hoped that these examples might convey the possibility that psychology is applicable to real life, just in case you ever thought it was only applicable to American students locked inside a laboratory inside the Ivory Tower.

Survival under extremes

There are many examples of both survival and failure to survive under extreme circumstances that can provide dramatic examples of how traits such as optimism can be fatal whereas pessimism, especially in its constructive form (such as the unfortunately labelled 'defensive pessimism'), can be the key to survival. The point we wish to make with these examples is the theme highlighted throughout this book that traits such as optimism or pessimism interact with a range of other factors in order to produce outcomes that involve extreme courage (Pury and Lopez, 2009). The aim is to show that there is no simple one-dimensional answer and that so much depends on a range of many other factors.

The Donner Party

Any Californian worth their salt will be able to tell you the harrowing story of the Donner Party, and may even have visited the sites in the Sierra Nevada mountains that now bear their names. The 'party' refers to a group of 87 pioneers who headed west from Illinois in April 1846 to reach the 'wonders of California' with all its great riches and beautiful climate (see e.g. George Stewart, *Ordeal by Hunger: The Story of the Donner Party*, 1988). For a variety of reasons, some of which we will consider, the party arrived at the great continental divide between east and west in the US, the Sierra Nevada, as winter was settling in, and they were caught in excessively heavy snows in the mountains. A few members of the group succeeded in getting through to California, and there they raised rescue teams, but by the time they got back to those trapped in the mountains in late February 1847 only 48 of the 87 survived, with many of those who had survived having resorted to cannibalism.

This ill-fated story of the pioneer migration westwards to the American promised land captures so much of the risks of fatal or unrealistic optimism. The Donner Party was organised by two relatively wealthy and successful Illinois businessmen who were in their sixties, George Donner and James Reed. Neither family needed to head west because they were already successful and well established in Springfield, Illinois, but in the age of pioneer fever they were motivated by the possibility that things could be even better. To emphasise that he was the wealthiest of the party, James Reed had specially constructed wagons made, including what his daughter Virginia referred to as the 'Pioneer Palace Car', which has become legendary in pioneer history. The wagon was two storeys high with an entrance from the side. It included spring-cushioned seats and bunks on the upper level for sleeping, and had its own stove for heating and cooking. The fact that it took eight oxen to pull the wagon, which was heavier and wider than anything that had ever headed west before, seems to have been overlooked by the wealthy optimist James Reed.

Reed's fellow optimist, who came to be the outright leader of the party, the genial George Donner, estimated that it would take them four months to reach California when they left Springfield on 14 April. However, even though they were following a well-used trail for the first part of their journey, they had only reached Fort Bridger in Wyoming after three months. At this stage, they had already diverted from a much larger group of pioneers at Fort Laramie, but now they made a second fatal mistake. Whereas the majority of the large group at Fort Bridger took the old established wagon route and actually all made it safely through to California, George and James decided to take an untried 'short cut', the so-called 'Hastings Route', which even the proposer of the route had not tried with a wagon at that stage. Indeed, at Fort Laramie, a friend of James Reed from Illinois, who had been along the route by horse, begged him not to try the Hastings Route because he said it would be impassable with wagons, especially those the size of the Reeds' wagon.

However, George and James believed what they wanted and that a 'short cut' had to be a short cut, even though it involved crossing the Great Salt Lake Desert and salt lakes before it hit the difficult high passes through Truckee Nevada. The short cut in fact took nearly a month longer than the normal route, and the group lost many of their oxen and other animals in the harsh conditions of the desert and salt lakes. By 28 October, the snows had arrived early in 1846 in the Sierra Nevada and the group were forced to set up a winter camp by Lake Truckee (now Lake Donner) because they were trapped by deep snow. During the winter, a bad gash to George's hand, sustained whilst trying to repair his wagon, turned gangrenous, so he became bedridden and was too weak to help the group. When the first rescue party arrived in late February, George was too weak to travel, so his wife Tamsen stayed with him, but both were dead when the final rescue party arrived in Truckee in April 1847, almost a year to the day that they had set out from Springfield.

The tragedy of the Donner Party has been captured in numerous histories, novels and films, each of which emphasises different features, such as the gruesome nature of the cannibalism that many of the survivors resorted to. However, in terms of the focus of this book, the most telling issues are the accumulation of small but significant errors that resulted from a fixed and inflexible way of thinking that is a consequence of unrealistic optimism. The wish to travel in luxury, to display wealth and status, to take a 'short cut', to ignore sensible advice – all of these characteristics add to the horror of the story. Yet in all of this one small detail stands out, which is that the group came to a halt by Lake Truckee in the Sierra Nevada, a lake that was still unfrozen and accessible at the time they stopped, and that was full of trout that they could have caught, eaten, smoked and preserved, but they did not know how to fish. For those of us brought up on survival television programmes, we have learned from survival experts such as Bear Grylls a dozen different ways of catching fish in the wild using spears, prongs, woven baskets, dams and whatever, made from products at hand in the wild. But these were well-equipped wagon trains in which one might have imagined that some means of fishing in rivers and lakes would have been standard. Everyone who knows the story of the Donner Party has their own morbid favourite piece of the horror, but being trapped by a lake full of trout and not knowing how to fish is especially tragic.

Roald Amundsen

The theme of survival and death under extreme winter conditions brings to mind the great polar explorers and some of the personality and other psychological differences that must have contributed to their great successes and failures. As with the leaders of the Donner Party, we do not have scores on a Life Optimism Test to help us decide definitively how optimistic or pessimistic the polar explorers were, so we can only base our guesstimates on their own personal accounts of themselves and on the accounts provided by others who knew them. In our search for an example of a successful pessimist, none seems to fit the bill better than the great Norwegian explorer Roald Amundsen, who has been described as 'taciturn under the best of circumstances' and, by a member of the British Royal Geographic Society who knew all the explorers, as 'the most unhappy of all the polar explorers he had ever met' (see e.g. Colman's *Amundsen of the Arctic*, 2011). Someone who slept with his bedroom window open as a teenager during the harsh Norwegian winters in order to prepare himself for polar exploration certainly sounds more like the defensive pessimist than the optimist. Amundsen also seems to have suffered from some very negative English press over the years. Some writers have never forgiven him for beating the great English polar explorer, Captain Scott, to the South Pole.

It is worth reminding ourselves of the scale of Amundsen's achievements before we consider further how some important aspects of his personality may have contributed to these successes. In his early thirties, Amundsen became the first person to traverse the notorious Northwest Passage that led from the Atlantic through to the Pacific across northern Canada. The journey took Amundsen and his crew 3 years, and the seas successively froze and thawed around them year after year as they slowly made their way through. Amundsen's next goal was to be the first to reach the North Pole. He was in fact preparing to sail there in 1910 when he heard that the American explorers, Robert Peary and Frederick Cook, had claimed, what may in fact have been falsely, to have reached the North Pole. If ever an explorer showed psychological flexibility, it was Amundsen, because he then switched his plans and headed to the South Pole instead, though it was not until he sailed into Madeira that he told his fellow explorers where they were going. They thought up to that point they were still heading to the North Pole! In later years, Amundsen did in fact become the first to fly over the North Pole in a balloon in 1926, after which he is reported to have said to a journalist 'If only you knew how splendid it is up there, that's where I want to die'. In fact, when flying over the Arctic on a rescue mission in 1928, his plane crashed somewhere north of Tromsø and it has never been recovered despite ongoing attempts to this day to find the wreckage.

In combination with Amundsen's notoriety as a taciturn and unhappy individual, what clearly comes through from his own writings and the writings of others about him is his psychological flexibility. This is evident not just in his capacity to switch to the South Pole when he had planned to head to the North Pole, but also in the small adaptations that he made to his approach to exploration following what he learned from his earlier voyages. For example, from the Northwest Passage experience he learned from the local Inuit that dogs and the dog sled were the most effective form of transport. Whereas Scott used mainly ponies (and mechanical sleds that did not work in the extreme temperatures) to travel to the South Pole, Amundsen used dogs. Similarly, he learned from the Inuit that, to survive the extreme low temperatures of winter, clothes made from animal skin and fur were far more effective against the cold than the heavier cotton and wool clothes used by Scott.

Amundsen's capacity for planning was renowned, as he himself stated:

> I may say that this is the greatest factor – the way in which the expedition is equipped – the way in which every difficulty is foreseen, and precautions taken for meeting or avoiding it. Victory awaits him who has everything in order. . . . Defeat is certain for him who has neglected to take the necessary precautions in time.
>
> (Amundsen, 1912, p. 222)

On the basis of his own writings and the accounts of him provided by others, Amundsen certainly seems to meet the criteria for the defensive pessimist, always trying to anticipate the difficulties and dangers ahead. However, his pessimism was accompanied by a great deal of psychological flexibility, which added considerably to why he was the greatest of all the polar explorers during the great age of polar exploration.

When pessimists are right

In our final example, we will move away from the frozen wastes of the Sierra Nevada and the polar regions in order to consider a very different example from more recent times. Based on Anthony Storr's well-known account, *Churchill's Black Dog* (1988), we have discussed elsewhere Winston Churchill's vulnerability to depression and how his gloomy pessimistic predictions about German rearmament were ignored until too late in the 1930s (Power and Dalgleish, 2015). Therefore, we will turn our attention to a much more recent, indeed current disaster, that of the current global financial crisis in which we will pick out one highlight – the role of property.

Happiness and optimism map well onto the economic bull market in that they reflect emotions brimming with confidence and positive biases. The associated risks of an excess of happiness, combined with over-confidence and unrealistic optimism, mean that the market characteristics now begin to shift more into the hypomania/mania extremes of happiness (see Chapter 2), in which the extreme can be followed by a crash or the bursting of an economic bubble. For example, Christie and colleagues carried out a qualitative interview study of house purchases following an Edinburgh house price boom in which people began paying excessive prices (Christie *et al.*, 2008):

> And love like fear has a material effect on price. It was out of love (or the hope for this affective tie to home) that the buyers undertook to pay high prices for specific properties, and which prices subsequently became a core element of the spiralling market uncertainty.
>
> *(p. 2307)*

House purchase cannot be modelled by any traditional economic approach because housing markets are driven as much by emotion as by economics. The reasons that people gave for paying exorbitant prices for the purchase of Edinburgh houses are not simply based on financial investment considerations, but also on a host of intense emotions about happiness, combined with fear and desperation that are as intense as many of the love infatuations that we discussed in Chapter 2.

A national example of a property bubble comes from Ireland, in which, during the period 2000 to a peak in 2006, Irish property prices tripled in value. The increase in property values led many Irish people to invest in property, both in Ireland and in other parts of the world, driven by over-optimism, greed and the belief that the property markets would continue to rise. However, the bubble burst in 2008, and by 2009 there were an estimated 230,000 vacant properties, approximately half of which were second homes and buy-to-rent properties. By 2012, the house prices in Dublin were only 56 per cent of what they were at their peak in 2007.

In the midst of the great Irish property boom, two Irish economists stood out from the pack in terms of their warnings that the Irish economy was unsustainable, based as it was on a major over-valuation of the property market, aided by poor decision-making in the banking sector. The two economists were Professor Morgan Kelly of University College Dublin and David McWilliams, who had worked as an economist with the Central Bank of Ireland but then moved into writing and broadcasting. Kelly published a research paper in 2006 stating that the property boom would soon burst and predicting accurately that house prices would fall by 60 per cent in the subsequent years. On the basis of this academic paper and a series of critical articles in the *Irish Times*, Kelly was denounced as 'Dr Doom' by the Irish media. The then Irish Taoiseach, Bertie Ahern, famously stated in response that people like Morgan Kelly who were on the sidelines should stop 'cribbing and moaning' and would be better off committing suicide! Strong words from a Taoiseach, and words that come back to haunt him, because it was the Irish economy that was on a suicide track. Professor Kelly has subsequently written that the Irish Central Bank Governor's miscalculation of the scale of bank losses was 'the costliest mistake ever made by an Irish person', with Ireland having become 'an object of international ridicule' and coming close to national bankruptcy as a consequence.

The point about these and other examples is that sometimes it is the pessimists amongst us who get it right, whilst everyone else is running wild with the positive biases and hypomania of the moment. Our argument, as we have stated previously, is not that pessimists are always right and optimists always wrong – or vice versa – but rather that we need to be aware as far as possible of the biases that characterise our thinking and that we need to approach situations with flexibility and foresight that maximise our chances of accurate predictions about the future, as we will summarise in the next section.

Flexibility, emotions and the self

In this section we will attempt to recap some of the arguments that we presented in earlier chapters about emotions and biases in human thinking. When different emotion states are examined in detail, they tend to be associated with different types of biases such that happiness tends to be associated with optimistic self-serving biases. However, each of the different basic emotions, as we argued in Chapter 3, serves important functions in our lives and, although they are sometimes unpleasant, like pain, these functions can be life-preserving. To give away our punch line again, part of our emotional development consists of learning about each of our emotions, about integrating these into the self, and then learning about the typical cognitive and other biases that each emotion is associated with. Ultimately, our meta-cognitive and meta-emotional skills develop to add flexibility to these emotion-driven processes. For example, we can overcome our action tendency to avoid and take flight in the face of anxiety, which may lead us to over-ride our automatic reactions in anxiety-provoking social situations and explicitly face up to these challenges. Such flexibility in the face of automatic biases is the stuff of emotional maturity.

Dual-process models

A number of recent formal models in different areas of psychology have come to be known as 'dual-process models', in that multi-level psychological processes are identified that operate both at a 'high level', with the possibility of conscious attention, and in parallel at a 'low level', typically automatically and unconsciously. For example, such dual-process models are evident in the study of attitudes and attitude formation, with the idea of explicit and implicit attitudes (Chaiken and Trope, 1999) in the area of visual attention (Corbetta and Shulman, 2002), in the area of reasoning (Johnson-Laird, 2006) and in the area of emotion, as we summarised in Chapter 3. Indeed, Daniel Kahneman himself released a book, *Thinking Fast and Slow*, in 2011, that is exactly about the topic of these two systems of thinking and their implications for psychology and economics. We will return to this later. First, however, we will summarise again our own dual-process account of emotion in order to illustrate how these dual-process theories offer a number of advantages over the earlier single-process theories.

The model of emotion that we have called SPAARS is presented in Figure 7.1. The figure shows the dual process to be incorporated in a multi-level model, with two routes to the production of emotion. The high-level route includes conscious appraisal of an event or situation in contrast to the low-level route in SPAARS, which is a fast and automatic route that typically occurs outside of awareness. A classic example in the emotion area is that of the 'fire alarm' emotion reaction. On hearing the fire alarm suddenly sound at work, the immediate and automatic reaction may be one of anxiety, interruption of ongoing work, and readiness to leave the building. However, a slower appraisal of the situation might include the fact that it is Thursday morning at 10 o'clock and that is when the memo said there

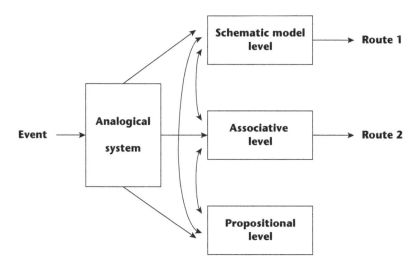

FIGURE 7.1 Two routes to emotion generation within the SPAARS model.

would be a fire alarm test, so anxiety quickly turns to relief and a resumption of ongoing activity. In this case, the high-level system serves to dampen down or down-regulate the fast automatic system. In other cases, the two systems can act synergistically to amplify or up-regulate the reaction, such as if the sound of the fire alarm were to be accompanied by the sound of people shouting and running down the corridor.

To continue with examples from the current self-inflicted global disaster of the economic and financial crisis, there are certain times in economic decision-making when processes can be solely high-level, solely low-level or some combination of the two. The dual-process account has been brought into popular economics, for example, in initial work by Sloman (2002), more recently by Gardner in his book *Risk* (2008), and by Kahneman (2011) as mentioned above. Gardner (2008) contrasts the two routes as 'head' versus 'gut', or as 'reason' versus 'feeling': contrasts that have immediate appeal in popular thinking. However, this contrast is not the correct one, because both routes within the SPAARS model can lead to the generation or incorporation of emotion or feelings. It is not correct to see one route as 'rational' and the other route as 'irrational'.

The so-called 'affect heuristic' is also based on the simplified assumption that the two routes can be likened to reason versus feeling. It is based on the proposal by Slovic and colleagues (e.g. Slovic *et al.*, 2002) that feelings, which are considered to be either positive (good) or negative (bad), have an impact on thinking and decision-making, especially under certain conditions. The affect heuristic received recent attention when it was used to explain the unexpected negative correlation between benefit and risk perception in behavioural economics. Finucane and colleagues (2000) argued that a good feeling towards a situation would lead to lower risk perception and higher benefit perception, even when this is not warranted for that situation. The affect bias shows that a strong emotional response to a word or other stimulus can alter a person's judgement. An example used by Slovic *et al.* (2002) to illustrate how words or names can have significant affective influences includes one of the reasons why performers use more positive-sounding stage names than their original names may convey, illustrating their point with the examples of John Denver (originally Henry Deutschendorf), Judy Garland (Frances Gumm) and Natalie Portman (Natalie Hershlag). In the spirit of Slovic *et al.*'s example, we might even suggest that such positive names may be more likely to achieve success in other areas of life, not just in the performing arts. Were the interview panel who appointed Frederick Goodwin as CEO of the Royal Bank of Scotland influenced unconsciously by the affect triggered by his name (Good-win!)? And Barclays Bank seem to have made the same mistake with Bob Diamond, who recently (3 July 2012) had to resign because of the bank interest rate-fixing scandal. Anyway, on this basis, the Michael Powers of the world perhaps should have gone into politics? (Except that the surname Power actually derives from the French word *pauvre*, which means poor!)

Another common situation involving the affect heuristic is where a strong, emotional first impression can inform a decision, even if subsequent facts weigh cognitively against the decision (e.g. Schwarz, 1996). House purchase is a good example; people have immediate first impressions, which can be good or bad, and which may run counter to subsequent information that is gained from careful examination, structural surveys and valuations. Indeed, there are numerous journalistic guides as to how to manipulate such first impressions, including adding a background smell of freshly ground coffee and having fresh-cut flowers in the window. In the qualitative study of the Edinburgh housing market during a phase of rapid price increase noted earlier, Christie *et al.* (2008) interviewed a number of people who had recently purchased Edinburgh properties. All of the study households conveyed their strong emotional reactions to the properties that they eventually bought. They spoke of their 'love of and feelings for the properties', of knowing that 'this is it, this is the one' (Christie *et al.*, 2008, p. 2306). Across the sample as a whole, the respondents described the process by which their emotional attachment to a house 'stuck them to the market and encouraged them to bid higher than seemed sensible to secure the sale' (p. 2308). Such examples highlight the consequences that affect can have on our economic and other decision-making.

It must be emphasised that the approach outlined here makes no inherent assumption that one route is inevitably right and that the other route is inevitably wrong. The two routes have evolved to serve a variety of survival functions, with one route that offers a fast 'gist' of a dynamic situation that can be acted on quickly (as in the fire-alarm system), and the other which allows a slower thinking-through of alternatives (as in the knowledge that it's 10 o'clock on Thursday and that is when the fire alarm test occurs). In this context, we will, therefore, next consider some of the conditions under which one of the routes is likely to predominate over the other and to consider some of the consequent implications for us with further examples from behavioural economics.

Conditions under which one or other route may prevail

The balance between high- and low-level processes changes under certain conditions, which can be generally summarised as shown in Figure 7.2. Thus, in low risk–low emotion scenarios, there is likely to be a preponderance of conscious high-level processes, but in high risk–high emotion scenarios there is likely to be a preponderance of low-level automatic processes. Specific factors that can produce the shifts between these finely balanced processes, as summarised in Figure 7.2, are outlined next.

1. *Perception of danger*: Danger, in the form of physical or social threat, leads to the generation of anxiety typically through activation of the fast associative route, though it can then be modulated via the high-level schematic route within the SPAARS model (see Figure 7.1).
2. *Exhaustion/fatigue*: Factors such as fatigue, exhaustion and tiredness seem to reduce the capacity of working memory and thereby decrease the likelihood of effortful processing via the schematic route. For example, under conditions of tiredness, people may be less able to counteract implicit prejudicial attitudes than when they are not fatigued (Chaiken and Trope, 1999).

3. *Time pressure*: The effect of time pressure can be similar to that of fatigue in that effects of prejudice and discrimination from implicit attitudes may be more apparent (e.g. Fiske *et al.*, 1999). The Finucane *et al.* (2000) study, noted earlier, showed how the inverse relationship that is observed between perceived risks and benefits increases under time pressure in a study in which people had to rate the perceived risks and perceived benefits of things such as pesticides, eating beef, railroads, etc.

4. *Working memory full because of other demands*: The impact of cognitive loads on working memory has been documented in a variety of contexts and may lead, for example, to the characteristic memory biases seen in depressed individuals in whom there are reductions in working memory capacity (Power and Dalgleish, 2015).

5. *Denial of low-level processes (e.g. over-confidence, beliefs of invulnerability and unrealistic optimism)*: Under certain circumstances, the outputs from low-level processes may be inhibited or rejected such that only high-level processes that are consistent with a particular model are pursued (Power and Dalgleish, 2015). There are numerous examples of self-deception and self-serving biases that may reflect the denial of low-level processes such as in the 'above average effect' in which the majority of people rate themselves as better than average for driving skill, health, productivity and managerial prowess (e.g. Svenson, 1981), even though such numbers are not possible, because, by definition, not everybody can be above average.

6. *Intensity of low-level process*: The more intense the low-level processes, the more likely that these processes will predominate, or as Lambie and Marcel (2002) stated, the more likely we are to be *immersed* in such processes.

7. *Novel, unfamiliar or unpredictable situations*: In chance-based gambling, for example, 'hunches', intuitions, lucky and unlucky numbers (e.g. Chinese lucky '8' versus unlucky '4') and 'feelings' come to be the source of decision-making. Ganzach (2001) reported that for unfamiliar stocks, financial analysts based their decisions more on global attitudes and feelings, whereas, for familiar stocks, a wider range of information about risks and returns is used. And the impact of numbers on markets is almost magical, as many commentators have observed, such that if the FTSE 100 index is standing, as it has been recently, at just below 7000, then it is worth buying the index stocks because markets are pushed to reach the 'magic round numbers' such as 7000, even though mathematically all numbers are equivalent (Rowe, 1997).

8. *Task difficulty*: For example, tasks that involve probabilistic reasoning and base rates are difficult. A simple demonstration of how bad we are at making use of probability comes from a study by Denes-Raj and Epstein (1994), who found that participants, when tasked to draw a red bean from a set of blue beans in a container, were more likely to choose a container with a greater absolute number of red beans (such as 7 in 100), in comparison to a container with a higher proportion but lower absolute number (such as 1 in 10). Kahneman

	Low emotion	**High emotion**
Low risk	Conscious processes ↑	Automatic processes ?
High risk	Conscious processes ?	Automatic Processes ↑

FIGURE 7.2   The interaction between risk and emotion processes.

and colleagues have a considerable number of such demonstrations of how we fail to take account of probability. In their well-known conjunction fallacy, Tversky and Kahneman (1984) demonstrated that participants often give higher ratings to statements of the form 'What percentage of men are over 55 years old and have had one or more heart attacks?' than to 'What percentage of men have had one or more heart attacks?' even though, by definition, the second statement includes all of the exemplars from the first statement plus all of those heart attacks under 55 years as well.

These examples all highlight how, under different conditions, the balance between controlled (high-level) and automatic (low-level) processes can be shifted in ways that have implications for a wide range of psychological phenomena, including memory, thinking, reasoning, perception and decision-making. In the next section, however, we will summarise the final piece of the jigsaw from the SPAARS model; namely, which one of the possible basic emotions is predominant in the system at a particular point in time.

The role of basic emotions

The second relevant part of the SPAARS model that we presented in detail in Chapter 3 is the notion of basic emotions, which draws on the work of psychologists such as Paul Ekman (1992, 1999), and Keith Oatley and Phil Johnson-Laird (1987). Although different theorists have offered different sets of basic emotions, there is general agreement that all such lists should contain at least the five emotions shown in Table 7.1, that is, happiness, sadness, anxiety, anger and disgust. The figure also shows the typical event/situation appraisals or evaluations that lead to the generation of that particular emotion.

TABLE 7.1 Appraisals for five basic emotions

Basic emotion	Appraisal
Sadness	Loss or failure (actual or possible) of valued role or goal
Happiness	Successful move towards or completion of a valued role or goal
Anger	Blocking or frustration of a role or goal through perceived agent
Fear	Physical or social threat to self or valued role or goal
Disgust	A person, object or idea repulsive to the self, and to valued roles and goals

One feature of the basic emotion approach is that all complex emotions are derived from an elaboration of one or more of the five basic emotions, as detailed in Chapter 3. This property is similar to the idea of a set of primary colours, from which all other colours are derivable (e.g. the colours blue and yellow when combined together produce green). Examples include a set of complex emotions, such as guilt and shame, which, according to the theory, are more complex forms of disgust, in which guilt is seen typically to be disgust applied to some action carried out by the self, and shame occurs when disgust is applied to the self as a whole (Power and Dalgleish, 2015). Other examples of complex emotions include nostalgia, which, although normally considered as a complex emotion derived from happiness, is in fact a blend of both happiness and sadness. Another such blended complex emotion that was prevalent at the beginning of the banking crisis was *Schadenfreude*, an enjoyable blend of happiness and contempt (in turn derivable from disgust and anger) over someone else's demise or failure, the word for which we must borrow from the German language.

One of the limitations of work on affect and the affect heuristic noted earlier is that, within the dimensional approach, affect or emotion tends to be dichotomised into positive (good) versus negative (bad). This simple dichotomy maps very well onto the bull versus bear description of economic markets, in which confidence and optimism in anticipation of future gains predominates in bull (rising) markets, in contrast to bear markets in which prices decline amidst gloom and pessimism. It is possible that this simple dichotomy might be sufficient, both psychologically and economically, to describe the interplay between affect and the behaviour of markets. However, it seems worthwhile to consider at least the possibility that a more sophisticated approach to emotion and affect, as represented by the basic emotions approach, might be able to offer a more sophisticated analysis for behavioural economics and for psychology more generally (see Power, 2013a, for a more detailed discussion). We will therefore consider each of the basic emotions in turn and what their implications might be, again with examples from economics because of its current relevance.

Happiness

As noted earlier, happiness maps on well to the economic bull market in that it reflects an emotion brimming with confidence and optimism, so we do not need to pursue this aspect of happiness to any great extent because of how much we have dealt with it already. Instead, we will return to the risk of an excess of happiness that we considered in Chapter 2, combined with over-confidence and unrealistic optimism. The market characteristics now begin to shift more into the hypomania/ mania extremes of happiness in which the extreme, for example, might be followed by a crash or the bursting of an economic bubble. The extent of the over-optimistic and self-promoting biases that are evident during happiness has led some cultures to socialise out happiness from an early age and has led the Bible to warn us of the 'sin of pride'. However, there is a danger of moving from a too positive to a too negative view of the biases that are typically associated with happiness, so we will simply remind the reader that it is the importance of *flexibility* of processes that we emphasise rather than promoting any extreme, as we will return to later.

Fear

As with happiness mapping onto bull markets, fear maps onto the bear market as an emotion descriptor of the pessimism and panic that can accompany this situation. There have been many dramatic fear-driven market collapses, none more dramatic than Black Monday on 19 October 1987, which saw the largest single-day decline in the value of the Dow Jones Index (22.6%) and other indices around the world. Whilst analysts still do not agree about the reasons for the collapse, there seem to have been conditions for a perfect storm, which, in the case of the London Stock Exchange, literally did include a perfect storm in the form of a hurricane that closed the Stock Exchange on Friday 16 October. Whatever the other reasons, the combination of a negative statement by the US Treasury Secretary, the attack by US warships on an Iranian oil platform, combined with an over-reliance on computer program trading, witnessed a mass panic as the herd raced to the exit.

The bursting of the 'dot.com bubble', based on the rapid growth and proliferation of internet-based companies between 1995 and 2000, beginning on Friday 10 March 2000, provides another example of fear and the bear market. In this case, the rapid increases in valuation of dot.com companies over the preceding 5 years were initially threatened by the *US versus Microsoft* court case, which declared Microsoft to be a monopoly. The destruction of the Twin Towers on 9/11 in 2001 added further to the bursting of the dot.com bubble. Again, we emphasise that those investors who do best, approach markets with a flexibility rather than optimism or pessimism, because they can stand aside from the biases caused by extreme emotions.

Sadness

The first two emotions of happiness and fear map on well to the notions of bull and bear markets, respectively, so it may be a problem for the remaining three basic emotions that such a global type of mapping may not be possible. Instead, we may need to consider more specific types of economic activity that reflect issues about loss, the anticipation of loss and the aversion to loss that have begun to be studied in psychology and behavioural economics. Of course, it is possible that major loss events, such as when the Japanese Emperor Hirohito died on 7 January 1989, could have had an impact on the Japanese markets, but this does not appear to have been the case. Instead, therefore, we will focus on two specific phenomena – loss aversion and anticipated regret – both of which are motivated by avoidance of loss and sadness.

Loss aversion is another challenge to classical economics because it reflects a non-rational and emotion-based behaviour. The phenomenon refers to the fact that most people avoid the risk of loss in circumstances where loss or gain are the possible outcomes, because, psychologically, 'losses loom larger than gains'. This can be illustrated with the example that most people would choose a 2 per cent pay rise with 4 per cent inflation over a 2 per cent pay cut with 0 per cent inflation (Shafir et al., 1997). The *disposition effect* in stock markets refers to the fact that loss aversion can lead to even greater losses because investors hold on too long to stocks that have decreased in value compared to their purchase price, but are too quick to sell stocks that have increased in price. Similarly, house owners are unwilling to sell their properties for less than the price at which they were purchased, so tend to hold on too long when the housing market is falling (Genesove and Mayer, 2001).

The phenomenon of anticipated regret is important in risk perception. Regret is a retrospective emotion that refers to something that one either has or has not done that leads to a perception of sadness and loss and to the wish that one had acted otherwise. Anticipatory regret, therefore, has received attention because sometimes the anticipation that one would feel regret leads to a course of action designed to avoid that feeling. For example, Zeelenberg (1999) has summarised a number of situations in which anticipated regret can motivate behaviour. The experience of regret is especially dependent on knowledge of the outcomes of the rejected alternatives, so that if you know you will receive feedback in the short term about your decision, you are more responsive to the effects of anticipated regret. Zeelenberg summarised a number of studies on choice between gambles, consumer decision-making and interpersonal decision-making, in which anticipated regret seemed to promote both risk-averse and risk-seeking choices in order to avoid later regret.

Anger

There is much less empirical evidence on the impact of anger on judgement and decision-making, though a study by Lerner and Keltner (2000) offers some clues. Lerner and Keltner asked their participants to complete a risk questionnaire in which the participants estimated the number of fatalities per year from a variety of causes (e.g. brain cancer, stroke, floods), given an anchoring value of 50,000 for car accidents. The participants were also required to complete self-report measures of anxiety and anger. Multiple regression analyses showed that, in contradiction to the negative affect hypothesis in which anger and anxiety should have similar negative effects on risk perception, those participants high in anger showed lower and more optimistic risk estimates, whereas those high on anxiety showed higher and more pessimistic risk estimates. Similar effects were found by Fischhoff *et al.* (2005), who used a mood-induction procedure with participants, so that they made risk estimates in angry or anxious moods, though the findings were extended to show effects of reduction of anger estimates for both past and future risk estimates.

Breakwell (2007) also notes the importance for risk management of *outrage*, which is an extreme form of anger with an attribution of blame to an external agent, whether the agent is an individual or a social organisation. The mismanagement of crises by governments can often be accompanied by a sense of outrage that can motivate people to action, as in the recent Arab Spring uprisings against dictatorships. Although, as we noted in Chapter 3, anger is often considered to be a negative and destructive emotion, it is clear that it can also have positive and potentially constructive impacts. Unfortunately, this aspect has been insufficiently researched to date.

An example of the consequences of national and international anger can be seen in the 1973 oil crisis. The surprise Israeli attack on Egypt and other Arab countries in the 1967 Six-Day War, which led to Israel occupying areas such as the Sinai and the Golan Heights, was followed by a surprise Syrian and Egyptian attack on Israel in early October 1973. The US Nixon administration intervened with substantial military and financial aid for Israel, which led to considerable anger in the Arab world. The Arab oil-producing countries subsequently agreed, on 16 October 1973, to an oil embargo and a substantial increase in oil prices. The embargo was not resolved until March 1974, when the US intervened to persuade Israel to withdraw from some of the disputed territories. However, oil prices remained high over the subsequent 10 years, peaking after further conflicts and tensions in Arab–Israeli relations in the 1970s.

Disgust

The basic emotion of disgust consists of a family of complex emotions that includes guilt, shame and contempt, and therefore includes a set of moral evaluations as well as the more specific disgust reactions. These emotions act at all levels from the most mundane (e.g. in response to the dog mess on the pavement) up to the highest levels of organisation (e.g. moral reactions towards banks, governments or religions). The Social Amplification of Risk Framework (SARF) proposed by Kasperson and colleagues (1988) includes *stigmatisation* as one of the key social processes by which reactions to risk communication and hazards can be modified or amplified. Stigmatisation is a process that is based on a moral disgust reaction towards individuals, groups or hazards, which sometimes includes the highlighting of some attribute with a powerful label, such as the labelling of genetically modified food as 'Frankenstein food'.

A final note on the impact of disgust and shame on economics is that the length of time that the impact and consequences hold force may be much longer than the impact of the other basic emotions that we have reviewed. For example, studies of consumer behaviour in the US show that Jewish Americans purchase significantly fewer German cars even 60 years after the Holocaust than do non-Jewish Americans, and that the impact is greater the more that Jewish Americans have direct links to the Holocaust (Podoshen, 2009). Of course, reactions to complex events such as the Holocaust involve many emotions such as fear and anger other than just shame and disgust, but, we argue, it is the moral outrage that leads to such a long-term impact, whereas the other basic emotions are more likely to have a shorter term impact.

In summary, the overall proposal made here is that the 'feelings' influencing psychological and other activity can be usefully divided more, not just into positive versus negative ones, as emphasised in the so-called 'affect heuristic'. The proposal is that the negative emotions of anger, fear, sadness and disgust may all have a differential impact, and that the positive emotions in the extreme, especially when they verge on mania or hypomania, lead in economics to market bubbles that are equally dysfunctional. The point is that all emotions, whether viewed as positive or negative, can have both functional and dysfunctional effects on thinking, reasoning and judgement according to the situation and circumstances in which we find ourselves.

Back to flexibility

We have taken this substantial detour through dual-process models and typical biases associated with different emotions in order to return to the point from which we first started – the notion of psychological flexibility. As we summarised in Chapter 6, there is now increasing interest in the concept of flexibility across a diverse range of areas of psychology, including studies of executive function in neuropsychology, coping and emotion regulation, and in personality psychology. For example, Hazlett et al. (2011) showed that people can shift between optimistic or pessimistic forecasts for their own future such that, when you are primarily concerned about growth and advancement, an optimistic stance can lead to better performance, whereas when you are focused on safety, security and prevention, then a more pessimistic stance leads to better performance. As we noted in Chapter 6, there may also be different functions for optimism and pessimism in older as opposed to younger adults, in that pessimism may have greater functionality for older adults. Thus, Palgi et al. (2011) found that combinations of low–low and high–high optimism and pessimism both lead to more emotionally adaptive lifestyles, such that many older adults report high levels of both optimism and pessimism according to different circumstances and situations. Research needs to consider, therefore, domain-specific aspects of optimism and pessimism, especially in older adults, because individuals may show considerable flexibility across domains so that concepts of 'dispositional' or trait optimism–pessimism fail to assess this situational flexibility.

Although we predict that the area of psychological flexibility will come to be of increasing applied and research importance in psychology and adjoining areas, there are some specific areas in psychology that have not been linked to the question of flexibility, but which would benefit from being approached from this perspective. Two of these areas – change in religious belief and posttraumatic growth – will be highlighted because we believe that further research in these areas would benefit from the concept of flexibility.

Apostasy and conversion

One area that has received surprisingly little consideration in psychology is that of apostasy (the loss of faith in a religious belief system), yet it potentially offers insights into fundamental aspects of our belief systems and the impact of development and change on them (Power, 2012). The equation of gods with parents in childhood leads to the interesting question of whether adolescents and young adults who lose their faith in god are more likely to have come from certain types of problematic families, from families who have been divorced, perhaps have had difficulties in attachment with their parents, or even have been more likely to have been abused by their parents (in the broadest sense of not just sexual or physical abuse, but including emotional abuse and neglect also). Before we address this question directly, we should note the appalling story told by Richard Dawkins in *The God Delusion* (2006) of the case of Sadiq Abdul Karim Malallah who, on 3 September 1992, was beheaded in Al-Qatif in Saudi Arabia after he was convicted of apostasy and blasphemy. Sadiq had been held in prison from April 1988 and had been told by the judge at his trial that he had to convert from Shi'a to Wahhabi Islam, but he failed to do so, and was eventually beheaded. Saudi Arabia is governed by an Islamic theocratic monarchy, which has imposed the strict Wahhabi Islamic code, in which the government-run religious police are designated to prevent the public practice of all non-Wahhabi Islamic religions. Amnesty International reported that at least 102 men and women were executed in Saudi Arabia in 2009, many for blasphemy and apostasy. Saudi Arabia is one amongst a number of Islamic countries in which apostasy is illegal and can therefore lead to severe punishment, including death.

As we mentioned earlier, the issue of apostasy is appallingly under-researched in psychology, but there are a couple of studies that can be cited. Bahr and Albrecht (1989) interviewed 30 former Mormons about why they had abandoned their faith. Most of them described themselves as having been on the periphery of belief, and so they had drifted away from the faith. However, a sub-group who had been fervent believers reported that the break-up of their families, such as through divorce and separation, had been key events that led to their loss of faith. Feelings of hypocrisy amongst believers and practitioners can also be important, as reported in a study by Altemeyer (2004). Lawton and Bures (2001) examined a much larger sample, using data from the US National Survey of Family and Households, of whom 11,372 were either Catholic or Protestant. The data showed that parental divorce was most predictive of apostasy for the Catholic and conservative Protestant groups, but less so for moderate Protestant groups. What these data highlight is that our religious beliefs are strongly related to how we view our parents whilst we are children, but that subsequent problems in those relationships can have a significant impact and can lead us to reject their belief systems.

William James was much taken with the issue of conversion. In *The Varieties of Religious Experience* (1902), he discussed different types of conversion and offered this observation:

> Emotional occasions, especially violent ones, are extremely potent in precipitating mental rearrangements. The sudden and explosive ways in which love, jealousy, guilt, fear, remorse, or anger can seize upon one are known to everybody. Hope, happiness, security, resolve, emotions characteristic of conversion, can be equally explosive. And emotions that come in this explosive way seldom leave things as they found them.
>
> *(p. 198)*

As James notes, probably the most famous of all sudden conversions was that of Saint Paul, formerly known as Saul of Tarsus. Paul was a Greek-speaking Jewish Pharisee who initially hated the new Christians:

> As for Saul, he made havock of the church, entering into every house, and haling men and women committed them to prison.
>
> *(Acts 8:3)*

The famous incident on the road to Damascus happened shortly after Paul had witnessed the stoning to death in Jerusalem of Stephen, the first Christian martyr:

> As he journeyed, he came near Damascus: and suddenly there shined round about him a light from heaven: And he fell to the earth, and heard a voice saying unto him, Saul, Saul, why persecutest thou me? . . . And Saul arose from the earth; and when his eyes were opened he saw no man. . . . And he was three days without sight, and neither did eat nor drink.
>
> *(Acts 9:3–9)*

The fact that Paul fell to the earth and saw a bright light has led some authors to speculate that he had experienced an epileptic seizure. However, such an explanation still does not explain the more important fact that Paul was suddenly converted from being a persecutor of Christians to becoming a Christian himself, and, moreover, that he became the leading proselytiser in bringing Christianity to Gentiles so that it was no longer merely a Jewish sect (Power, 2012).

Sudden conversions, such as that of Saint Paul, are just one of the types of conversion that have been identified. In her discussion of conversion in *The Psychology of Religion* (2000), Kate Loewenthal has summarised a number of studies showing that sudden conversions are a rare form of conversion because most conversions are gradual and occur over a long period of time, in which individuals struggle both at an intellectual level and at an emotional level with which religious belief system is best for them. Furthermore, conversions need not consist only of individual personal struggle, but can also result from group pressure. For example, of the recent new religious movements, the Unification Church (Moonies) has been studied in most detail. Members of the Church target young, lonely-looking individuals on the high street, and invite them back for a meal to their communities where they are 'love-bombed' by the whole group. The new convert is then gradually disconnected from previous family and friends in order to become more dependent on the religious group. Such procedures highlight the fact that some people are more vulnerable to 'conversion' than others, with factors such as early problems in attachment relationships, stress and unhappiness in the pre-conversion period, and the degree of intrinsic religiosity that the person has also being of importance (Loewenthal, 2000).

Posttraumatic growth

A further area in which the concept of psychological flexibility is likely to be of importance is that of so-called posttraumatic growth, though it has not traditionally been considered from this perspective. The concept is a wide-ranging one that is still in development. Three areas of positive change have been noted in the relevant literature (Tedeshi and Calhoun, 2004). First, relationships can become enhanced following significant traumatic experiences. For example, people may come to value their friends and family more importantly, they may feel an increased sense of compassion towards others and have a longing for more intimate relationships, whilst perhaps having less interest in work activity. Second, people's views of themselves can change, for example, that they have an increased sense of personal resiliency, wisdom and strength, perhaps coupled with a greater acceptance of their vulnerabilities and limitations, as a consequence of working through the trauma. Third, people can describe changes in their belief systems and philosophy, for example, finding a new appreciation for day-to-day situations and experiences and changing their understanding of what matters to them in life.

Positive changes have been generally reported by people following significant trauma. A number of studies have now shown that growth is common for survivors of a range of traumatic events, including transport-related accidents (shipping disasters, plane crashes, car accidents, train crashes), natural disasters (hurricanes, earthquakes, floods), interpersonal experiences (combat, violence, rape, sexual assault, child abuse), medical problems (cancer, coronary problems, brain injury, spinal cord injury) and other life experiences (divorce, bereavement, asylum, emigration). Typically, 30–70 per cent of survivors will say that they have experienced positive changes of one form or another (Joseph et al., 2012).

Research has shown that greater posttraumatic growth is associated with a range of factors that include emotional stability, extraversion, openness to experience, optimism and self-esteem; and ways of coping such as acceptance, positive reframing, seeking social support, turning to religion, problem solving and social support. Theories of posttraumatic growth have largely drawn on Ronnie Janoff-Bulman's (1992) theory of shattered assumptions, in that posttraumatic growth can arise from the individual's struggle to resolve his or her challenged assumptive world. These theories propose an understanding of how posttraumatic growth can arise out of the interaction of personality, coping and social support variables, in which we believe psychological flexibility may play an as yet relatively unexplored important role.

Butler *et al.* (2005), in a study following the 9/11 attack in New York in September 2001, reported that increased posttraumatic stress was associated with greater posttraumatic growth, but only up to an optimum point, beyond which posttraumatic growth declined. They therefore proposed that there may be a curvilinear or inverted-U relationship between posttraumatic stress and posttraumatic growth. Low levels of posttraumatic stress reactions indicate that the person has been minimally affected, thus, one would expect minimal posttraumatic growth. A moderate level of posttraumatic stress is indicative that the individual's assumptive world has in some way been challenged, triggering the intrusive and avoidant experiences, but the person remains able to cope, think clearly and engage flexibly in the processing needed to work through the traumatic experience. However, a high level of posttraumatic stress may lead to the person's coping ability being overwhelmed, with their ability to process and work through the experience being limited (Power and Dalgleish, 2015).

Prati and Pietrantoni (2009) reported on a meta-analysis of 103 different studies of posttraumatic growth and found that optimism, social support, acceptance coping, reappraisal coping, religious coping and seeking social support were associated with posttraumatic growth. The important point to note may be that so many different types of coping may be tried following traumatic stress and, therefore, it is people's flexibility, in which they are prepared to try new approaches if the previous one does not work, that may be more important for recovery and growth.

Existential questions, fulfilment and lifestyle

As we approach the end of this book, we must return to the question we started with: that of happiness. You may rightly ask that if we, along with Daniel Kahneman and others, propose to 'retire' the word happiness, then what are we proposing in its place? Remember, we have argued that 'happiness' is simply a momentary emotion state that seems to have become confused not only in English but in other languages with a final point to which one should direct one's life.

Even worse, many religions tell us that we should even be aiming for happiness in the *afterlife*, in order to spend eternity in blissful paradise, entry into which became the focus of life for the Ancient Egyptians. However, as we argued in Chapter 5 and have considered in detail elsewhere (Power, 2012), it takes courage to give up on the seductive illusions of the false promises of religion. But, again, you will ask, if we give up on these powerful illusions of happiness and the afterlife, what do we put in their place that can provide us with a sufficient sense of purpose and meaning and not just abandon us to the nihilistic equivalent of hell on earth? In fact, this question reminds me of when I used to work clinically with people with severe drug and alcohol problems. Life for them centred around drugs and alcohol, which, when taken away, left a vacuum into which something more meaningful than drugs and alcohol had to be placed.

The first questions that have to be answered are, therefore, existential ones. Why are we here? What is our purpose? What is the meaning of life? Of course, religions offer wonderful solutions to these puzzles, but these solutions are wrong. Science has shown us that we are not at the centre of a narcissistic religious universe that has been designed just for us. We are the accidents of a tendency towards complexity, given our universe's laws of physics and chemistry. There is no eternal meaning for our existence, but this is a truth that requires courage to face and to live with. Ultimately, the purpose and meaning of our lives is *other people*. If you strip away the illusions, as we have attempted to throughout this book, then what is left at the core of our existence is ourselves in relation to other people. Our goals, ambitions, hopes and dreams are set in the context of others and how we contribute to their lives and, reciprocally, how they contribute to us. In *Adieu to God* (2012), we spelled out just what such humanism looks like at its best, but we will summarise these proposals again in the following paragraphs.

Meaning and purpose

Many people find meaning and purpose in the religious belief systems to which they subscribe, but as we have stated in Chapter 5 and elsewhere (Power, 2012), modern science has challenged these belief systems such that agnosticism and atheism have substantially increased in many cultures. For example, amongst a range of statistics reported on the British Humanist Association website (www.humanism.org.uk), surveys have shown that there has been an increase in the number of people in the UK who report themselves to be 'non-religious', from 31 per cent in 1983 to 50 per cent in 2009. Over that time period, membership of the Church of England has halved from 40 per cent to 20 per cent of the population. It is important that new belief systems based on truth come to replace these religious-based illusory systems. The development of meaning and purpose that places humanity and humanistic values at its centre is a necessary first step that requires existential courage.

Fulfilment

We progress through life enmeshed in a matrix of goals and plans about ourselves and ourselves in relation to other people. These goals and plans range from the immediate, such as what to have for dinner this evening, to the medium term, such as where to go on holiday next summer, to the long term, such as how many children you want to have, and who to have them with. Andy MacLeod (e.g. MacLeod *et al.*, 1993) has shown that those at risk of suicide have few, if any, constructive goals for the future, or that the most valued goals have been lost or abandoned. Across the lifespan, the nature of this matrix of goals contributes to our sense of fulfilment as we create new goals and plans that build on previous goals and plans according to our strengths (cf. Wright and Lopez, 2002).

Generativity

One important aspect of these goals and plans is that we have a sense of generativity that contributes to our feelings of fulfilment as we progress through life. The most obvious form of evolutionary generativity, and the one that many people value the most, is that of having children and contributing to successive generations. However, as a species we also value many sublimated forms of generativity as well, including contributions to the arts, to the sciences, to political life, to business, and so on. The important thing is that a sense of generativity can be obtained from a wide range of different domains, but our focus groups with older adults worldwide (Power *et al.*, 2005) emphasised how important generativity is.

Creativity

Linked to generativity is the feeling of creativity, but, again, creativity can be defined across a wide range or number of different domains. Activity in the arts provides one obvious source of creative satisfaction, but any hobby, sport or other activity, can provide a sense or feeling of creativity.

Regret and talents

A simple and quick self-assessment will soon tell you about how many regrets you may have accumulated in your life. These regrets could be about past lost loves and relationships that might have been and about which nothing can be done, though one hopes that current relationships make up sufficiently for what might have been. Sometimes people have a different set of regrets that can focus more on a sense of wasted talent rather than relationships. If there is one thing that we should ask our universal education systems to leave us with, it is a sense of what we can do well, what we have some talents at and how we can incorporate these talents in an ongoing way into our lives. Of course, you might say you were talented at football but can now play no more because of age, so what is the point? You regret that you did not work hard enough to develop your talent at the time. But we know from our work with older adults that the healthiest learn new languages, they learn how to play musical instruments, they travel if that is what they have never had a chance to do, and they take up new sports and activities.

A strengths-based approach not only to early education, but to lifelong learning, is one of the contributions that can help reduce a sense of regret in people's lives (Clifton and Harter, 2003). Lifelong learning is also a key to health and longevity, and contributes to the development of wisdom (e.g. Baltes *et al.*, 2002).

Intimacy

As a social species, and one that is heavily dependent on our primary caregivers for many years for our survival from birth onwards, the presence of intimacy is crucial to our survival and healthy development. Work on attachment theory (e.g. Bowlby, 1969) has demonstrated how early attachment problems can be linked to later problems in or avoidance of intimate relations in life, together with the problems that are consequent upon the absence of intimate relations. Physical and emotional intimacy contribute significantly to health and well-being and help us to adapt both to the expected and the unexpected (e.g. see Sonja Lyubomirsky's recent *The Myths of Happiness,* 2013).

Nurturance

Again, a related issue to generativity and intimacy is that of our need to be able to nurture others, and of course be nurtured ourselves in return. The obvious form of nurturance is the provision of care and protection for our children. However, the ownership of pets emphasises how important nurturance is, not just of our own species, but of certain other species too, with dogs and cats being the most popular. There are an estimated 78.2 million dogs and 86.4 million cats in the US; an estimated 35 per cent of Canadian households have a dog and 38 per cent a cat; an estimated 26 per cent of UK households have a cat and 31 per cent a dog (see e.g. www.petques tions.com). There is now good evidence that owning pets can have positive emotional and health benefits for the owners.

Connection

Researchers such as Robert Putnam (2003) have emphasised how important social capital is to all aspects of health and well-being, and we were particularly interested, in Chapter 1, in the impact of indicators of social inequality in different social groups. Social and political factors impact on the health and well-being of a nation, factors that often require coordinated social action for which we all must take responsibility. In Chapter 1 we highlighted the work of Wilkinson and Pickett (2010) on the consequences of inequality at a national level, with a range of consequences for life satisfaction, health and well-being. The austerity politics and economics of the post-financial crisis have led to increases in inequality in countries such as the UK, with the poorest getting poorer because of cuts to welfare benefits, whilst the rich get richer because of cuts to taxes (e.g. see Joseph Stiglitz's *The Price of Inequality*, 2013). The politics of happiness for the few and misery for the majority seems to be an inevitable consequence of this neoliberalism. In contrast, one thing that we can learn from the inequality data is that the Scandinavian countries with more socialist policies do better on the measures of happiness, well-being and health in national surveys.

Belonging

A factor related to connection and social capital is that of belonging. In Chapter 4, we reviewed in Chapter 4 how social identity, that is, our membership of certain groups, has an important impact on our values and belief systems, but also has impact on other outgroups and can contribute to social conflict if these outgroups are viewed in devalued or negative ways. It is important for own identity that we belong to different work, personal value, interest-related and cultural groups, but the membership should not be accompanied with the devaluation of outgroups.

Healthy lifestyle

Ultimately, whether or not you smoke, drink too much alcohol, eat too much fatty food, drink too much cola, travel everywhere by car, never take exercise and fart in public (which pretty accurately describes my then Head of Department at Sussex University when I was a postgraduate student!) is a personal choice that each of us must make as adults. However, if we choose such a lifestyle, we must do so fully cognisant of the fact that, like my unfortunate Head of Department, life will end up painful and relatively short. Indeed, under some social care systems, you will end up punished as well because you may not be able to get the care that you need when you develop obesity-, alcohol- and smoking-related diseases such as cardiac problems, diabetes, arthritis and certain types of cancer. A healthy approach to lifestyle is a personal choice, but it is one that needs to be supported by our family and socio-political systems in order to improve our health and well-being, as cultures experience the general demographic changes associated with greater longevity. There are bookshops full of self-help guides out there, but Friedman and Martin's (2011) *The Longevity Project: Surprising Discoveries for Health and Long Life from the Landmark Eight-Decade Study* provides an interesting starting point based on findings from the landmark eight-decade Longevity Project.

In summary, we must all deal with our existential questions in ways that either face up to them or ways that avoid them. There are many proffered solutions, of which the religious ones were the most popular until the impact of science over the past 200 years. However, the scientific revolution has re-presented its supporters with those existential questions because it points us to the need to find meaning and purpose in what we do now, rather than in the pursuit of some illusory dodgy afterlife. In the midst of these existential questions, we can choose to generate, to be creative, to connect, to belong, to be healthy or to be unhealthy. We have characterised these choices in Chapter 1 as whether to be a HAS or a HAS-not; that is, we all need to make choices about Healthy lifestyle, Adaptability and Support, and the various ways that we have outlined in this section on how a wide range of issues impact on these factors. Health, meaning, longevity and the general success and survival of our species depend on such choices.

Conclusions

At the core of thousands of years of different human cultures has lain the illusory pursuit of happiness. However, this simple pursuit is fraught with philosophical and psychological complexity, and modern scientific evidence that is inconsistent with its overly positive proposals. How, for example, can we account for the findings that defensive pessimists often perform better than optimists? That older people who are pessimistic and who experience health events often do better than older people who are optimists? Why do great leaders such as Churchill, or great explorers such as Amundsen, not come from the ranks of the optimists but are numbered amongst life's great pessimists? How have greed and unrealistic optimism contributed to our current global financial crisis? Before we labour this list for too long, and before you get the impression that we are claiming that pessimism is best, let us remind you that we are not proposing either pessimism or optimism as best. Instead, our argument is that there is another high-level psychological capacity called *flexibility*, which means that sometimes optimism may be better, sometimes pessimism and sometimes even realism itself when reality is knowable. Truth is better than illusion. And realism is better than optimism or pessimism. However, our futures are mostly uncertain and fundamentally unknowable, so whether realism, optimism or pessimism is more accurate may depend on a range of other personal and social factors for which flexibility is required. If you want to be a great leader and win a world war, you have to show great flexibility over a sustained period of time. If you want to be the first to the North Pole but you believe someone has just beaten you there, then there is always the South Pole to be the first to instead. As we noted earlier, the study of psychological flexibility may be at a relatively early stage, yet there are a number of different areas of psychology that are pointing in a similar direction. In addition to a prediction that there will be much more research in this area, we also expect to see flexibility explicitly incorporated into therapeutic developments as an explicit component, and not just in acceptance and commitment therapy, which has already grasped the importance of the concept.

So, and in order to end on a low note about happiness and its illusory pursuit, psychological interventions to counter hyper-positivity will become increasingly necessary if Western cultures continue their preoccupation with happiness and its illusory associated utopias. However, there are important political, moral and ethical issues that arise from the illusions and promises of the happiness industry. In a country such as the US, in which there are some of the greatest health and wealth inequalities of any developed nation, telling people to think positively when they are suffering in poverty in the underbelly of society, misquoting the evidence on the links between wealth, health and well-being, is a morally bankrupt approach which blames the individual and exonerates the social systems which should be there to protect rather than to exploit. Get your facts and your theories right, then your social systems can be developed for the benefit of all and not just the elite theocrats, plutocrats and fat-cats. From each according to his ability, to each according to his need, as somebody once said, and to which psychology has a moral and ethical duty to contribute. Happiness is a simple transitory momentary state so cannot and should not be an endpoint or life goal in itself, for if happiness is pursued you will become one of its many victims, trapped in its blinding illusions.

REFERENCES

Allport, G.W. and Ross, J.M. (1967). Personal religious orientation and prejudice. *Journal of Personality and Social Psychology*, 5, 432–443.

Altemeyer, B. (2004). The decline of organized religion in Western civilization. *International Journal for the Psychology of Religion*, 14, 77–89.

Amelang, M., Hasselbach, P. and Sturmer, T. (2004). Personality, cardiovascular disease, and cancer: first results from the Heidelberg cohort study of the elderly. *Zeitschrift fur Gesundheitspsychologie*, 12, 102–115.

American Psychiatric Association (2013). *Diagnostic and statistical manual of mental disorders* (5th edn). Washington, DC: APA.

Amundsen, R. (1912). *The South Pole*. Readaclassic.com.

Andrews, F.M. and Withey, S.B. (1976). *Social indicators of well-being: America's perception of life quality*. New York: Plenum.

Ano, G.G. and Vasconcelles, E.B. (2005). Religious coping and psychological adjustment to stress: a meta-analysis. *Journal of Clinical Psychology*, 61, 461–480.

Argyle, M. (2001). *The psychology of happiness* (2nd edn). New York: Routledge.

Aristotle (1947). Nicomachean ethics (W.D. Ross, Trans.). In R. McKeon (Ed.), *Introduction to Aristotle*, pp. 300–543. New York: Modern Library.

Assanangkornchai, S., Tangboonngam, S., Sam-Angsri, N. and Edwards, J.G. (2007). A Thai community's anniversary reaction to a major catastrophe. *Stress and Health*, 23, 43–50.

Augustine, A.A., Larsen, R.J., Walker, M.S. and Fisher, E.B. (2008). Personality predictors of the time course for lung cancer onset. *Journal of Research in Personality*, 42, 1448–1455.

Averill, J.R. and Moore, T.A. (2000). Happiness. In M. Lewis and J.M. Haviland-Jones (Eds), *Handbook of emotions* (2nd edn). New York: Guilford.

Baetz, M. and Toews, J. (2009). Clinical implications of research on religion, spirituality, and mental health. *Canadian Journal of Psychiatry*, 54, 292–301.

Bahr, H.M. and Albrecht, S.L. (1989). Strangers once more: patterns of disaffiliation from Mormonism. *Journal for the Scientific Study of Religion*, 28, 180–200.

Baker, J. (2008). An investigation of the sociological patterns of prayer frequency and content. *Sociology of Religion*, 69, 169–185.

Baltes, P.B., Gluck, J. and Kunzmann, U. (2002). Wisdom: its structure and function in regulating successful life span development. In C. Snyder and S.J. Lopez (Eds), *The Oxford handbook of positive psychology*. Oxford: Oxford University Press.

Barbui, C., Cipriani, A., Patel, V., Ayuso-Mateos, J.L. and Van Ommeren, M. (2011). Efficacy of antidepressants and benzodiazepines in minor depression: systematic review and meta-analysis. *British Journal of Psychiatry*, 198, 11–16, suppl 1.

Baron-Cohen, S. (2004). *The essential difference*. London: Penguin Books.

Barraclough, J. (1999). *Cancer and emotion* (3rd edn). Chichester: Wiley-Blackwell.

Barrett, K.C., Zahn-Waxler, C. and Cole, P.M. (1993). Avoiders versus amenders: implications for the investigation of guilt and shame during toddlerhood? *Cognition and Emotion*, 7, 481–505.

Bartholomew, K. (1990). Avoidance of intimacy: An attachment perspective. *Journal of Social and Personal Relationships*, 7, 147–178.

Berkowitz, L. (1999). Anger. In T. Dalgleish and M.J. Power (Eds), *Handbook of cognition and emotion*. Chichester: Wiley.

Blair, J., Mitchell, D. and Blair, K. (2005). *The psychopath: emotion and the brain*. Oxford: Blackwell.

Bleil, M.E., McCaffery, J.M., Muldoon, M.F., Sutton-Tyrrell, K. and Manuck, S.B. (2004) Anger-related personality traits and carotid artery atherosclerosis in untreated hypertensive men. *Psychosomatic Medicine*, 66, 633–639.

Bodenhausen, G.V., Kramer, G.P. and Susser, K. (1994). Happiness and stereotypic thinking in social judgement. *Journal of Personality and Social Psychology*, 66, 621–632.

Bonnano, G.A., Davis, P.J., Singer, J.L. and Schwartz, G.E. (1991). The repressor personality and avoidant information processing: a dichotic listening study. *Journal of Research in Personality*, 25, 386–401.

Bowlby, J. (1969). *Attachment and loss: Vol. 1, Attachment*. London: Hogarth Press.

Bowlby, J. (1973). *Attachment and loss: Vol. 2, Separation*. London: Hogarth Press.

Bowlby, J. (1980). *Attachment and loss: Vol. 3, Sadness and depression*. London: Hogarth Press.

Breakwell, G.M. (2007). *The psychology of risk*. Cambridge: Cambridge University Press.

Breuer, J. and Freud, S. (1895/1974). *Studies on hysteria*. The Pelican Freud Library, Vol. 3. Harmondsworth: Penguin.

Brickman. P., Coates, D. and Janoff-Bulman, R. (1978). Lottery winners and accident victims: is happiness relative? *Journal of Personality and Social Psychology*, 36, 917–927.

Brown, N.J.L., Sokal, A.D. and Friedman, H.L. (2013). The complex dynamics of wishful thinking: the critical positivity ratio. *American Psychologist*, 801–813.

Bryant, F.B., Smart, C.M. and King, S.P. (2005). Using the past to enhance the present: boosting happiness through positive reminiscence. *Journal of Happiness Studies*, 6, 227–260.

Bullinger, M., Power, M.J., Aaronson, N.K., Cella, D.F. and Anderson, R.T. (1996). Creating and evaluating cross-cultural instruments. In B. Spilker (Ed.), *Quality of life and pharmacoeconomics in clinical trials* (2nd edn). Hagerstown, MD: Lippincott-Raven.

Burton, C.L., Yan, O.H., Pat-Horenczyk, R., Chan, I.S.F., Ho, S. and Bonanno, G.A. (2012). Coping flexibility and complicated grief: a comparison of American and Chinese samples. *Depression and Anxiety*, 29, 16–22.

Buss, D.M. (2001). *The dangerous passion: why jealousy is as necessary as love or sex*. London: Bloomsbury.

Butler, L.D., Blasey, C.M., Garlan, R.W., *et al*. (2005). Posttraumatic growth following the terrorist attacks of September 11, 2001: cognitive, coping, and trauma symptom predictors in an internet convenience sample. *Traumatology*, 11, 247–267.

Bylsma, L. M., Morris, B. H. and Rottenberg, J. (2008). A meta-analysis of emotional reactivity in major depressive disorder. *Clinical Psychology Review*, 28, 676–691.

Byrne, D. (1964). Repression-sensitization as a dimension of personality. In B.A. Maher (Ed.), *Progress in Experimental Personality Research*, Vol. 1, pp. 169–220. New York: Academic Press.

Campbell-Sills, L., Barlow, D.H., Brown, T.A. and Hofmann, S.G. (2006). Effects of suppression and acceptance on emotional responses of individuals with anxiety and mood disorders. *Behaviour Research and Therapy*, 44(9), 1251–1263.

Cappellanus, A. (1186/1960). *The art of courtly love*. New York: Columbia University Press.

Carrico, A.W. Ironson, G., Antoni, M.H., *et al.* (2006). A path model of the effects of spirituality on depressive symptoms and 24-h urinary-free cortisol in HIV-positive persons. *Journal of Psychosomatic Research*, 61, 51–58.

Carson, J., Chander, A., Muir, M., Wakely, E. and Clark, S. (2010). 'Silent gratitude isn't much use to anyone': piloting a gratitude intervention in a community mental health team. *Clinical Psychology Forum*, 212, 27–31.

Carstensen, L.L. (2006). The influence of a sense of time on human development. *Science*, 312, 1913–1915.

Carver, C.S. and Scheier, M.F. (1990). Origins and functions of positive and negative affect: a control process view. *Psychological Review*, 97, 19–35.

Carver, C.S., Scheier, M.F. and Segerstrom, S.C. (2010). Optimism. *Clinical Psychology Review*, 30, 879–889.

Casey, R.J. (1996). *Emotional development in atypical children*. Mahwah, NJ: Erlbaum.

Caspi, A., Moffitt, T.E., Newman, D.L. and Silva, P.A. (1995). Behavioural observations at age 3 years predict adult psychiatric disorders: longitudinal evidence. *Archives of General Psychiatry*, 53, 1033–1039.

Cassidy, F. and Carroll, B.J. (2001). The clinical epidemiology of pure and mixed manic episodes. *Bipolar Disorders*, 3, 35–40.

Cavanagh, J., Schwannauer, M., Power, M.J. and Goodwin, G.M. (2009). A novel scale for measuring mixed states in bipolar disorder. *Clinical Psychology and Psychotherapy*, 16, 497–509.

Chaiken, S. and Trope, Y. (Eds) (1999). *Dual-process theories in social psychology*. New York: Guilford.

Chang, E.C., Sanna, L.J. and Yang, K.M. (2003). Optimism, pessimism, affectivity, and psychological adjustment in US and Korea: a test of a mediation model. *Personality and Individual Differences*, 34, 1195–1208.

Chang, J. and Halliday, J. (2005). *Mao: the unknown story*. London: Vintage.

Chang, W.C. and Sivam, R.W. (2004). Constant vigilance: heritage values and defensive pessimism in coping with severe acute respiratory syndrome in Singapore. *Asian Journal of Social Psychology*, 7, 35–53.

Chen, Y.Y. and Koenig, H.G. (2006). Do people turn to religion in times of stress? An examination of change in religiousness among elderly, medically ill patients. *Journal of Nervous and Mental Disease*, 194, 114–120.

Chentsova-Dutton, Y.E., Chu, J.P., Tsai, J.L., Rottenberg, J., Gross, J.J. and Gotlib, I.H. (2007). Depression and emotional reactivity: variation among Asian Americans of East Asian descent and European Americans. *Journal of Abnormal Psychology*, 116, 776–785.

Chentsova-Dutton, Y.E., Tsai, J.L. and Gotlib, I.H. (2010). Further evidence for the cultural norm hypothesis: positive emotion in depressed and control European American and Asian American women. *Cultural Diversity and Ethnic Minority Psychology*, 16, 284–295.

Cheung, R.Y., and Park, I.J. (2010). Anger suppression, interdependent self-construal, and depression among Asian American and European American college students. *Cultural Diversity and Ethnic Minority Psychology*, 16, 517–525.

Chomsky, N. (1959). A review of B.F. Skinner's verbal behavior. *Language*, 35, 26–58.

Chomsky, N. (1965). *Aspects of the theory of syntax*. Cambridge, MA: MIT Press.

Christie, H, Smith, S.J. and Munro, M. (2008). The emotional economy of housing. *Environment and Planning*, 40, 2296–2312.

Cipriani, A., Furukawa, T.A., Salanti, G., *et al*. (2009). Comparative efficacy and acceptability of 12 new-generation antidepressants: a multiple-treatments meta-analysis. *Lancet*, 373, 746–758.

Clark, A.E. (2003). Unemployment as a social norm: psychological evidence from panel data. *Journal of Labour Economics*, 21, 323–351.

Clifton, D.O. and Harter, J.K. (2003). Strengths investment. In K.S. Cameron, J.E. Dutton and R.E. Quinn (Eds), *Positive organizational scholarship*. San Francisco, CA: Berrett-Koehler.

Cohen, A.B. and Hill, P.C. (2007). Religion as culture: religious individualism and collectivism among American Catholics, Jews and Protestants. *Journal of Personality*, 75, 709–742.

Cohen, F., Kearney, K.A., Zegans, L.S., Kemeny, M.E., Neuhaus, J.M. and Stites, D.P. (1999). Differential immune system changes with acute and persistent stress for optimists vs pessimists. *Brain, Behavior, and Immunity*, 13, 155–174.

Colman, C.H. (2011). *Amundsen of the arctics*. Cincinnati, OH: Fancourt Publications.

Colman, W. (1994), Love, desire and infatuation. *Journal of Analytical Psychology*, 39, 497–514.

Compton, M.T. and Nemeroff, C.B. (2000). The treatment of bipolar depression. *Journal of Clinical Psychiatry*, 61(suppl 9), 57–67.

Corbetta, M. and Shulman, G.L. (2002). Control of goal-directed and stimulus-driven attention in the brain. *Nature Reviews: Neuroscience*, 3, 201–215.

Coyne, J.C., Stefanek, M. and Palmer, S.C. (2007). Psychotherapy and survival in cancer: the conflict between hope and evidence. *Psychological Bulletin*, 133, 367–394.

Darwin, C. (1859). *On the origin of species*. Oxford: Oxford University Press.

Darwin, C. (1871). *The descent of man*. London: Penguin.

Dattore, P.J., Shontz, F.C. and Coyne, L. (1980). Premorbid personality differentiation of cancer and noncancer groups: a test of the hypothesis of cancer proneness. *Journal of Consulting and Clinical Psychology*, 48, 388–394.

David, R. (1998). *The Ancient Egyptians: beliefs and practices*. Brighton: Sussex Academic Press.

Davies, M., Stankov, L. and Roberts, R.D. (1998). Emotional intelligence: in search of an elusive construct. *Journal of Personality and Social Psychology*, 75, 989–1015.

Davis, P.J. (1987). Repression and the inaccessibility of affective memories. *Journal of Personality and Social Psychology*, 53, 585–593.

Davis, P.J. (1990). Repression and the inaccessibility of emotional memories. In J.L. Singer (Ed.), *Repression and Dissociation*. Chicago: University of Chicago Press.

Davis. P.J. and Schwartz G.E. (1987). Repression and the inaccessibility of affective memories. *Journal of Personality and Social Psychology*, 52, 155–162.

Davis, P.J., Singer, J.L., Bonnano, G.A. and Schwartz, G.E. (1988). Repression and reponse bias during an affective memory recognition task. *Australian Journal of Psychology*, 40, 147–157.

Dawkins, K. and Furnham, A. (1989). The colour naming of emotional words. *British Journal of Psychology*, 80, 383–389.

Dawkins, R. (1976). *The selfish gene*. Oxford: Oxford University Press.

Dawkins, R. (2006). *The god delusion*. London: Bantam Press.

Deaton, A. (2008). Income, health, and well-being around the world: evidence from the Gallup World Poll. *Journal of Economic Perspectives*, 22, 53–72.

De Botton, A. (2012). *Religion for atheists a non-believer's guide to the uses of religion*. London: Hamish Hamilton.

Del Valle, C.H.C. and Mateos, P.M. (2008). Dispositional pessimism and optimism: the effect of induced mood on prefactual and counterfactual thinking and performance. *Cognition and Emotion*, 22, 1600–1612.

Denes-Raj, V. and Epstein, S. (1994). Conflict between intuitive and rational processing: when people behave against their better judgment. *Journal of Personality and Social Psychology*, 66, 819–829.

Dennett, D. (1991). *Consciousness explained*. Boston, MA: Little Brown.

Denollet, J., Martens, E.J., Nyklicek, I., Conraads, V. and Gelder, B. de (2008). Clinical events in coronary patients who report low distress: adverse effect of repressive coping. *Health Psychology*, 27, 302–308.

Derakshan, N. and Eysenck, M.W. (2001). Effects of locus of attention on physiological, behavioural, and reported state anxiety in repressors, low-anxious, high-anxious, and defensive high-anxious individuals. *Anxiety, Stress, and Coping*, 14, 285–299.

Derakshan, N., Eysenck, M.W. and Myers, L.B. (2007). Emotional information processing in repressors: the vigilance-avoidance theory. *Cognition and Emotion*, 21, 1585–1614.

Descartes, R. (1649/1989). *The passions of the soul*. Indianapolis, IN: Hackett.

Diener, E. (1984). Subjective well-being . *Psychological Bulletin*, 95, 542–575.

Diener, E. (2003). What is positive about positive psychology: the curmudgeon and Pollyanna. *Psychological Inquiry*, 14, 115–120.

Diener, E. and Biswas-Diener, R. (2008). *Happiness: unlocking the mysteries of psychological wealth*. New York: John Wiley & Sons.

Diener, E., Emmons, R.A., Larsen, R.J. and Griffin, S. (1985). The Satisfaction with Life Scale. *Journal of Personality Assessment*, 49, 71–75.

Diener, E., Lucas, R.E. and Scollon, C.N. (2006). Beyond the hedonic treadmill: revisions to the adaptation theory of well-being. *American Psychologist*, 61, 305–314.

Diener, E., Sandvik, E. and Pavot, W. (1991). Happiness is the frequency, not the intensity, of positive versus negative affect. In F. Strack, M. Argyle and N. Schwarz (Eds), *Subjective well-being: an inter-disciplinary perspective*. Elmsford, NY: Pergamon Press.

Diener, E., Tay, L. and Oishi, S. (2013). Rising income and the subjective well-being of nations. *Journal of Personality and Social Psychology*, 104, 267–276.

DiGiuseppe, R. and Tafrate, R.C. (2007). *Understanding anger disorders*. Oxford: Oxford University Press.

Dixon, N. (1976). *On the psychology of military incompetence*. London: Futura.

Dolan, P. (2014). *Happiness by design: finding pleasure and purpose in everyday life*. London: Allen Lane.

Drevenstadt, G.L. (1998). Race and ethnic differences in the effects of religious attendance on subjective health. *Review of Religious Research*, 37, 19–32.

Dupuy, H.J. (1984). The Psychological General Well-Being (PGWB) Index. In N.K. Wenger, M.E. Mattson, C.D. Furberg and J. Elinson (Eds), *Assessment of quality of life in clinical trials of cardiovascular therapies*. New York: Le Jacq.

Eckersley, R. (2006). Is modern western culture a health hazard? *International Journal of Epidemiology*, 35, 252–258.

Ehrenreich, B. (2009). *Smile or die: how positive thinking fooled America and the world*. London: Granta.

Ehring, T., Tuschen-Caffier, B., Schnülle, J., Fischer, S. and Gross, J.J. (2010). Emotion regulation and vulnerability to depression: spontaneous versus instructed use of emotion suppression and reappraisal. *Emotion*, 10, 563–72.

Ekman, P. (1992). An argument for basic emotions. *Cognition and Emotion*, 6, 169–200.

Ekman, P. (1999). Basic emotions. In T. Dalgleish and M.J. Power (Eds), *Handbook of cognition and emotion*. Chichester: John Wiley & Sons.

Ekman, P. (2003). *Emotions revealed: understanding faces and feelings*. London: Weidenfeld and Nicolson.

Emmons, R.A. (2009). Greatest of the virtues? Gratitude and the grateful personality. In D. Narvaez and D. Lapsley (Eds), *Personality, identity, and character: explorations in moral psychology*. New York: Cambridge University Press.

Emmons, R.A. and McCullough, M.E. (2003). Counting blessings versus burdens. *Journal of Personality and Social Psychology*, 84, 377–389.

Emmons, R.A. and Shelton, C. S. (2002). Gratitude and the science of positive psychology. In C.R. Snyder and S.J. Lopez (Eds), *Handbook of positive psychology*. New York: Oxford University Press.

Erdelyi, M.H. (2006). The unified theory of repression. *Behavioral and Brain Sciences*, 29, 499–551.

Eysenck, M. (1990). *Happiness: facts and myths*. Hove: Psychology Press.

Eysenck, M.W. and Keane, M.T. (2015). *Cognitive psychology: a student's handbook* (7th edn). Hove: Psychology Press.

Fenix, J.B., Cherlin, E.J., Prigerson, H.G., Johnson-Hurzeler, R., Kasl, S.V. and Bradley, E.H. (2006). Religiousness and major depression among bereaved family caregivers: a 13-month follow-up study. *Journal of Palliative Care*, 22, 286–292.

Finucane, A., Whiteman, M.C. and Power, M.J. (2010). The effect of happiness and sadness on alerting, orienting, and executive attention. *Journal of Attention Disorders*, 13, 629–639.

Finucane, M.L., Alhakami, A.S., Slovic, P. and Johnson, S.M. (2000). The affect heuristic in judgments of risk and benefits. *Journal of Behavioural Decision making*, 13, 1–17.

Fischer, P., Gretemeyer, T. and Kastenmuller, A. (2007). What do we think about Muslims? The validity of Westerners' implicit theories about the associations between Muslims' religiosity, religious identity, aggression potential, and attitudes towards terrorism. *Group Processes and Intergroup Relations*, 10, 373–382.

Fischhoff, B., Gonzalez, R.M. and Lerner, J.S. (2005). Evolving judgments of terror tasks: foresight, hindsight, and emotion. *Journal of Experimental Psychology: Applied*, 11, 124–139.

Fiske, S.T., Lin, M. and Neuberg, S.L. (1999). The continuum model: ten years later. In Chaiken, S. and Trope, Y. (Eds), *Dual-process theories in social psychology*. New York: Guilford.

Flavell, J.H. (1979). Metacognition and cognitive monitoring: A new area of cognitive developmental inquiry. *American Psychologist*, 34, 906–911.

Fox, E. (1993). Allocation of visual attention and anxiety. *Cognition and Emotion*, 7, 207–215.

Fox, E. (1994). Attentional bias in anxiety: a defective inhibition hypothesis. *Cognition and Emotion*, 8, 165–195.

Fox, J.R.E. and Harrison, A. (2008). The relation of anger to disgust: the potential role of coupled emotions within eating pathology. *Clinical Psychology and Psychotherapy*, 15, 86–95.

Fox, J.R.E., Smithson, E., Kellett, S., Ferreira, N., Mayr, I. and Power, M.J. (2013). Emotion coupling and regulation in anorexia nervosa. *Clinical Psychology and Psychotherapy*, 16, 240–267.

Frances, A. (2013). *Saving normal: an insider's revolt against out-of-control psychiatric diagnosis, DSM-5, big pharma, and the medicalization of ordinary life*. New York: William Morrow.

Franklin, S.S. (2010). *The psychology of happiness: a good human life*. Cambridge: Cambridge University Press.

Franzini, L.R. and Grossberg, J.M. (1995). *Eccentric and bizarre behaviors*. New York: John Wiley & Sons.

Frasure-Smith N, Lesperance F, Gravel G, *et al.* (2002). Long-term survival differences among low-anxious, high-anxious and repressive copers enrolled in the Montreal heart attack readjustment trial. *Psychosomatic Medicine*, 64, 571–579.

Fredrickson, B.L. (1998). What good are positive emotions? *Review of General Psychology*, 2, 300–319.

Fredrickson, B.L. (2005). The broaden-and-build theory of positive emotions. In F.A. Huppert, N. Baylis and B. Keverne (Eds), *The science of well-being*. Oxford: Oxford University Press.

Fredrickson, B.L. (2013). Updated thinking on positivity ratios. *American Psychologist*, 68, 814–822.

Fredrickson, B.L. and Branigan, C.A. (2005). Positive emotions broaden the scope of attention and thought-action repertoires. *Cognition and Emotion*, 19, 313–332.

Fredrickson, B.L. and Losada, M.F. (2005). Positive affect and the complex dynamics of human flourishing. *American Psychologist*, 60, 678–686.

Fredrickson, B.L., Mancuso, R.A., Branigan, C. and Tugade, M.M. (2000). The undoing effect of positive emotions. *Motivation and Emotion*, 24, 237–258.

Freud, A. (1937). *The ego and the mechanisms of defence*. London: Hogarth Press.

Freud, S. (1914). *On the history of the psychoanalytic movement*. Pelican Freud Library, Vol. 15. Harmondsworth: Penguin.

Freud, S. (1915/1949). *The unconscious*. In J. Strachey (Ed. and Trans.), The standard edition of the complete psychological works of Sigmund Freud, Vol. 14. London: Hogarth Press.

Freud, S. (1926/1979). *Inhibitions, symptoms and anxiety*. Pelican Freud Library, Vol. 10. Harmondsworth: Penguin.

Friedman, H.S. and Martin, L.S. (2011). *The Longevity Project: surprising discoveries for health and long life from the landmark eight-decade study*. London: Hay House.

Friedman, L.C., Kalidas, M., Elledge, R., *et al.* (2006). Optimism, social support and psychosocial functioning among women with breast cancer. *Psycho-Oncology*, 15, 595–603.

Friedman, M. and Rosenman, R.H. (1959). Association of specific overt behavior pattern with blood and cardiovascular findings. *Journal of the American Medical Association*, 169, 1286–1296.

Frith, U. (2003). *Autism: explaining the enigma* (2nd end). Oxford: Blackwell.

Ganzach, Y. (2001). Judging risk and return of financial assets. *Organizational Behaviour and Human Decision Processes*, 83, 353–370.

Gardner, D. (2008). *Risk: the science and politics of fear*. London: Virgin Books.

Gardner, H. (1983). *Frames of mind: the theory of multiple intelligences*. New York: Basic Books.

Geddes, J.R., Carney, S.M., Davies, C., *et al.* (2003). Relapse prevention with antidepressant drug treatment in depressive disorders: a systematic review. *Lancet,* 361, 653–661.

Genesove, D. and Mayer, C. (2001). Loss-aversion and seller behavior: evidence from the housing market. *Quarterly Journal of Economics*, 116, 1233–1260.

Gibbons, R.D., Brown, C.H., Hur, K., Davis, J.M. and Mann, J.J. (2012). Suicidal thoughts and behavior with antidepressant treatment: reanalysis of the randomized placebo-controlled studies of fluoxetine and venlafaxine. *Archives of General Psychiatry*, 69, 580–587.

Gibson, B. and Sanbonmatsu, D.M. (2004). Optimism, pessimism, and gambling: the downside of optimism. *Personality and Social Psychology Bulletin*, 30, 149–160.

Gilbert, P. (1998). What is shame? Some core issues and controversies. In P. Gilbert and B. Andrews (Eds), *Shame: interpersonal behavior, psychopathology and culture*. New York: Oxford University Press.

Goldstein, A.J. and Chambless, D.L. (1978). A reanalysis of agoraphobia. *Behavior Therapy*, 9, 47–59.

Goleman, D. (1995). *Emotional intelligence*. New York: Bantam Books.

Goodwin, F.K. and Jamison, K.R. (2007). *Manic-depressive illness: bipolar disorders and recurrent depression* (2nd edn). New York: Oxford University Press.

Green, A. (1993). *On private madness*. Madison, CT: International Universities Press.

Green, M. and Elliott, M. (2010). Religion, health, and psychological well-being. *Journal of Religion and Health*, 49, 149–163.

Greyson, B. (1990). Near-death encounters with and without near-death experiences: Comparative NDE Scale profiles. *Journal of Near Death Studies*, 8, 151–161.

Gross, J.J. (1998). The emerging field of emotion regulation: an integrative review. *Review of General Psychology*, 2, 271–299.

Gross, J.J. (Ed.) (2007). *Handbook of emotion regulation*. New York: Guilford.

Gruber, J. (2011). Can feeling too good be bad? Positive emotion persistence (PEP) in bipolar disorder. *Current Directions in Psychological Science*, 20, 217–221.

Gruber, J., Mauss, I.B. and Tamir, M. (2011). A dark side of happiness? How, when and why happiness is not always good. *Perspectives on Psychological Science*, 6, 222–233.

Gudjonsson, G.H. (1981). Self-reported emotional disturbance and its relation to electrodermal reactivity, defensiveness and trait anxiety. *Personality and Individual Differences*, 2, 47–52.

Haidt, J. (2003). The moral emotions. In R.J. Davidson, K.R. Scherer and H.H. Goldsmith (Eds), *Handbook of affective sciences*. Oxford: Oxford University Press.

Hansen, C.H., Hansen, R.D. and Shantz, D.W. (1992). Repression at encoding: discrete appraisals of emotional stimuli. *Journal of Personality and Social Psychology*, 63, 1026–1035.

Hardin, E.E. and Leong, F.T.L. (2005). Optimism and pessimism as mediators of the relations between self-discrepancies and distress among Asian and European Americans. *Journal of Counseling Psychology* 52, 25–35.

Hatfield, E. and Rapson, R.L. (1993). *Love, sex, and intimacy: their psychology, biology, and history*. New York: Harper Collins.

Hatfield, E. and Sprecher, S. (1986). Measuring passionate love in intimate relations. *Journal of Adolescence*, 9, 383–410.

Hatfield, E., Cacioppo, J. and Rapson, R.L. (1994). *Emotional contagion*. New York: Cambridge University Press.

Hayes, S.C., Strosahl, K. and Wilson, K.G. (1999). *Acceptance and commitment therapy: an experimental approach to behavior change*. New York: Guilford.

Hazan, C. and Shaver, P. (1987). Romantic love conceptualised as an attachment process. *Journal of Personality and Social Psychology*, 52, 511–524.

Hazlett, A., Molden, D.C. and Sackett, A.M. (2011). Hoping for the best or preparing for the worst? Regulatory focus and preferences for optimism and pessimism in predicting personal outcomes. *Social Cognition*, 29, 74–96.

Healy, D. (2002). *The creation of psychopharmacology*. Cambridge, MA: Harvard University Press.

Helliwell, J.F. and Putnam, R.D. (2005). The social context of well-being. In F.A. Huppert, N. Baylis and B. Keverne (Eds), *The science of well-being*. Oxford: Oxford University Press.

Higham, C. (2001). *The civilization of Angkor*. London: Phoenix.

Hills, P. and Argyle, M. (1998). The Oxford Happiness Questionnaire: a compact scale for the measurement of psychological well-being. *Personality and Individual Differences*, 33, 1071–1082.

Hobson, P. (1995). *Autism and the development of mind*. Hove: Psychology Press.

Hochschild, A. (1983). *The managed heart: commercialization of human feeling*. Berkeley, CA: University of California Press.

Hoigard, C. and Finstad, L. (1992). *Backstreets: prostitution, money and love*. Philadelphia, PA: Pennsylvania State University Press.

Hummer, R.A., Ellison, C.G., Rogers, R.G., Moulton, B.E. and Romero, R.R. (2004). Religious involvement and adult mortality in the United States: Review and perspective. *Southern Medical Journal*, 97, 1223–1230.

Humphrey, N. (2008). *The mind made flesh: essays from the frontier of psychology and evolution.* Oxford: Oxford University Press.

Hutton. J. (1795). *A theory of the earth with proofs and illustrations.* Amazon: Kindle Edition.

Idler, E.L. and Kasl, S.V. (1992). Religion, disability, depression and the timing of death. *American Journal of Sociology*, 97, 1052–1079.

Isaacowitz, D.M. and Seligman, M.E.P. (2001). Is pessimism a risk factor for depressive mood among community-dwelling older adults? *Behaviour Research and Therapy*, 39, 255–272.

Isaacowitz, D.M. and Seligman, M.E. (2002). Cognitive style predictors of affect change in older adults. *International Journal of Aging and Human Development*, 54, 233–253.

Isen, A.M. (1993). Positive affect and decision making. In M. Lewis and J.M. Haviland (Eds), *Handbook of emotions.* New York: Guilford.

Isen, A.M. (1999). Positive affect. In T. Dalgleish and M.J. Power (Eds), *Handbook of cognition and emotion.* Chichester: John Wiley & Sons.

Isen, A.M. (2008). Some ways in which positive affect influences decision making and problem solving. In M. Lewis, J.M. Haviland-Jones and L.F. Barrett (Eds), *Handbook of emotions* (3rd edn). New York: Guilford.

Isen, A.M., and Reeve, J.M. (1992). The influence of positive affect on intrinsic motivation. Unpublished manuscript. Cornell University.

Isen, A.M., and Reeve, J. (2005). The influence of positive affect on intrinsic and extrinsic motivation: facilitating enjoyment of play, responsible work behavior, and self-control. *Motivation and Emotion*, 29, 297–325.

Isen, A.M., Niedenthal, P.M., and Cantor, N. (1992). An influence of positive affect on social categorization. *Motivation and Emotion*, 16, 65–78.

Isen, A.M., Rosenzweig, A.S. and Young, M.J. (1991). The influence of positive affect on clinical problem solving. *Medical Decision Making*, 11(3), 221–227.

Isen, A.M., Shalker, T., Clark, M.S. and Karp, L. (1978). Affect, accessibility of material and behaviour: a cognition loop? *Journal of Personality and Social Psychology*, 36, 1–12.

Izard, C.E. (1991). *Psychology of Emotions.* New York: Plenum.

Izard, C.E. (2001). Emotional intelligence or adaptive emotions? *Emotion,* 1, 249–257.

James, W. (1902). *The varieties of religious experience.* New York: Longman Green.

Jamison, K.R. (1993). *Touched with fire.* New York: Free Press.

Janoff-Bulman, R. (1992). *Shattered assumptions: towards a new psychology of trauma.* New York: Free Press.

Jauhar, S. and Cavanagh, J. (2013). Classification and epidemiology of bipolar disorder. In M.J. Power (Ed.), *The Wiley-Blackwell handbook of mood disorders* (2nd edn). Chichester: Wiley-Blackwell.

Johnson, S. (2005). Life events in bipolar disorder: Towards more specific models. *Clinical Psychology Review*, 25, 1008–1027.

Johnson, S.C. and Spilka, B. (1991). Outcome research and religious psychotherapies: Where are we and where are we going? *Journal of Psychology and Theology*, 21, 297–308.

Johnson-Laird, P.N. (1988). *The computer and the mind: an introduction to cognitive science.* London: Fontana.

Johnson-Laird, P.N. (2006). *How we reason.* Oxford: Oxford University Press.

Jones, S. (2001). Circadian rhythms, multilevel models of emotion and bipolar disorder – an initial step towards integration? *Clinical Psychology Review*, 21, 1193–1209.

Joormann, J. and Gotlib, I.H. (2010). Emotion regulation in depression: relation to cognitive inhibition. *Cognition and Emotion*, 24(2), 281–298.

Joseph, S., Murphy, D. and Regel, S. (2012). An affective-cognitive processing model of post-traumatic growth. *Clinical Psychology and Psychotherapy*, 19, 316–325.

Kagan, J. (2012). *Psychology's ghosts: the crisis in the profession and the way back*. New York: Yale University Press.

Kahneman, D. (2011). *Thinking fast and slow*. London: Allen Lane.

Kahneman, D. (2012). Interview with Daniel Kahneman. *Monitor on Psychology*, February 2012.

Kahneman, D. and Deaton, A. (2010). High income improves evaluation of life but not emotional well-being. *Psychological and Cognitive Sciences*, 107, 16489–16493.

Kammann, R. (1982). Personal circumstances and life events as poor predictors of happiness. Paper presented at the annual convention of the American Psychological Association, Washington, DC.

Kashdan, T.B. and Biswas-Diener, R. (2014). *The upside of your dark side*. New York: Hudson Street Press.

Kashdan, T.B. and Rottenberg, J. (2010). Psychological flexibility as a fundamental aspect of health. *Clinical Psychology Review*, 30, 865–878.

Kasperson, R.E., Renn, O., Slovic, P., *et al.* (1988). The social amplification of risk: a conceptual framework. *Risk Analysis*, 8, 177–187.

Kasser, T. and Ahuvia, A. (2002). Materialistic values and well-being in business students. *European Journal of Social Psychology*, 32, 137–146.

Kato, T. (2012). Development of the Coping Flexibility Scale: evidence for the coping flexibility hypothesis. *Journal of Counseling Psychology*, 59, 262–273.

Kenez, P. (2006). *A history of the Soviet Union from the beginning to the end* (2nd edn). Cambridge: Cambridge University Press.

Kitayama, S. Markus, H.R. and Kurokawa, M. (2000). Culture, emotion, and well-being: good feelings in Japan and the United States. *Cognition and Emotion*, 14, 93–124.

Koenig, H.G. (2009). Research on religion, spirituality, and mental health: a review. *Canadian Journal of Psychiatry*, 54, 283–291.

Kozma, A. and Stones, M.J. (1980). The measurement of happiness: development of the Memorial University of Newfoundland Scale of Happiness (MUNSCH). *Journal of Gerontology*, 35, 906–912.

Kurtz, M.E., Kurtz, J.C., Given, C.W. and Given, B.A. (2008). Patient optimism and mastery – Do they play a role in cancer patients' management of pain and fatigue? *Journal of Pain and Symptom Management*, 36, 1–10.

Laidlaw, K., Power, M.J., Schmidt, S. and the WHOQOL-OLD Group (2007). The Attitudes to Ageing Questionnaire (AAQ): development and psychometric properties. *International Journal of Geriatric Psychiatry*, 22, 367–379.

Lambie, J.A. and Marcel, A.J. (2002). Consciousness and the varieties of emotion experience: a theoretical framework. *Psychological Review*, 109, 219–259.

Larsen, R.J. (2000). Toward a science of mood regulation. *Psychological Inquiry*, 11, 129–141.

Larsen, R.J. and Fredrickson, B.L. (1999). Measurement issues in emotion research. In D. Kahneman, E. Diener and N. Schwarz (Eds), *Well-being: the foundations of hedonic psychology*. New York: Russell Sage Foundation.

Lawton, L.E. and Bures, R. (2001). Parental divorce and the 'switching' of religious identity. *Journal for the Scientific Study of Religion*, 40, 99–111.

Layard, R. (2011). *Happiness: lessons from a new science* (2nd edn). London: Penguin.

LeDoux, J.E. (1996). *The emotional brain: the mysterious underpinnings of emotional life*. New York: Simon and Schuster.

Lee, J.A. (1976). Forbidden colours of love: patterns of gay love love and gay liberation. *Journal of Homosexuality*, 1, 401–418.

Lerner, J.S. and Keltner, D. (2000). Beyond valence: toward a model of emotion-specific influences on judgment and choice. *Cognition and Emotion*, 14, 473–493.

Leslie, A.M. (1994). ToMM, ToBY and agency: Core architecture and domain specificity. In L.A. Hirschfield and S.A. Gelman (Eds), *Mapping the mind*. New York: Cambridge University Press.

Levav, I., Kohn, R., Golding, J.M. and Weissman, M.M. (1997). Vulnerability of Jews to affective disorders. *American Journal of Psychiatry*, 154, 941–947.

Levin, I. (1972). *The Stepford wives*. New York: Random House.

Levi-Strauss, C. (1962). *The savage mind*. Chicago: University of Chicago Press.

Lewis-Williams, D. (2010). *Conceiving God: the cognitive origin and evolution of religion*. London: Thames and Hudson.

Loewenthal, K. (2000). *The psychology of religion: a short introduction*. Oxford: Oneworld.

Loewenthal, K.M. (2008). The alcohol–depression hypothesis: gender and the prevalence of depression among Jews. In L. Sher (Ed.), *Comorbidity of depression and alcohol use disorders*. New York: Nova Science.

Loewenthal, K.M. (2011). Religion, spirituality and culture. In K.I. Pargament *et al.* (Eds), *APA handbook of psychology, religion, and spirituality*. Washington, DC: APA.

Loewenthal, K.M., MacLeod, A.K., Goldblatt, V., Lubitsh, G. and Valentine, J.D. (2000). Comfort and joy? Religion, cognition, and mood in Protestants and Jews under stress. *Cognition and Emotion*, 14, 355–374.

Long, A.A. and Sedley, D.N. (1987). *The Hellenistic philosophers*. Cambridge: Cambridge University Press.

Long, J. (2005). *Biblical nonsense: a review of the Bible for doubting Christians*. New York: iUniverse.

Looby, A. and Earleywine, M. (2007). The impact of methamphetamine use on subjective well-being in an internet survey: preliminary findings. *Human Psychopharmacology*, 22, 167–172.

Lopez, S.J. and Snyder, C.R. (Eds) (2009). *The Oxford handbook of positive psychology* (2nd edn). Oxford: Oxford University Press.

Lucas, R.E., Clark, A.E., Georgellis, Y. and Diener, E. (2003). Reexamining adaptation and the set point model of happiness: reactions to changes in marital status. *Journal of Personality and Social Psychology*, 84, 527–539.

Luo, J. and Isaacowitz, D.M. (2007). How optimists face skin cancer information: risk assessment, attention, memory, and behavior. *Psychology and Health*, 22, 963–984.

Lutz, C.A. (1988). *Unnatural emotions: everyday sentiments on a Micronesian atoll and their challenge to Western theory*. Chicago, IL: University of Chicago Press.

Lyubomirsky, S. (2013). *The myths of happiness: what should make you happy, but doesnt, what shouldnt make you happy, but does*. New York: Penguin.

Lyubomirsky, S. and Dickerhoof, R. (2005). Subjective well-being. In J. Worrell (Ed.), *Handbook of girls and womens psychological health: Gender and well-being across the life span*. New York: Oxford University Press.

Lyubomirsky, S. and Lepper, H. (1999). A measure of subjective happiness: preliminary reliability and construct validation. *Social Indicators Research*, 46, 137–155.

Lyubomirsky, S., Sousa, L. and Dickerhoof, R. (2006). The costs and benefits of writing, talking, and thinking about life's triumphs and defeats. *Journal of Personality and Social Psychology*, 90, 692–708.

MacDonald, R. (2003). Finding happiness in wisdom and compassion – the real challenge for an alternative development strategy. *Journal of Bhutan Studies*, 9, 1–22.

Machiavelli (1532/2003). *The prince*. London: Penguin.

MacLeod, A., Rose, G.S. and Williams, J.M.G. (1993). Components of hopelessness about the future in parasuicide. *Cognitive Therapy and Research*, 17, 441–455.

MacLeod, A.K., Andersen, A. and Davies, A. (1994). Self-ratings of positive and negative affect and retrieval of positive and negative affect memories. *Cognition and Emotion*, 8, 483–488.

MacLeod, C., Mathews, A. and Tata, P. (1986). Attentional biases in emotional disorders. *Journal of Abnormal Psychology*, 95, 15–20.

Macritchie, K. and Blackwood, D. (2013). Neurobiological theories of bipolar disorder. In M.J. Power (Ed.), *The Wiley-Blackwell handbook of mood disorders* (2nd edn). Chichester: Wiley-Blackwell.

Main, M. and Solomon, J. (1986). Discovery of an insecure-disorganized/disoriented attachment pattern. In T.B. Brazelton and M.W. Yogman (Eds), *Affective development in infancy*. Westport, CT: Ablex Publishing.

Malatynska, E. and Knapp, R.J. (2005). Dominant-submissive behavior as models of mania and depression. *Neuroscience and Biobehavioral Reviews*, 29, 715–737.

Mallandain, I. and Davies, M.F. (1994). The colours of love: personality correlates of love styles. *Personality and Individual Differences*, 17, 557–560.

Marmot, A.F., Eley, J., Stafford, M., Stansfeld, S.A., Warwick, E. and Marmot, M.G. (2006). Building health: an epidemiological study of 'sick building syndrome' in the Whitehall II study. *Occupational and Environmental Medicine*, 63, 283–289.

Maslow, A.H. (1968). *Toward a psychology of being* (2nd eedn). New York: Van Nostrand Reinhold.

Matthews, G., Yousfi, S., Schmidt-Rathjens, C. and Amelang, M. (2003). Personality variable differences between disease clusters. *European Journal of Personality*, 17, 157–177.

Mauss, I. B., Cook, C. L. and Gross, J.J. (2007). Automatic emotion regulation during anger provocation. *Journal of Experimental Social Psychology*, 43, 698–711.

McCrae, R.R. and Costa, P.T. (1997). Conceptions and correlates of openness to experience. In R. Hogan, J. Johnson and S. Briggs (Eds), *Handbook of personality psychology*. San Diego, CA: Academic Press.

McCullough, M.E., Hoyt, W.T., Larson, D.B., Koenig, H.G. and Thoresen, C.E. (2000). Religious involvement and mortality: a meta-analytic review. *Health Psychology*, 19, 211–222.

McGreal, R. and Joseph, S. (1993). The Depression-Happiness Scale. *Psychological Reports*, 73, 1279–1282.

McGregor, I., Nash, K. and Prentice, M. (2010). Reactive approach motivation (RAM) for religion. *Journal of Personality and Social Psychology*, 99, 148–161.

McIntosh, D.N., Silver, R.C. and Wortman, C.B. (1993). Religion's role in adjusting to a negative life event: coping with the loss of a child. *Journal of Personality and Social Psychology*, 65, 812–821.

McIntosh, W.D. and Martin, L.L. (1991). The cybernetics of happiness: the relation of goal attainment, rumination and affect. In M.S. Clark (Ed.), *Review of personality and social psychology*, Vol. 13. Newbury Park, CA: Sage.

McKenna, M.C. Zevon, M.A., Corn, B. and Rounds, J. (1999). Psychosocial factors and the development of breast cancer: a meta-analysis. *Health Psychology*, 18, 520–531.

McMahon, D. (2006). *The pursuit of happiness: a history from the Greeks to the present*. London: Penguin.

McNulty, J.K. and Fincham, F.D. (2012). Beyond positive psychology? Toward a contextual view of psychological processes and well-being. *American Psychologist*, 67, 101–110.

McNulty, J.K. and Karney, B.R. (2004). Positive expectations in the early years of marriage: should couples expect the best or brace for the worst? *Journal of Personality and Social Psychology*, 86, 729–743.

McNulty, J.K. and Russell, V.M. (2010). When 'negative' behaviors are positive: a contextual analysis of the long-term effects of problem-solving behaviors on changes in relationship satisfaction. *Journal of Personality and Social Psychology*, 98, 587–604.

Melnechuk, T. (1988). Emotions, brain, immunity and health: a review. In M. Clynes and J. Panksepp (Eds), *Emotions and psychopathology*. New York: Plenum Press.

Michalczuk, R., Bowden-Jones, H., Verdejo-Garcia, A. and Clark, L. (2011). Impulsivity and cognitive distortions in pathological gamblers attending the UK National Problem Gambling Clinic: a preliminary report. *Psychological Medicine*, 41, 2625–2635.

Mischel, W. (1993). *Introduction to personality* (5th edn). Fort Worth, TX: Harcourt Brace.

Mols, F., Thong, M.S.Y., de Poll-Franse, L.V., Roukema, J.A. and Denollet, J. (2012). Type D (distressed) personality is associated with poor quality of life and mental health among 3080 cancer survivors. *Journal of Affective Disorders*, 136, 26–34.

Morris, H. and Whitcomb, J. (1961). *The Genesis flood*. New York: Presbyterian and Reformed Publishing.

Mund, M. and Mitte, K. (2012). The costs of repression: a meta-analysis on the relation between repressive coping and somatic diseases. *Health Psychology*, 31, 640–649.

Myers, L.B. (1993). Repression and autobiographical memory. Unpublished doctoral dissertation, University of London.

Myers, L.B. (2000). Identifying repressors: a methodological issue for health psychology. *Psychology and Health*, 15, 205–214.

Myers, L.B. (2010). The importance of the repressive coping style: findings from 30 years of research. *Anxiety, Stress and Coping*, 23, 3–17.

Myers, L.B. and Brewin, C.R. (1994). Recall of early experience and the repressive coping style. *Journal of Abnormal Psychology*, 103, 288–292.

Myers, L.B. and Derakshan, N. (2004). To forget or not to forget: what do repressors forget and when do they forget? *Cognition and Emotion*, 18, 495–511.

Myers, L.B., Brewin, C.R. and Power, M.J. (1992). Repression and autobiographical memory. In M.A. Conway, D.C. Rubin, H. Spinnler and W.A. Wagenaar (Eds), *Theoretical perspectives on autobiographical memory*. Dordrecht: Kluwer.

Myers, L.B., Brewin, C.R. and Power, M.J. (1998). Repressive coping and the directed forgetting of emotional material. *Journal of Abnormal Psychology*, 107, 141–148.

Nakaya, N., Tsubono, Y., Hosokawa, T., *et al.* (2003). Personality and the risk of cancer. *Journal of the National Cancer Institute*, 95, 799–805.

Neisser, U. (1976). *Cognition and reality*. San Francisco, CA: Freeman.

Nemeroff, C.B., Evans, D.L., Gyulai, L., *et al.* (2001). Double-blind, placebo-controlled comparison of imipramine and paroxetine in the treatment of bipolar depression. *American Journal of Psychiatry*, 158, 906–912.

Newman, L.S., Nibert, J.A. and Winer, S.E. (2009). Mnemic neglect is not an artefact of expectancy: the moderating role of defensive pessimism. *European Journal of Social Psychology*, 39, 477–486.

NICE (2005). *Depression in children and young people*. London: NICE.

NICE (2009). *Depression in adults*. London: NICE.

Nixon, D. (2009). 'I can't put a smiley face on': working-class masculinity, emotional labour and service work in the 'new economy'. *Gender, Work and Organization*, 16, 300–322.

Norem, J. (2002). *The positive power of negative thinking*. New York: Basic Books.

Nozick, R. (1974). *Anarchy, state and utopia*. New York: Basic Books.

Ntoumanis, N., Taylor, I.M. and Standage, M. (2010). Testing a model of antecedents and consequences of defensive pessimism and self-handicapping in school physical education. *Journal of Sports Sciences*, 28, 1515–1525.

Oatley, K. (1992). *Best laid schemes: the psychology of emotion*. Cambridge: Cambridge University Press.

Oatley, K. (2005). *Emotions: a brief history*. Oxford: Blackwell.

Oatley, K. and Johnson-Laird, P.N. (1987). Towards a cognitive theory of emotions. *Cognition and Emotion*, 1, 29–50.

O'Connor, L.E., Berry, J.W., Weiss, J. and Gilbert, P. (2002). Guilt, fear, submission, and empathy in depression. *Journal of Affective Disorders*, 71(1–3), 19–27.

O'Gorman, J. (2010). Construct validity of components of the type A behaviour pattern. In R.E. Hicks (Ed.), *Personality and individual differences: current directions*. Queensland: Australian Academic Press.

Okun, M.A. and George, L.K. (1984). Physician and self-ratings of health, neuroticism and subjective well-being among men and women. *Personality and Individual Differences*, 5, 533–539.

Olds, J. and Milner, P. (1954). Positive reinforcement produced by electrical stimulation of septal area and other regions of the rat brain. *Journal of Comparative and Physiological Psychology*, 47, 419–427.

O'Neill, M. (2001). *Prostitution and feminism*. Cambridge: Cambridge University Press.

Oxman, T.E., Freeman, D.H. and Manheimer, E.D. (1995). Lack of social participation or religious strength and comfort as risk factors for death after cardiac surgery in the elderly. *Psychosocial Medicine*, 57, 5–15.

Palgi, Y., Shrira, A., Ben-Ezra, M., Cohen-Fridel, S. and Bodner, E. (2011). The relationship between daily optimism, daily pessimism, and affect differ in young and old age. *Personality and Individual Differences*, 50, 1294–1299.

Pargament, K.I. (1997). *The psychology of religion and coping: theory, research, practice*. New York: Guilford.

Pateman, C. (1988). *The sexual contract*. Redwood City, CA: Stanford University Press.

Peale, N.V. (1953). *The power of positive thinking*. New York: Vermilion.

Petersen, T., Harley, R., Papakostas, G. I., Montoya, H. D., Fava, M. and Alpert, J.E. (2004). Continuation cognitive-behavioural therapy maintains attributional style improvement in depressed patients responding acutely to fluoxetine. *Psychological Medicine*, 34, 555–561.

Philipp, A. and Schupbach, H. (2010). Longitudinal effects of emotional labour on emotional exhaustion and dedication of teachers. *Journal of Occupational Health Psychology*, 15, 494–504.

Philippot, P. (2007). *Emotion et psychotherapie*. Wavre: Mardaga.

Philippot, P. and Feldman, R.S. (Eds) (2004). *The regulation of emotion*. Mahwah, NJ: Erlbaum.

Phillips, K.F.V. and Power, M.J. (2007). A new self-report measure of emotion regulation in adolescents: the Regulation of Emotions Questionnaire. *Clinical Psychology and Psychotherapy*, 14, 145–156.

Phipps, S. (2007). Adaptive style in children with cancer: Implications for a positive psychology approach. *Journal of Pediatric Psychology*, 32, 1055–1066.

Piaget, J. (1954). *The construction of reality in the child*. New York: Basic Books.

Pinker, S. (2011). *The better angels of our nature: the decline of violence in history and its causes*. London: Allen Lane.

Plath, S. (1963). *The bell jar*. New York: Heinemann.

Plath, S. (1965). *Ariel*. London: Faber and Faber.

Plato (1977). The Phaedo. In S.M. Cahn (Ed.), *The classics of Western philosophy* (3rd edn). Indianapolis, IN: Hackett.

Podoshen, J. (2009). Distressing events and future purchase decisions: Jewish consumers and the Holocaust. *Journal of Consumer Marketing*, 26, 263–276.

Power, M.J. (1997). Conscious and unconscious representations of meaning. In M.J. Power and C.R. Brewin (Eds), *The transformation of meaning in psychological therapies*. Chichester: John Wiley & Sons.

Power, M.J. (1999). Sadness and its disorders. In T. Dalgleish and M.J. Power (Eds), *Handbook of cognition and emotion*. Chichester: John Wiley & Sons.

Power, M.J. (2003). Quality of life. In S.J. Lopez and C.R. Snyder (Eds), *Positive psychological assessment: a handbook of models and measures*. Washington, DC: American Psychological Association.

Power, M.J. (2005). Psychological approaches to bipolar disorders: a theoretical critique. *Clinical Psychology Review*, 25, 1101–1122.

Power, M.J. (2006). The structure of emotion: an empirical comparison of six models. *Cognition and Emotion*, 20, 694–713.

Power, M.J. (2010). *Emotion focused cognitive therapy*. Chichester: Wiley-Blackwell.

Power, M.J. (2012). *Adieu to god: why psychology leads to atheism*. Chichester: Wiley-Blackwell.

Power, M.J. (2013a). Well-being, quality of life, and the naive pursuit of happiness. *TOPOI: An International Review of Philosophy*, 32, 145–152.

Power, M.J. (Ed.) (2013b). *Wiley-Blackwell handbook of mood disorders*. Chichester: Wiley-Blackwell.

Power, M.J. (2014). *Madness cracked*. Oxford: Oxford University Press.

Power, M.J. and Brewin, C.R. (1991). From Freud to cognitive science: a contemporary account of the unconscious. *British Journal of Clinical Psychology*, 30, 289–310.

Power, M.J. and Champion, L.A. (2000). Models of psychological problems: an overview. In L.A. Champion and M.J. Power (Eds), *Adult psychological problems: an overview*. Hove: Psychology Press.

Power, M.J. and Dalgleish, T. (1997). *Cognition and emotion: from order to disorder*. Hove: Psychology Press.

Power, M.J. and Dalgleish, T. (2008). *Cognition and emotion: from order to disorder* (2nd edn). Hove: Psychology Press.

Power, M.J. and Dalgleish, T. (2015). *Cognition and emotion: from order to disorder* (3rd edn). Hove: Psychology Press.

Power, M.J. and Fyvie, C. (2013). The role of emotion in PTSD: two preliminary studies. *Behavioural and Cognitive Psychotherapy*, 41, 162–172.

Power, M.J. and Tarsia, M. (2007). Basic and complex emotions in depression and anxiety. *Clinical Psychology and Psychotherapy*, 14, 19–31.

Power, M.J. and Wykes, T. (1996). The mental health of mental models and the mental models of mental health. In J. Oakhill and A. Garnham (Eds), *Mental models in cognitive science: essays in honour of Phil Johnson-Laird*. Hove: Psychology Press.

Power, M.J., Bullinger, M., Harper, A. and WHOQOL Group (1999). The World Health Organization WHOQOL-100: tests of the universality of quality of life in 15 different cultural groups worldwide. *Health Psychology*, 18, 495–505.

Power, M.J., de Jong, F. and Lloyd, A. (2002). The organisation of the self-concept in bipolar disorders: an empirical study and replication. *Cognitive Therapy and Research*, 26, 553–561.

Power, M.J., Quinn, K., Schmidt, S. and the WHOQOL-OLD Group (2005). Development of the WHOQOL-OLD module. *Quality of Life Research,* 14, 2197–2214.

Prati, G and Pietrantoni, L. (2009). Optimism, social support, and coping strategies as factors contributing to posttraumatic growth: a meta-analysis. *Journal of Loss and Trauma*, 14, 364–388.

Prien, R.F., Kupfer, D.J., Mansky, P.A., *et al.* (1984). Drug therapy in the prevention of recurrences in unipolar and bipolar affective disorders. Report of the NIMH

Collaborative Study Group comparing lithium carbonate, imipramine, and a lithium carbonate-imipramine combination. *Archives of General Psychiatry*, 41, 1096–1104.

Prosen, H., Martin, R. and Prosen, M. (1972). The remembered mother and the fantasised mother. *Archives of General Psychiatry*, 27, 791–794.

Pury, C.L.S. and Lopez, S.J. (2009). Courage. In Lopez, S.J. and Snyder, C.R. (Eds). *The Oxford handbook of positive psychology* (2nd edn). Oxford: Oxford University Press.

Putnam, R. (2003). *Bowling alone: the collapse and revival of American community*. New York: Simon and Schuster.

Rachman, S.J. (2003). *The treatment of obsessions*. Oxford: Oxford University Press.

Reicher, S.D. (2001). Crowds and social movements. In M. Hogg and S. Tindale (Eds), *Blackwell handbook of social psychology: group processes*. Oxford: Blackwell.

Reynolds, J., Stewart, M., MacDonald, R. and Sischo, L. (2006). Have adolescents become too ambitious? High school seniors' educational and occupational plans, 1976 to 2000. *Social Problems*, 53, 186–206.

Richards, J.M., Butler, E.A. and Gross, J.J. (2003). Emotion regulation in romantic relationships: the cognitive consequences of concealing feelings. *Journal of Social and Personal Relationships*, 20, 599–620.

Rilke, R.M. (1986). *Rilke*. London: Penguin.

Ringdal, G.I. (1996). Religiosity, quality of life, and survival in cancer patients. *Social Indicators Research*, 38, 193–211.

Rizzolatti, G. and Craighero, L. (2004). The mirror-neuron system. *Annual Review of Neuroscience*, 27, 169–192.

Roberts, R.D., Zeidner, M. and Matthews, G. (2001). Does emotional intelligence meet traditional standards for intelligence? Some new data and conclusions. *Emotion*, 1, 196–231.

Rose, J.P., Endo, Y., Windschitl, P.D. and Suls, J. (2008). Cultural differences in unrealistic optimism and pessimism: the role of egocentrism and direct versus indirect comparison measures. *Personality and Social Psychology Bulletin*, 34, 1236–1248.

Ross, J.M. (1991). A psychoanalytic essay on romantic, erotic love. *Journal of the American Psychoanalytic Association,* 39 (S), 439–474.

Rowe, D. (1997). *The real meaning of money*. London: Harper Collins.

Rozin, P. (1999). Preadaptation and the puzzles and properties of pleasure. In D. Kahneman, E. Diener and N. Schwarz (Eds), *Well-being: the foundations of hedonic psychology*. New York: Russell Sage Foundation.

Rozin, P. and Fallon, A.E. (1987). A perspective on disgust. *Psychological Review*, 94, 23–41.

Rozin, P., Haidt, J. and McCauley, C.R. (1999). Disgust: the body and soul emotion. In T. Dalgleish and M.J. Power (Eds), *Handbook of cognition and emotion*. Chichester: John Wiley & Sons.

Ruini, C. and Fava, G.A. (2012). Role of well-being therapy in achieving a balanced and individualized path to optimal functioning. *Clinical Psychology and Psychotherapy*, 19, 291–304.

Russell, G.W. (2004). Sport riots: a social-psychological review. *Aggression and Violent Behavior*, 9, 353–378.

Ryan, R.M. and Deci, E.L. (2001). On happiness and human potential: a review of research on hedonic and eudaimonic well-being. *Annual Review of Psychology*, 52, 141–166.

Ryff, C.D. (1989). Happiness is everything, or is it? Explorations on the meaning of psychological well-being. *Journal of Personality and Social Psychology*, 6, 1069–1081.

Ryff, C.D. and Singer, B.H. (2008). Know thyself and become what you are: a eudaimonic approach to psychological well-being. *Journal of Happiness Studies*, 9, 13–39.

Salovey, P. and Mayer, J.D. (1990). Emotional intelligence. *Imagination, Cognition, and Personality*, 9, 185–211.

Sanders, T. (2005). 'It's just acting': Sex workers' strategies for capitalizing on sexuality. *Gender, Work and Organization*, 12, 319–342.

Sandvik, E., Diener, E. and Seidlitz, L. (1993). Subjective well-being: the convergence and stability of self-report and non-self-report measures. *Journal of Personality*, 61, 317–342.

Scheff, T. (2001). Individualism and alienation in popular love songs 1930–1999. www.soc. ucsb.edu/faculty/thomas-scheff Scheier, M.F. and Carver, C.S. (1985). Optimism, coping, and health: assessment and implications of generalized outcome expectancies. *Health Psychology*, 4, 219–247.

Scherer, K.R., Schorr, A. and Johnstone, T. (Eds) (2001). *Appraisal processes in emotion: theory, methods, research*. Oxford: Oxford University Press.

Schwartz, G.E. (1982). Physiological patterning and emotion: implications for the self-regulation of emotion. In K.R. Blankstein and J. Polivy (Eds), *Self control and self-modification of emotional behaviour*. New York: Plenum.

Schwarz, N. (1996). *Cognition and communication: judgmental biases, research methods, and the logic of conversation*. Mahwah, NJ: Erlbaum.

Schwartz, R.M. (1992). States of mind model and personal construct theory: implications for psychopathology. *International Journal of Personal Construct Psychology*, 5, 123–143.

Searle, J. (1997). *The mystery of consciousness*. London: Granta.

Seligman, M.E.P. (1998). *Learned optimism: how to change your mind and your life*. New York: Pocket Books.

Seligman, M.E.P. (2002). *Authentic happiness: using the new positive psychology to realize your potential for lasting fulfillment*. London: Nicholas Brealey.

Seligman, M.E.P., Steen, T.A., Park, N. and Peterson, C. (2005). Positive psychology progress: empirical validation of interventions. *American Psychologist*, 60, 410–421.

Sen, A. (2001). Economic progress and health. In D.A. Leon and G. Watt (Eds), *Poverty, inequality, and health: an international perspective*. Oxford: Oxford University Press.

Shafir, E., Diamond, P. and Tversky, A. (1997). Money illusion. *Quarterly Journal of Economics*, 112, 341–374.

Shaver, P.R. and Hazan, C. (1988). A biased overview of the study of love. *Journal of Personal and Social Relationships*, 5, 474–501.

Shaver, P.R., Wu, S. and Schwartz, J.C. (1991). Cross-cultural similarities and differences in emotion and its representation: a prototype approach. In M.S. Clark (Ed.), *Review of personality and social psychology*, Vol. 13. Newbury Park, CA: Sage.

Shipley, B.A., Weiss, A., Der, G., Taylor, M.D. and Deary, I.J. (2007). Neuroticism, extraversion, and mortality in the UK Health and Lifestyle Survey: a 21-year prospective cohort study. *Psychosomatic Medicine*, 69, 923–931.

Shushan, G. (2009). *Conceptions of the afterlife in early civilizations*. London: Continuum International.

Simonton, D.K. (2009). Creativity. In S.J. Lopez and C.R. Snyder (Eds), *Oxford handbook of positive psychology* (2nd edn). Oxford: Oxford University Press.

Sin, N.L. and Lyubomirsky, S. (2009). Enhancing well-being and alleviating depressive symptoms with positive psychology interventions: A practice-friendly meta-analysis. *Journal of Clinical Psychology*, 65, 467–487.

Sincoff, J.B. (1992). Ambivalence and defense: Effects of a repressive style on normal adolescents' and young adults' mixed feelings. *Journal of Abnormal Psychology*, 101, 251–256.

Singer, J.L. and Sincoff, J.B. (1990). Beyond repression and the defenses. In J.L. Singer (Ed.), *Repression and dissociation: implications for personality theory, psychopathology and health*. Chicago: University of Chicago Press.

Skinner, B.F. (1957). *Verbal behavior*. Acton: Copley Publishing Group.

Sloman, S.A. (2002). Two systems of reasoning. In T. Gilovich, D. Griffin and D. Kahneman (Eds.), *Heuristics and biases: the psychology of intuitive judgment.* Cambridge: Cambridge University Press.

Slovic, P., Finucane, M., Peters, E. and MacGregor, D.G. (2002). The affect heuristic. In T. Gilovich, D. Griffin and D. Kahneman (Eds), *Heuristics and biases: the psychology of intuitive judgment.* Cambridge: Cambridge University Press.

Smith, T.B., McCullough, M.E. and Poll, J. (2003). Religiousness and depression: Evidence for a main effect and the moderating influence of stressful life events. *Psychological Bulletin,* 129, 614–636.

Snowdon, D. (2001). *Aging with grace.* London: Fourth Estate.

So, S.H., Freeman, D., Dunn, G., *et al.* (2012). Jumping to conclusions, a lack of belief flexibility and delusional conviction in psychosis: a longitudinal investigation of the structure, frequency, and relatedness of reasoning biases. *Journal of Abnormal Psychology,* 121, 129–139.

Spencer, S.M., Schulz, R., Rooks, R.N., *et al.* (2009). Racial differences in self-rated health at similar levels of physical functioning: an examination of health pessimism in the Health, Aging, and Body Composition study. *Journals of Gerontology: Series B: Psychological Sciences and Social Sciences,* 64B, 87–94.

Spiegel, D., Bloom, J.R., Kraemer, H.C. and Gottheil, E. (1989). Effect of psychosocial treatment on survival of patients with metastatic breast cancer. *Lancet,* 2, 888–891.

Spielberger, C.D., Gorsuch, R.L. and Lushene, R. (1970). *Trait Anxiety Scale.* Palo Alto, CA: Consulting Psychologists Press.

Spilker, B. (1990). *Quality of life assessments in clinical trials.* New York: Raven Press.

Spilker, B. (1996). Introduction. In B. Spilker (Ed.), *Quality of life and pharmacoeconomics in clinical trials.* New York: Raven Press.

Sternberg, R. (1986). A triangular theory of love. *Psychological Review,* 93, 119–135.

Sternberg, R. (1988). Triangulating love. In R.J. Sternberg and M.L. Barnes (Eds), *The psychology of love.* New Haven: Yale University Press.

Stevenson, R.L. (1876/1988). *The strange case of Dr Jekyll and Mr Hyde.* Harmondsworth: Penguin.

Stewart, G. (1988). *Ordeal by hunger: the story of the Donner Party.* Boston, MA: Houghton Mifflin.

Stiglitz, J.E. (2013). *The price of inequality.* London: Penguin.

Stone, M., Laughren, T., Jones, M.L., *et al.* (2009). Risk of suicidality in clinical trials of antidepressants in adults: analysis of proprietary data submitted to US Food and Drug Administration. *British Medical Journal,* 339, b2880.

Storbeck, J. and Clore, G.L. (2005). With sadness comes accuracy, with happiness, false memory: mood and the false memory effect. *Psychological Science,* 16, 785–791.

Storr, A. (1979). *The art of psychotherapy.* London: Heinemann.

Storr, A. (1988). *Churchill's black dog, Kafka's mice, and other phenomena of the human mind.* New York: Grove Weidenfeld.

Sun-Tzu (2002). *The art of war.* London: Penguin Books.

Svenson, O. (1981). Are we all less risky and more skilful than our fellow driver? *Acta Psychologica,* 47, 143–148.

Sweeny, K. and Shepperd, J.A. (2010). The costs of optimism and the benefits of pessimism. *Emotion,* 10, 750–753.

Tajfel, H. and Turner, J. (1979). An integrative theory of intergroup conflict. In Austin, W.G. and Worchel, S. (Eds), *The social psychology of intergroup relations.* Monterey: Brooks/Cole.

Tallis, F. (2004). *Love sick: love as a mental illness.* London: Century.

Tangney, J.P. (1999). The self-conscious emotions: shame, guilt, embarrassment and pride. In T. Dalgleish and M.J. Power (Eds), *Handbook of cognition and emotion*. Chichester: John Wiley & Sons.

Tedeshi, R.G. and Calhoun, L.G. (2004). *Helping bereaved parents*. London: Routledge.

Tennov, D. (1979). *Love and limerance*. New York: Stein and Day.

Tiihonen, J., Lonnqvist, J., Wahlbeck, K., Klaukka, T., Tanskanen, A. and Haukka, J. (2006). Antidepressants and the risk of suicide, attempted suicide, and overall mortality in a nationwide cohort. *Archives of General Psychiatry*, 63, 1358–1367.

Turvey, C. and Salovey, P. (1994). Measures of repression: converging on the same construct? Imagination. *Cognition and Personality*, 13, 279–289.

Tversky, A. and Kahneman, D. (1984). Extensional versus intuitive reasoning: the conjunction fallcy in probability judgment. *Psychological Review*, 90, 293–315.

Twenge, J.M. (2006). *Generation me*. New York: Free Press.

Tycocinski, O.E. and Steinberg, N. (2005). Coping with disappointing outcomes: Retroactive pessimism and motivated inhibition of counterfactuals. *Journal of Experimental Social Psychology*, 41, 551–558.

Tyldesley, J. (2011). *The Penguin book of myths and legends of Ancient Egypt*. London: Penguin.

Vaillant, G.E. (1990). Repression in college men followed for half a century. In J.L. Singer (Ed.), *Repression and dissociation*. Chicago, IL: University of Chicago Press.

Van Dijk, P.A. and Kirk, A. (2007). Being somebody else: emotional labour and emotional dissonance in the context of the service experience at a heritage tourism site. *Journal of Hospitality and Tourism Management*, 14, 157–169.

Van Hiel, A., Hautman, L., Cornelis, I. and De Clercq, B. (2007). Football hooliganism: comparing self-awareness and social identity theory explanations. *Journal of Community and Applied Social Psychology*, 17, 169–186.

Van Lommel, P., van Wees, R., Meyers, V. and Elfferich, I. (2001). Near-death experience in survivors of cardiac arrest: a prospective study in the Netherlands. *The Lancet*, 358, 2039–2045.

Vatsyama, M. (1962). *The Kama Sutra*. London: East-West Publications.

Veenhoven, R. (1984). *Conditions of happiness*. Dordrecht, The Netherlands: D. Reidel.

Veenhoven, R. (2000). The four qualities of life: ordering concepts and measures of the good life. *Journal of Happiness Studies*, 1, 1–39.

VFA (2015). *The international pharmaceutical market*. www.vfa.de/en/statistics/statistics-2012-am-international1

Vitterso, J., Roysamb, E. and Diener, E. (2002). The concept of life satisfaction across cultures: exploring its diverse meaning and relation to economic wealth. In E. Gullone and R.A. Cummins (Eds), *The universality of subjective wellbeing indicators*. Social Indicators Research Series, Vol. 16. Dordrecht: Kluwer.

Wall, P. (1999). *Pain: the science of suffering*. London: Weidenfeld and Nicolson.

Wann, D.L., Grieve, F.G., Waddill, P.J. and Martin, J. (2008). Use of retroactive pessimism as a method of coping with identity threat: the impact of group identification. *Group Processes and Intergroup Relations*, 11, 439–450.

Watson, M., Greer, S., Young, J., Inayat, Q., Burgess, C. and Robertson, B. (1988). Development of a questionnaire measure of adjustment to cancer: The MAC scale. *Psychological Medicine*, 18, 203–209.

Weber, M. (1978) *Economy and society: an outline of interpretive sociology*, Vols 1 and 2. Berkeley, CA: University of California Press.

Webster, J.D. (2002). Reminiscence functions in adulthood: age, race, and family dynamics correlates. In J.D. Webster and B.K. Haight (Eds), *Critical advances in reminiscence work: from theory to application*. New York: Springer.

Weinberger, D.A., Schwartz, G.E. and Davidson. R.J. (1979). Low-anxious, high anxious and repressive coping styles: psychometric patterns and behavioural responses to stress. *Journal of Abnormal Psychology*, 88, 369–380.

Weinstein, N.D. (1984). Why it won't happen to me: perceptions of risk factors and susceptibility. *Health Psychology*, 3, 431–457.

Wells, A. (1997). *Cognitive therapy of anxiety: a practice manual and conceptual guide*. Chichester: John Wiley & Sons.

Wells, H.G. (2007). *The country of the blind*. London: Penguin.

Wessman, A.E. and Ricks, D.F. (1966). *Mood and personality*. New York: Holt, Rinehart and Winston.

Westerhof, G.J., Bohlmeijer, E.T., van Beljouw, I.M. and Pot, A.M. (2010). Improvement in personal meaning mediates the effects of a life review intervention on depressive symptoms in a randomized controlled trial. *Gerontologist*, 50, 541–549.

WHOQOL Group (1995). The World Health Organization Quality of Life assessment (WHOQOL): position paper from the World Health Organization. *Social Science and Medicine*, 41, 1403–1409.

WHOQOL Group (1998a). The World Health Organization Quality of Life Assessment (WHOQOL): development and general psychometric properties. *Social Science and Medicine*, 46, 1569–1585.

WHOQOL Group (1998b). Development of the World Health Organization WHOQOL-BREF Quality of Life Assessment. *Psychological Medicine*, 28, 551–558.

Wilkinson, R. and Pickett, K. (2010) *The spirit level: why equality is better for everyone*. London: Penguin.

Wilkinson, T. (2010). *The rise and fall of Ancient Egypt*. London: Bloomsbury.

Woodward, M., Oliphant, J., Lowe, G. and Tunstall-Pedoe, H. (2003). Contribution of contemporaneous risk factors to social inequality in coronary heart disease and all causes mortality. *Preventive Medicine*, 36, 561–568.

World Health Organization (1958). *The first ten years of the World Health Organization*. Geneva: World Health Organization.

Wright, B.A. and Lopez, S.J. (2002). Widening the diagnostic focus: a case for including human strengths and environmental resources. In C. Snyder and S.J. Lopez (Eds), *The Oxford handbook of positive psychology*. Oxford: Oxford University Press.

Zeelenberg, M. (1999). Anticipated regret, expected feedback and behavioural decision making. *Journal of Behavioural Decision Making*, 12, 93–106.

Zimbardo, P. (2007). *The Lucifer effect: understanding how good people turn evil*. London: Rider.

AUTHOR INDEX

SUBJECT INDEX